THE STEAM SHAVING MACHINE. [See p. 32.

BORDER

REMINISCENCES.

BY

RANDOLPH B. MARCY,

U. S. Army;

AUTHOR OF "THE PRAIRIE TRAVELLER," "THIRTY YEARS OF ARMY LIFE ON THE BORDER," ETC.

NEW YORK:

HARPER & BROTHERS, PUBLISHERS,

FRANKLIN SQUARE.

1872.

By GENERAL R. B. MARCY.

ARMY LIFE ON THE BORDER. Thirty Years of Army Life on the Border. Comprising Descriptions of the Indian Nomads of the Plains; Explorations of New Territory; a Trip across the Rocky Mountains in the Winter; Descriptions of the Habits of Different Animals found in the West, and the Methods of Hunting them; with Incidents in the Life of different Frontier Men, &c., &c. By Brevet Maj.-General R. B. Marcy, U.S.A. 8vo, Cloth, Beveled Edges, $3 00.

THE PRAIRIE TRAVELLER. A Hand-Book for Overland Emigrants. With Maps, Illustrations, and Itineraries of the Principal Routes between the Mississippi and the Pacific. By Brevet Maj.-General R. B. Marcy, U.S.A. Published by Authority of the War Department. 16mo, Cloth, $1 00.

PREFACE.

Although not in exact accord with my own inclination, I have been induced, by the solicitations of friends in the army and in civil life, to permit the publication of the following pages.

The very kind and flattering reception given to my other books by the public and the press encourages me to hope that an equally indulgent greeting may be extended to this volume, which is a miscellany of fugitive recollections—a compilation of random sketches written in leisure hours during a period of several years, and which will be found somewhat desultory and disconnected; yet, as they, for the most part, are records of the results of long personal experience in a sphere of life that has hitherto found but few chroniclers, they may hereafter possess some historic significance. However this may be, if they have no other value, they can be relied upon as truthful memoirs of persons with whom the writer has been thrown in contact during a protracted military career in the Far West, and as faithful delineations of incidents and adventures without the coloring of romance, excepting in the few instances where the fact is expressly stated.

Should any of the individual specimens of frontiersmen, the traits of whose characters I have endeavored to depict in bold relief, seem unnatural or overdrawn, I beg the reader to remember that the life, habits, and associations of the borderer are necessarily of such a peculiar nature as to produce strange types of character and remarkable developments of humanity. The fact should also be borne in mind that my illustrations have been drawn from the most anomalous and salient specimens of those types.

In preparing the manuscript for publication, I have endeavored to collate and arrange the different parts in as connected, homogeneous, and attractive a form as possible, and if the book serves to while away pleasantly the ennui of a dull hour, my chief object will have been accomplished, and I shall be content.

CONTENTS.

CHAPTER V.

CHAPTER VI.

PIONEERS OF THE WEST.

CHAPTER VII.

PIONEERS OF THE WEST.

CHAPTER VIII.

CHAPTER IX.

PRAIRIE INDIANS.

CHAPTER X.

ILLUSTRATIONS.

BORDER REMINISCENCES.

CHAPTER I.

A Major of the Old Regime.—Quadroon Ball.—High Game of Faro. —Lafitte the Pirate.—Whaling Voyage.—Absence without leave. —Post-fund Controversy.—Novel Shaving Machine.—Extraordinary Shot.—Musk-rat Hunting.—American Sovereignty.

A MAJOR OF THE OLD REGIME.

Doubtless every one who has read Marryatt's works will remember Captain Kearney, who is introduced as a prominent actor in that entertaining romance, "Peter Simple," and whose propensity for dealing in hyperbole was so irrepressible that even on his death-bed, with the rattle in his throat, and when he was almost speechless, he said to the hero of the story, who was leaning over him to catch the last sentences that with great effort gurgled from his lips, "Peter, I'm going now—not that the rattle—in my throat—is a sign of death—for I once knew a man—to live with—the rattle in his throat —for six weeks," when he fell back and died.

Whether this character was exclusively ideal, begotten and conceived solely in the author's imagination, or whether he was designed to represent an individual, or a class of British naval officers, is left for the reader to determine. However this may have been, many of the traits in this man's character, so vividly delineated by the writer, afforded so striking a concurrence with those of a real, veritable old army officer whom I once encountered, that immediately after reading the book I sat down and wrote the following. Before proceeding with my narrative, however, I take occasion to remark, as an act of justice to the service, that I am proud in giving my attestation to the fact that the Munchausen *genus-homo* has hitherto found but a meagre representation in the army. Nevertheless, it must be admitted that a lone specimen has now and then, at wide intervals, made his appearance, as the individual I am about introducing to the reader, and whose dominant propensity was proverbial among his contemporaries, clearly shows.

Many years since I was stationed at a frontier post with an officer by the name of C***s, who, during the War of 1812, enlisted in the regular army as a private soldier, and who, for gallant conduct in action, was rewarded with an ensign's commission.

This officer served under General Jackson in the

Creek Indian Campaign, and at New Orleans, besides having performed meritorious service elsewhere.

When I first met him he had been advanced to the grade of major, and was then verging upon the mature age of "threescore and ten," yet he still preserved an exceedingly social disposition, and never seemed more happy than when fighting his battles over again, and recounting the prominent incidents in his life to an appreciative audience by the fireside or at the mess-table.

I verily believe he would not, for his right hand, have perpetrated a deliberate misrepresentation of facts or circumstances which would in the slightest degree have tended to injure any person, for the milk of human kindness predominated largely in his nature. At the same time, his conceptive faculties were eminently fertile and vivid, while his memory was far from being reliable. Moreover, the marvelous held such absolute sway over every other attribute in his composition, that it often impelled him to "draw a prodigiously long bow," and, by a most astonishing coincidence, he was himself invariably the hero of his wonderful adventures, which seemed to be stereotyped upon the tablets of his imagination, ready for rehearsal to every one who felt inclined to listen to them.

As may be conjectured, these legends lost none of their romance by repetition; on the contrary, it was quietly whispered about among the officers that they had become so much changed and exaggerated by time and reiteration that but little, if any thing, of the original plots remained.

He always maintained a most grave and dignified cast of countenance when speaking of his exploits, and, as he was eminently pugnacious, it was seldom that any one in his presence, with the exception of his "better half," ever presumed to throw the slightest shadow of incredulity upon the truth of the narrations. His wife, however, often assumed the privilege of expressing her opinions in the rather abrupt form of "*Now; C***s, you know you lie.*" The old man was one of those imperturbable persons who never manifested surprise at the narration of the most startling facts by others, and invariably had at his tongue's end an apposite incident, purporting to be connected with his own experience, that may not in all cases have been original, but which threw all others far into the background.

In order to render the memoir of this remarkable romancer more complete, I have ventured to embody in the following sketch a few striking incidents in his memorable career.

QUADROON BALL.

The major seemed to derive especial satisfaction from relating the circumstances connected with his personal adventures in New Orleans, and, among others, he informed me that, shortly after his arrival in that city, having a desire to gain as much information as possible concerning the peculiar habits of the people, he paid a visit to a quadroon ball, where he encountered a large concourse of persons of all classes, and among them were quite a number of Spanish Creole young men, who evinced rather an unfriendly disposition toward army officers generally, and were particularly pointed in their deportment toward him. He endeavored to avoid them for some time, but they seemed determined to draw him into a quarrel, and at length their insults became so personal that, to repeat his own language, "I was compelled to smash three or four chairs over their heads; but this did not settle the difficulty, and I drew from my vest pockets a pair of 'Derringers' that I carried, and fired them into the crowd; but this did not prove sufficient, and I was obliged to draw from my coat pockets a pair of holster-pistols which I happened to have, and discharged them also."

At this stage of the narrative some inquisitive

individual inquired if the police did not interfere to quell the disorderly proceedings. He said no; that in the *mêleé* which ensued the lights were extinguished, and this gave him an opportunity to make his escape to his quarters. Then, leaning toward us, and at the same time placing his hand around his mouth so as to prevent the disclosure from escaping in any other direction, he added, in a low tone of voice, "I say nothing about the sequel of this affair, gentlemen, excepting I was informed that *dead Spaniards* were found in the ball-room on the following morning."

VISITING A FARO-BANK.

During the period that the major remained in New Orleans, the pay of the army was so small, and the paymaster so seldom in funds, that the officers for the most part were obliged to depend for a subsistence upon the slender fare derived from the commissary's store. They rarely had an opportunity of indulging in the expensive luxuries that the market afforded, unless, perchance (which did not often occur), they received an invitation to dine out with some friend who was so fortunate as to possess means aside from his pay. According to his own account, an invitation was upon a certain occasion extended to himself and his room-mate, a brother officer named Tom ———, to join a party of officers who were to dine with Colonel Croghan. They gladly accepted the invitation, and went to the dinner, during which the wine circulated briskly, and every one seemed to enjoy the sumptuous fare which the colonel's long purse enabled him to spread before his guests.

At a late hour, when all were competent to give direct evidence as to the superior quality of the wine that had been so bountifully supplied by their hospitable host, and at a time when some of the guests appeared about taking their departure, a bottle of Champagne was placed at each plate, and an intimation given by the colonel that he expected every one to finish his bottle before leaving the table. The major said he regarded this as a peremptory mandate, drank off his quota at once, and retired, with the intention of hurrying to his quarters and going to bed before he became seriously affected by it. On his way, however, he was passing the door of a gambling saloon, and, having a dollar in his pocket, he resolved to try his fortune with it. Accordingly he entered, and placed his money upon a card which won for him several times, and he in a short time accumulated quite a "pile of chips," and he continued betting, until at length the room began to revolve as upon an axis, the cards and counters multiplied into many times their original numbers, and every thing in the establishment seemed to wax dim and misty, and finally he lost all recollection of events, until late on the following morning he was awakened by his messmate Tom ———, when, to his astonishment, he found himself in his own room, and suffering from a most excruciating headache. After rubbing his eyes and collecting his wandering senses, he was informed by his friend that their larder was completely exhausted, and if they were to have any dinner it would be necessary to replenish it, but as for himself, he had no money. The major replied that it was likely his finances were in the same condition of depletion, as he had paid a visit to the faro-bank, and was somewhat oblivious as to the result; but, if there was any thing, he presumed it would be found in his pockets; whereupon his clothes were examined, and, to their utter amazement and delight, every pocket of coat, vest, and trowsers was crammed full of doubloons and bank-notes, amounting in the aggregate to something like ten thousand dollars.

"Now, Tom, my boy," said the major, "as we have been roughing it for a good while on commissary tack, I propose that you go to market and lay in a good stock of luxuries, and from this time out we'll live like gentlemen." Whereupon his friend took money and went in quest of the supplies.

Now Tom, be it known, was himself very fond of his grog, and would at any time sooner have dispensed with his dinner than his liquor. After he had been absent for a while, the major heard a heavy rumbling noise like the rolling of logs across the hall, and, on going to the door, found his friend engaged in superintending the unloading of barrels from a huge wagon. He was in the most exuberant spirits, and, rubbing his hands together, informed the major, with a most gratified expression of countenance, that he had secured a magnificent lot of supplies.

In reply to the inquiry as to the character of the articles purchased, he said there were *thirteen barrels of whisky, two hams, and a loaf of bread.* He said he would have purchased a little coffee and sugar, but he thought they did not care about such flummery so long as they had a good stock of the substantials of life.

LAFITTE THE PIRATE.

I once inquired of the major if, while he was with the army at New Orleans, he ever chanced to meet the renowned pirate whose name heads this sketch.

He said he had seen him often, and knew him intimately; indeed, that General Jackson had once sent him for the express purpose of capturing the outlaw. It appeared some one had reported that the redoubtable buccaneer, with but three or four followers, was then lying concealed among the islands in the vicinity of Fort Livingston, and the major, with a detachment of twenty men, was directed to search out his hiding-place, and, if possible, secure him. Accordingly, with his party in two barges, he proceeded down the river to the Balize, thence turned west, and skirted along the numerous bayous for a long distance without seeing any trace of the pirates, and was upon the point of abandoning the search, when suddenly, as he rounded a high projecting point, he came directly into immediate proximity with a fleet of seven raking, suspicious-looking vessels lying quietly at anchor.

Being then too close to retreat with safety, he adopted the only alternative that occurred to him. Putting on a bold face, he rowed directly up to the gangway of the flag-ship, and inquired for the commanding officer, who soon made his appearance in the person of the veritable Lafitte himself, and who very courteously saluted him, calling him by name, and invited him on board his vessel. He accepted the invitation, and took an early occasion to observe that, having learned the fleet was in that vicinity, it occurred to him that he would come and pay his respects to the renowned commander. He was cordially received, invited into the luxurious cabin, and treated with the most distinguished consideration and hospitality. A sumptuous dinner was served upon the most costly plate, accompanied by the best wines and liquors, of which he partook freely. Afterward he smoked the most recherche segars while indulging a luxurious siesta in a gorgeous hammock suspended in the coolest part of the deck, and every thing was done by the courteous pirate to render his visit agreeable.

When the time arrived for him to take his departure, he found his boats stocked with baskets of Champagne, jars of rare sweetmeats, and other delicacies in the greatest profusion.

As he was about leaving the ship, Lafitte informed him that he was perfectly well aware of the object of his visit, and suggested that when he next started out for the purpose of capturing the commander of a fleet of seven vessels completely armed and manned, he should take a greater force than twenty men. He thought the advice good, and resolved to profit by it; then, bidding adieu to the buccaneer, whom he pronounced a most generous fellow, he returned to New Orleans.

WHALING VOYAGE.

The major, I was aware, had at one time been stationed at Portsmouth, New Hampshire; and as I had been told that a whale was once killed in that vicinity, I incidentally asked him if he ever heard of the circumstance. "Why, my dear fellow," said he, "I was the very man that killed him."

I was not a little surprised at this, and requested him to give me an account of the affair, which he did in the following words:

"It was reported to me one day that a large sperm whale had been seen spouting about two miles below Portsmouth, and there was every indication to induce the belief that he was coming up to the town; whereupon I called out my boat's crew, manned my barge, and, seizing a harpoon that I happened to have, set off in pursuit, and soon came alongside him, and I fortunately succeeded, at the very first cast, in fastening the harpoon into him.

"The monster made some terrific struggles to extricate himself, but not succeeding, set off furiously up the river with the barge in tow. At length, however, he turned down stream for a few miles, then, coming about again, he went up the river, and in this manner he continued carrying us up and down stream for three successive days and nights, during all of which time I stood at the bow of the boat, axe in hand, ready to cut the harpoon-rope in case he should take us out to sea. This contingency did not occur, however, and, at the expiration of the time specified, the whale became so much exhausted that he was easily killed and landed, and he afforded an enormous amount of oil."

I inquired of the major if he did not suffer from hunger during all those three days and nights. He replied, "No; our friends threw provisions into the boat as we swiftly passed back and forth under the bridge at Portsmouth."

A DAY'S DUCK-SHOOTING.

As I remarked before, the memory of the major was sometimes at fault.

One evening I came in from a duck-shooting excursion, when I had been successful in bagging an unusually large number of birds. I reported my return to the major, and gave him an account of the most interesting incidents of the hunt, and, among other things, mentioned that I had killed nine ducks at a single shot.

"Why, my dear fellow," said he, "when I was with Old Hickory at New Orleans, I took a day's duck-shooting on Lake Pontchartrain, and I pledge you my word, sir, that two of us bagged six hundred and ninety-one duck and mallard. I myself, with my large-bored 'Joe Manton,' that Pakingham presented me, at a single shot brought down seventy-seven ducks, which we picked up, besides wounding many others that got away."

One of the officers present gave a prolonged low whistle of incredulity at this marvelous statement, when the major turned upon him, and, with a most indignant air, asked if he presumed to doubt the correctness of what he had asserted. "By no means," answered the young man. "Certainly not. I haven't the slightest doubt upon the subject."

The major continued: "You may rest perfectly assured, sir, that every word I have advanced is absolutely and literally true, and, as I said before, we bagged eight hundred and ninety-three duck and mallard, and I myself killed eighty-seven of them at a single shot with my 'Purdy,' which Andrew Jackson insisted upon my accepting as a Christmas present. *Moreover, let me tell you, sir, that it was an infernally bad day for duck-shooting too.*"

ABSENCE WITHOUT LEAVE.

While commanding a post in Louisiana, the major upon a certain occasion gave permission for one of his officers to visit New Orleans, and the young man, finding the city very attractive, overstaid his leave, and expected to be called to account for it.

Immediately after his return he called at the quarters of the commanding officer to report his arrival, and, not finding him in at the moment, he endeavored to place himself on as favorable a footing as possible with the lady of the house. He described to her the latest fashions, related the most recent gossip circulating among the "*haut-ton*" of the city, and was ingratiating himself rapidly into favor with her, when the major entered, and in a very dignified manner asked him the news from New Orleans.

Now the major possessed no *penchant* for literary pursuits. He seldom read books of any description, but poetry was his abhorrence—he could not endure it. He had, however, accomplished the task of wading entirely through the four ponderous volumes of Emmons's epic, "The Fredoniad," in the vain effort of finding his own name mentioned in connection with the events of the campaign of 1812–14. Instead of appreciating the merits of the work, he seemed most essentially disgusted with it, and even went so far as to pronounce the author "a humbug."

The lieutenant, aware of this unjust prejudice against the writer of the historical effusion, replied to the question as follows:

"Indeed, major, there is but little news in the city, excepting I heard that Mr. Emmons had issued a new edition of his poem."

"He has, has he?" said the major. "Well, Mr. ———, I'll tell you what it is, sir, that man Emmons I take to be a consummate ass, sir."

"Why, major," said the lieutenant, "do you know he has introduced you into this edition?"

"The devil he has! What, I should like to know, has he got to say about me?"

"Well, sir, he says,

> "'And there was Major C***s in a blaze of fire,
> *He* caused the British for to retire.'"

The major's face lighted up with a most gratified expression immediately, and he observed that, upon reflection, he believed "Emmons was a d—d sight more of a knave than fool."

The adroit lieutenant escaped without arrest, or even a reprimand.

POST-FUND CONTROVERSY.

Upon another occasion, when the major was stationed at a military post in the Northwest, he encountered a good deal of perplexity and annoyance in getting his accounts of the post fund adjusted to the satisfaction of the authorities at Washington, and a protracted correspondence between himself and the adjutant general ensued, in which a wide discrepancy of opinion was exhibited regarding the proper manner of disbursing and accounting for the money.

The major conceived that he had not in this discussion been treated with that amenity and respect which was due to his rank and services, and that the adjutant general had given expression to his views in an arbitrary and dictatorial manner altogether unjustifiable under the circumstances. This for a time seemed to give him considerable uneasiness, as he prided himself specially upon his reasoning powers. He talked about the matter constantly, and threatened to give the adjutant general a severe epistolary castigation for his want of courtesy. In his own words, he "intended to apply the *argumentum ad hominum* to him." That something very severe was intended by the use of this expression is quite certain, yet no one for a moment supposed he had the remotest idea of its signification.

After a few days had elapsed, the major asserted that he had written and forwarded such a caustic letter as would probably end the discussion, and forever afterward prevent the Washington officials from giving him any farther trouble.

About this time an inspector general visited the post, and was solicited by the major to examine the correspondence, and give his views upon the vexed and unsettled question at issue. He assented, read over the letters carefully, and gave it as his candid judgment that the adjutant general had decidedly the best of the argument.

The major was disappointed at this unexpected decision, but soon rallied, and exultingly said, "You may think so now, but you have not yet seen my last letter to the adjutant general; read that, if you please, sir, and then tell me what your opinion is." He then handed him another letter, officially headed, briefed, and signed, in strict conformity with the requirements of the regulations, which proved to be a tissue of acrimonious comments and harsh reflections upon the course pursued by the adjutant general, besides being highly indecorous and disrespectful not only to the officer to whom it was addressed, but to the general commanding the army.

After the inspector general had read it over attentively, the major asked him what he thought of it, to which the inspector replied, "The thing which astonishes me most in this matter is that you were not ordered in arrest the moment this document was received at the head-quarters of the army, for it is throughout eminently defiant and disrespectful toward your superior officers."

The major at once perceived that he had committed himself a little too far, as the inspector might think it his duty to make a note of the case and investigate it on his return to Washington, which would be likely to prove seriously embarrassing to him.

In view of this, he smilingly replied: "Now, my dear general, you certainly will allow us to have our little amusements and jokes at such a remote frontier station as this. It is very true I wrote that letter, but I never intended to send it to the War Department, and no such communication ever was sent; for you may be assured I have always entertained the most profound respect not only for the general-in-chief, but for the adjutant general."

PATENT SHAVING MACHINE.

At another time, while the major was stationed at New Orleans, he said he was ordered by General

Jackson to proceed to Havana for the purpose of transacting important business with the Spanish authorities. According to his own statement, he made the voyage in a war vessel, arrived safe in the harbor, and, on going ashore, to his surprise, found awaiting his coming the governor general, who at once ordered his luggage to the palace, and insisted upon his making that his home during his sojourn in the city. He would have preferred taking his quarters at a hotel, but it seemed the invitation was so pressing as to leave him no discretion; he was forced, *nolens volens*, to accept.

After having been ushered into a gorgeous suite of apartments, where numerous servants were placed at his command, he was informed that dinner would be served as soon as he had completed his toilet. As he had had no opportunity of shaving while at sea, and as his beard required trimming, he inquired of the major domo if there was a barber's shop near where he could be shaved expeditiously. He was informed that there was an establishment within the court of the palace where his beard could be taken off in something like two seconds, and was immediately conducted to a spacious apartment, where, to his astonishment, he found a steam shaving machine, to which was attached an enormous razor about four feet in length, with other dimensions corresponding. The first glance at this formidable instrument, he acknowledged, caused him to feel a little perturbation; but, after the engineer had explained to him the manner in which it operated, he willingly consented to try the novel invention, and seated himself in a huge arm-chair directly under the razor, when the operator let on the steam, the piston moved, and the ponderous instrument made two revolutions, each one of which took the beard from a side of his face as clean as if he had been a woman, and the operation was completed.

One of the officers asked if the process was attended with any pain or pulling of the beard. He replied, "Not the slightest; on the contrary, I assure you, gentlemen, that it was the most comfortable shave I ever had in my life. And I really think it would conduce to the interest of the service if it was adopted into the army, as a regiment might be marched up after the reveille, and every man be shaved before breakfast."

Another inquisitive individual remarked that he would imagine but few persons could resist the impulse of dodging when the huge razor came whirling around in close contact with their faces, and that they might thereby incur the risk of having their heads instead of their beards taken off. This unexpected query seemed to puzzle the old man a little, but his ready resources soon supplied him with an extrication from the dilemma in these words: "*How in h—l would a man dodge, I'd like to know, when his head was screwed into a vice?*"

A CAPITAL SHOT.

Of all the events in the history of this irrepressible devotee of fiction, none seemed to be preserved by him with more vivid and pleasant remembrances than his hunting adventures.

Although his contemporaries never knew him to fire a shot, yet he professed to have been in his younger days an ardent disciple of Nimrod; and he possessed an inexhaustible fund of sporting incident, from which illustrations of his marvelous achievements in that line were continually drawn.

The theatre of his exploits was often located in Florida, and, according to his own statement, the catalogue of his performances in that country embraced a vast aggregate of small game of all descriptions, besides a large number of bears and panthers, which had been slaughtered by him under every conceivable aspect of danger and excitement.

He was at one time asked if hunting such formidable animals as bears and panthers was not very exciting sport, to which he replied that he had found the sport rather interesting, except now and then the animals had taken it into their heads to hunt him, when the excitement became rather too intense to be agreeable.

In this connection he observed that a most remarkable circumstance once happened in his experience while hunting in East Florida.

Upon the occasion alluded to, it appeared that he had gone out to a large *hammock* a short distance from camp for the purpose of woodcock shooting, and, as bears were known to frequent that particular locality, he took the precaution, before entering the jungle, to load the right barrel of his fowling-piece with a ball, while the left barrel was charged with the smallest sized woodcock shot. Thus prepared, he sent his dogs into the hammock and followed closely behind. They beat the cover thoroughly for some time without finding game; at length, however, one of the dogs made a stanch point, and was soon backed up by the others. He advanced cautiously with both barrels cocked and ready for use, but nothing moved until he "*hied on*" the dogs, and they rushed forward, flushing the game suddenly upon both sides, and, under the impulse of nervous excitement, he made snap shots to the right and left in quick succession. In reference to the results, he said, "I was confident I saw the game fall to the ground simultaneously with the discharge of the gun, but was ignorant of what I had achieved until I recharged my fowling-piece and went to bag the game, when on the right hand I found a woodcock, and, to my surprise, on the left a huge bear was lying gasping in the agonies of death; but imagine my utter astonishment, gentlemen, when, upon examination, I discovered that I had killed the woodcock with the two-ounce bullet, and the bear with the woodcock shot!"

One of his auditors remarked that he was unable to comprehend how it was possible for a mustard-seed shot to go through the tough hide of a large bear, and penetrate to the vitals.

The old man was considerably exercised at this manifestation of incredulity, and, with a good deal of acerbity, responded: "Your remark would seem to imply that you doubt the truth of my statement, sir. I'll have you to know that I am not in the habit of exaggerating, sir; and I can inform you furthermore that the bear was not only killed with the smallest-sized bird-shot, but I took occasion to pace the distance at which I stood from the animal when I fired, and found it to be just ninety-seven yards."

The inquisitive individual said that, in making his queries, he disclaimed any intention of doubting the major's word, but that he was animated solely by a desire to obtain correct information; and added, "How could you see the bear at the distance you have named in a thicket so dense as to render it impossible to discern a man only twenty yards off?"

The major said he was ready to admit that neither a bear nor any other animal could be seen at the distance mentioned by looking directly through the tangled jungle of a Florida hammock, but, said he, "I'll explain to you how it was: I took him, as it were, upon the wing, while he exposed his body in the act of leaping over a palmetto-tree."

MUSK-RAT HUNTING.

One winter, when the major was stationed at a military post in a high northern latitude, he was ordered out with a detachment of soldiers in pursuit of a party of hostile Indians who had committed depredations upon the border settlements. In compliance with his instructions, he took the trail, and followed it rapidly for a long distance, expecting every day to overtake the marauders. This led them so far away from the fort into the wilderness that all their provisions were consumed long before they got back, and the party was forced to resort to every available expedient in order to obtain sustenance.

One evening, after they had killed and eaten their last pack animal, and devoured every thing else they could find that afforded the least nutriment, they bivouacked upon the border of a lake which was frozen over, and above the ice appeared a large number of musk-rat houses.

It is a fact in natural history, familiar almost to every one, that the musk-rat selects his tenement in shallow water, covering a soft morass difficult of access in the summer season. The structure is then erected, and projects in a semi-spherical form several feet above the water, with an entrance opening at the bottom, which enables the animals to enter unseen, and reach the part of their habitation that is above the surface; and here they pass the cold months of winter.

The Indians, understanding this fact perfectly, are in the habit of crawling up to the houses upon the ice, and suddenly driving a long, slender lance through them, which not unfrequently impales three or four animals. The grassy superstructure is then torn off, and the rats taken from the lance.

The major was cognizant of these facts, and when he saw the houses upon the lake near his bivouac, resolved to make an effort to replenish his larder therefrom. Accordingly, with a knife and pole, he soon improvised a lance, and cautiously upon the ice approaching one of the largest houses, he, with all his might, drove the instrument entirely through it, with the intention of killing as many of the unsuspecting victims as possible at the first thrust.

There were several officers present at the time he was relating the story, all anxiously listening to hear the sequel, which they were confident would prove one of the major's loftiest flights of fancy. He continued: "After my lance had passed through the house, there seemed to be quite a commotion among the occupants indicative of a successful coup; whereupon I called some of my men, who removed the superstructure, and disclosed to us the result; and now, gentlemen, I would like to have your opinions as to the number of musk-rats you think I found spitted upon that one lance."

Various random conjectures were given in compliance with the request, some placing their estimates at five or six, others going as high as eight or ten. All gave their opinions cheerfully excepting Captain H***e, who was a thorough sportsman, and had often endeavored to contrast his real, *bonâ fide* hunting exploits with the major's fancy sketches; but whenever he was the first to relate any circumstance connected with his own experience, the major either invariably had in reserve, or manufactured for the occasion, an exploit which threw him far into the background.

As may be imagined, this did not augment his regard for the old man, and he determined to have satisfaction the first opportunity that offered. When he was asked how many musk-rats he imagined they took from the house, he replied, "I really can not say."

"But," said the major, "you certainly can have no objections to hazarding a conjecture."

"Certainly not," said he. "If I were to make an estimate based upon the data you have presented to us, I should say about five hundred and fifty-nine."

This ironical response, uttered with the most imperturbable gravity, caused a general laugh among all present excepting the major, who for an instant manifested considerable displeasure, but soon rallied, and very urbanely asked the captain if he did not think that five hundred and fifty-nine musk-rats would be rather crowded upon a single lance. "Not at all," replied he; "and, if I were to be called upon to make another conjecture, I really believe I should be inclined to increase rather than diminish the number."

The major then, with a most quizzical expression of countenance, said, "Oh no, my dear fellow, you are very far from the mark this time. I assure you, upon my honor, sir, that after we had demolished the house, and exposed the lance to view, *there was not the first musk-rat upon it.*"

It is needless to add that the laugh was turned upon the captain.

AMERICAN SOVEREIGNTY.

Major C***s and Captain H***e were once present at a dinner-party, when an animated discussion arose as to which particular district of the United States possessed the greatest agricultural attractions, and much diversity of sentiment was manifested during the agitation of the question.

One of the party, who had traveled extensively, expressed the opinion that the Rock River Valley was more productive and beautiful than any he had seen. Another declared the "Missouri Bottoms" more favorable for tillage; and several other alluring localities were mentioned as being pre-eminently adapted to the requirements of husbandry, the advocates of each claiming precedence over the others.

Captain H***e said the district of country from which he hailed presented to the planters more advantageous conditions than any he had visited, and, as an evidence of this, mentioned some enormous yields of grain that had been grown there.

The major, who was a native of New England, observed that, with all deference to the judgment of his friend, Captain H***e, he was compelled to differ with him in his exalted estimate of the advantages of the locality of his nativity (a Southern state), as he believed the Connecticut River Valley, with its excellent soil, contiguity to railroads, close proximity to markets, with other local attractions, rendered this more desirable to the planter than any other section.

The captain remarked that he had never visited the Northeastern States, and could not, therefore, from personal observation, give direct evidence as to their tillable features, but he had always been under the impression that the climate of the New England States was so cold and inhospitable, the soil so thin and barren, and so covered with rocks, that it was next to impossible for a planter to subsist in that region. So notorious were these facts, that he had heard it asserted, hyperbolically, that the farmers of New England were in the habit of sharpening the noses of their sheep to enable them to pick out the straggling blades of grass that here and there forced their growth within the interstices of the rocks. He had also been told, but would not vouch for its literal truth, that they were compelled during the planting season to shoot their grain into the flinty soil with a cannon before it would take root.

Major C***s said he had never witnessed any agricultural operations with heavy ordnance in the Connecticut River Valley, and as there were but few rocks in that section, he hardly thought it necessary; "but," added he, "I have the advantage of Captain H***e in having, shortly after the Creek War, had occasion to travel through the district of country where he was nurtured, which afforded me a good opportunity to judge of its merits. While upon this journey, I stopped one night at a small log tavern in what was regarded as about the most fertile portion of the state, and during the evening a number of the neighboring farmers collected in the bar-room of the shanty, where, after indulging in sundry drinks of 'apple-jack,' they lit their cob-pipes and entered into conversation upon the subject of their crops, from which it appeared that the season had proved unusually favorable. One of them, who assumed quite a consequential bearing, and seemed to be the nabob of the party, with an air of decided self-gratulation, took occasion to observe that his plantation had yielded that season something like ten bushels of corn, five bushels of white beans, two loads of pumpkins, besides a fair average of other less important products, which would enable his family to subsist bounteously during the approaching winter.

"Another man remarked that, although he had not been so munificently blessed by Providence as his neighbor who had just spoken, yet he was happy to say that his garners were sufficiently stocked to afford a reasonable guarantee that his household would not suffer until the new crop came in. All the others of the coterie, in succession, enumerated the products of their plantations voluntarily, with the exception of one exceedingly tall, lank, haggard, and unwashed, but eminently independent-looking individual, who, seated upon a rude bench in a corner of the cabin, with his feet resting against the logs above his head, and with his scanty apparel hanging in shreds and tatters about his loosely-jointed and bony person, continued ejecting the smoke in dense clouds toward the roof, while his blear, smoke-stained, and expressionless optics were turned up in the same direction, indicative of a total indifference to, and abstraction from, the frivolities of all mundane concerns; and as he evinced no disposition to communicate to the assembly the results of his agricultural experience, one of the party said to him,

'Mister Jeemes, has you been a'croppin o'nt much this seezing?'

"The only response that the *distrait* individual condescended to make to this query was an emphatic ejaculation of the interrogative pronoun '*Which?*'

"The question was then repeated in the following form:

"'Mister Jeemes, has you *pre*-ducted a tollible pee-'urt chance o' crops this yere seezing?'

"This formal inquiry caused him slowly to depress the elevated line of his vision from his sky-scraping contemplations until it rested upon the interrogator, when, with an air of consequential importance, he responded,

"'I'll tell ye, gente*men*, how it war. Me an my ole woman (Mistress Jeemes), we put in a far sprinklin o' corn, an taters, an other truck, this yere seezing, an we 'low'd we mought *per*-duce right smart o' craps. But one mornin, jist afore sun-up, a ole he-bar he brake inter the corn-patch, an after browsin round considdible, and destructin a heap o' corn, he ups an makes sign for the house. Then Mistress Jeemes she 'low'd she'd skeer the varmint off; but when that consarned ole he-bar git sight o' her a cummin, he look sorter bothered, an he sot up, an he turn his head this-a-way and that-a-way, like he never seen a femenine woman afore. Then he slap his right paw on his heart, an he wink his eyes, an make sign with his left paw, jist like a human, fur Mistress Jeemes to come that-a-way; but Mistress Jeemes is tollible pee'urt, an she pre-farded not to 'cept that sort o' invite. Then that kantankeratious ole cuss he git mad, an he gist comes a *tar*in at my ole woman (Mistress Jeemes), who tuk the agur powerful that mornin, an it shock the strenth all outen 'er. An when she seen the critter a chargin on 'er, she clean guv up, an she git the hysteericks, an she cavorted, an she howled so *tre*mendus, that that ole he-bar he git skurt hisself wosser nur Mistress Jeemes, an he turn tail an brake fur the timber.

"'Then the dog-ond weeds they comes inter the corn, and choked it so like h—ll that we didn't gether narry 'n ear. We got shut o' corn. But, gente-*men*, we has *pre*-ducted a half bushel o' white beans this seezing, an we reckons as how, with what possums an other varmints we ken kotch, they'll do us till blackberry an percimmon time. Then white beans may jist go to thunder, an I don't keer a dod durn pickayune ef I never raise narry 'nuther nubbin.' Then, turning to me, he added, 'Stranger, will ye liquor?'"

CHAPTER II.

Education in the Army.—Any Thing in Reason.—Toledo Blade.—The Mess-table.—Hard Fare.—The handsomest Man.—The ugliest Man.—Old Beeswax.—Captain Forbes Britton.—His Patriotism illustrated.—Tally-ho!—Colonel T*****.—Perfect Police.—Colonel Morgan.—Bad Wine.—Short Pants.—Review and Inspection.—Colonel Ben. Bell.—Long Time between Drinks.—Come to stay.

EDUCATION IN THE ARMY.

THE officers of the army, previous to the Rebellion, were for the most part educated at the Military Academy, and it must be admitted that they were generally men of intelligence and culture, who entertained the most exalted conceptions of integrity and moral personal responsibility. These attributes were cherished and cultivated in the service with an *esprit du corps* truly commendable.

The numerous examples where these men, during the late war, were intrusted with the disbursement of vast sums of public money, and could, perhaps, had they been so disposed, have swindled the government and covered their tracks, as some others are said to have done, but who, instead of this, guarded the public interests with zealous care, and are now entirely dependent upon their limited pay for subsistence from month to month, most strikingly evinces the truth of what has been stated. Moreover, the appropriations made for Indians by the Congress of 1868, wherein army officers were required to witness the disbursements of civilian agents and certify to their accuracy, conclusively shows the confidence reposed in their integrity by our national Legislature.

But, alas for the good of the nation, the greater part of these pure and noble spirits laid down their lives, were crippled, or ruined their constitutions in the service of their country during the protracted continuance of the sanguinary Rebellion, so that but few of them now remain upon the active service list.

In the army, as with other classes of people, may probably be found an occasional representative of almost every conceivable type of humanity, but the characters I propose introducing to the reader's notice under the above heading must not be understood as having constituted any appreciable element in the old military establishment. Far from it. They have been selected specially on account of their anomalous idiosyncratic peculiarities, and as rare exceptions to the great mass of their comrades.

There were in the old establishment a few officers

who for gallant service had been promoted from the ranks, or who, through the influence of political friends, had obtained commissions, and I am happy to say that the majority of these were accomplished gentlemen, honorable men, and excellent officers; but it must be admitted that the education of some of them had been sadly neglected, and, indeed, one was occasionally found who entertained supreme contempt for any literature save the Army Regulations and the Tactics.

ANY THING IN REASON.

Upon a certain occasion, the precise date of which it is not necessary to mention, when a detachment of troops was about setting out from the Missouri River upon a long march across the Plains, and when the limited amount of transportation had rendered it necessary to reduce the officers' baggage to the minimum regulation allowance, the commanding officer, who was never known to consume much time over books, but seldom declined a pressing invitation to participate in a social glass, was applied to by a young subaltern just from West Point for permission to carry along a small package of books which he had provided himself with to while away the dull monotony of garrison life. The commander replied that he was always ready and willing to do any thing *in reason* for all his officers, but when transportation was so very limited, as in that particular instance, he did not feel authorized to encumber his wagons with such useless trumpery as books. He was very sorry to refuse, but it was impossible to comply with the request. The young gentleman went away greatly disappointed; and shortly afterward another officer, a particular friend of the commander, came up and made application to have a barrel of whisky transported in the wagons, which probably weighed ten times as much as the lieutenant's rejected little parcel of books. To this request he received the following reply:

"Certainly, lieutenant — certainly, sir; of course you can take along a barrel or two of whisky, or any thing else *in reason;* but the idea of lumbering up my wagons with books is most preposterous, and I must say that I am astonished at such an unreasonable request coming from any officer of my command."

This same officer was once presented with a sword by a friend, who assured him that it was a genuine specimen of the rare Toledo blade. He himself, it is true, had not a very clear conception of what was meant by this peculiar designation of the weapon, as will appear in the sequel; but he was confident that it was something better than the regulation sabre, and prized it highly. He often exhibited the present to his friends, who generally concurred with him in the discussion of its merits; but upon one occasion an officer, who professed to be a connoisseur in such matters, ventured to express a doubt as to the quality of the metal, remarking, at the same time, that but very few well-authenticated old Toledo or Damascus blades could now be found in any part of the world, and that probably the most of these were in the possession of rich Spanish hidalgos, who could not be induced to part with them at any price. Moreover, added he, the secret of manipulating the steel from which these rare specimens of art were produced was lost in the seventeenth century.

The proprietor of the weapon, at this attempt to cast a shadow of doubt upon its genuineness, became quite excited, and, jumping to his feet, exclaimed, in a loud tone of voice, "Spanish hidalgo—h—l! I tell you, sir, this is no counterfeit, but a real Simon pure Toledo blade; and I pledge you my word, sir, that a friend of old Toledo himself assured me that this was the very last sword the old man made before he took sick and died."

THE MESS-TABLE.

The —— regiment of —— was a superior organization, composed of excellent material, as every body connected with the old army establishment very well knew, and a great amount of arduous and meritorious service was performed by this regiment in the Indian country long before the breaking out of the rebellion Some of the officers made their marks in the Florida and Mexican campaigns; others distinguished themselves in prominent positions during the late war, while many others of them have been killed in battle or have died in the service of their country, so that now, alas! like some of the old war frigates, although the name, configuration, and model remain, the original material has almost entirely disappeared.

For some years after this regiment was first called into service the officers bore the reputation of being about the most hospitable, generous, and convivial set of good fellows in the army, and wherever they were quartered, either in barracks or in camp, there was certain to be gayety and festivity, and it may truly be said of them "that their latch-strings were never drawn in, and their purse-strings seldom ever tied." Indeed, they were noted for spending their money freely so long as it lasted; but some of them were so prodigal that they were rarely ever known to be in funds during the last half of a month, or, at all events, until the paymaster came around. The itinerant, gipsy-like locomotion that the troops on the frontier are continually subjected to, even in time of profound peace, precludes the possibility of their forming permanent household arrangements, as they can never tell to-day where they may be ordered to-morrow.

The regiments are usually so widely dispersed in small garrisons that it is difficult for them to establish any thing like regimental messes, such as are found in the English army. Yet at one station in Texas quite a respectable mess was formed, and a majority of the officers of the regiment joined it. But, unfortunately for the aspirations of some of the young subalterns, their finances had become so low, and they were so deeply involved in debt, as to be unable to pay the somewhat extravagant mess bills of the large association, and they were obliged to "rough it" by themselves in a more frugal manner, chiefly upon supplies obtained at low rates from the commissary. Indeed, I heard of one lieutenant (but I will not vouch for its literal authenticity) whose purse became so perfectly depleted at one time that for several weeks he was compelled to subsist upon rice alone. During this period of fasting it unfortunately so fell out that a friend of his from a neighboring post paid him a most unseasonable visit, not having the slightest previous conception or warning of the scanty fare he was destined to encounter.

The impoverished lieutenant put the best possible face upon the meagre condition of his larder, and received him with his usual urbane hospitality at about the hour for dinner, when it was too late, however, even had it been in his power, to have made much change in his bill of fare, except to borrow a little mustard from a brother officer, which he imagined might make the rice diet more palatable. The dinner was soon announced, the two friends seated themselves at the pine camp-table, when the host raised the solitary cover, and, in a very beseeching way, inquired of his guest if he should help him to rice. The latter, conceiving this dish to be the preliminary course, like "raw oysters on the half shell," replied, "No, I thank you; I never eat rice." "Then," said the lieutenant, not a little perplexed as to what he should do or say next, and as a desperate *dernier ressort* under the exceedingly embarrassing circumstances, "help yourself to mustard, for, if you can get any thing else in this ranch, you are smarter than I am."

The finances of the officers of the general mess were in a more flourishing condition, and their table was usually supplied with the best dishes the market afforded. Indeed, they sometimes even indulged in the luxury of a bottle of wine at dinner, and, in order to give zest to its flavor, and to contribute excitement against the heavy monotony of garrison life, they occasionally resorted to the stimulating influences of wagers, and other ingenious devices, involving results that invariably added to their stock of wine.

Some of these novel expedients were superlatively ludicrous. For example: Quite an animated and somewhat acrimonious discussion arose one day as to who was the handsomest man in the mess, and a wide diversity of opinion was evinced upon the subject, without any prospect of a satisfactory solution of the question, until some one suggested that it should be decided by disinterested ladies, who were acknowledged to be much more competent judges of such matters than men. As there were no ladies at the post, the greater part of the officers being in a state of "single blessedness," it was proposed, as the only alternative for feminine arbitration, that three camp-women should be sent for, and whoever they decided to be the best-looking of the party should be required to pay for a basket of Champagne.

This suggestion seemed to meet the approbation of the party, and there was a unanimous accord in submitting to the ordeal. The laundresses were immediately called in, the proposition fully explained to them, and they at once commenced a modest but scrutinizing examination of each officer at the table in succession. When this was finished they retired to a corner of the room, where they held a protracted consultation in whispers, after which they delegated one of their number, by the name of Nancy, to announce the result, which she did in the following words:

"Ef the gentlemen please, the ladies of the board has to report that they has examined all the officers of this 'ere mess, and they has 'rived to the 'nanimous 'clusion that Colonel M—— is the most *millenary*-looking man, but that Captain M—— is the most handsomest man."

This decision was quite unexpected, for Captain M—— was generally admitted to be by all odds the ugliest man in the mess. He, however, was not exactly that way of thinking himself, and believing the verdict to be perfectly fair and disinterested, he was highly elated at the compliment, and most cheerfully paid the wine.

A few days subsequent to this another discussion arose as to who was the ugliest man in the mess, and after arguing the question in all its possible bearings, they agreed to call another board of camp-women to decide it, and the unfortunate individual was to suffer the penalty of paying for another basket of Champagne. Accordingly the referees were called, consisting of Nancy, with two new members, who, after going through an inspection and consultation similar to the one before described, delegated one of their number to communicate the decision, which was as follows:

"The ladies of this 'ere board has 'cluded that Major G—— is the most *onmillenariest*-looking man, but that Captain M——" (the same officer that had been selected before) "is the most *ornariest* and the most *ugliest* man of the hull party."

This announcement so astounded M—— that he jumped from his seat at the table in a highly excited state, and demanded to know of the startled laundresses why they had presumed to make such an inconsistent decision, when only a few days before this, as they very well knew, he had been pronounced the handsomest man of the entire mess.

The exponent of the referees, with a timid, simpering smile, in the midst of peals of laughter from the other officers, undertook to explain the discrepancy in the two decisions. She said:

"The cap'n must consider that two new members has been detailed on this 'ere board; besides," she added, "the cap'n must also 'member that we ladies is priv'leged to change our 'pinions sometimes."

He was not satisfied with the explanation, and appealed from the decision, but a prompt and unanimous *viva voce* vote of the mess was adverse to him, and he was compelled to suffer the infliction of the penalty involved. He paid for the second basket of wine, but under protest, and with the emphatic declaration that he would not submit to any more inspections of the kind in future. Moreover, he even hinted that in his opinion the two adverse decisions had been brought about by the machinations of certain officers of the mess.

BOTTLED BEESWAX.

There was one officer of high rank in the regiment who seemed to possess an irresistible natural penchant for practical joking, and although, like most other men of similar tendencies, he was wonderfully sensitive upon the subject of being quizzed himself, he was continually seeking opportunities to run his rigs upon others.

As an illustration of this, upon a certain occasion a young officer, who had been acting assistant commissary for a short period, found himself in a state of perplexity by the return of his accounts from the Treasury Department, from which it appeared that he was deficient in a considerable amount of sugar that had been charged against him by the auditor. He was a good deal troubled upon the subject, and, having but little experience in such matters, applied to the facetious colonel for advice, acknowledging that he was deficient in the amount of sugar charged, but stating, at the same time, that he had on hand a large surplus of soap, and it seemed to him a very hard case that he should be held responsible for the loss of the sugar when the value of the soap was more than sufficient to cover it.

The colonel, with an air of the utmost apparent sincerity, assured him that it was really very unjust on the part of the auditor to impose upon him in that manner, but that, in his judgment, it was the easiest thing imaginable to set the matter right, and that possibly he might even have a small balance in his favor if he would only insert at the foot of the return as follows: "*Nota bene.*—For *sugar*, read *soap*."

I am not positive whether the return, corrected as suggested, was sent back to the auditor; my impression is that it was; but whether the alchemic powers of the laboratory of the Treasury Department have ever succeeded in transmuting the saponaceous constituent of the ration into the more saccharine component has never, that I am aware of, been promulgated.

The colonel did not always come off unscathed in his attempts to perpetrate jests upon others, as the reader will perceive from what follows:

The sutler at Fort ———, who was a kind and obliging man, but rather primitive and literal in his perceptions, was once about leaving the post for New Orleans, where he designed purchasing his annual supply of goods, and just before starting he called on the colonel to ascertain if he could do any thing for him in the city. The colonel replied that he did not at that moment think of any particular commissions for him to execute, but directly afterward something seemed to occur to his mind, and, giving a sly wink to some officers near, said to the sutler that he would confer an especial favor if he would purchase for him some bottled beeswax.

This being a commodity the sutler had never before heard of, he requested the colonel to enlighten him, and was informed that it was a very rare and expensive article, that could only be obtained in a few places, and that he would not be surprised if he failed to find it even in New Orleans. He was anxious to oblige the commanding officer, and assured him that he should spare no pains to obtain it if it was to be found in the city, and left.

Some of the young officers who were present and overheard the conversation, and for whose especial delectation the joke had been concocted, thought this a good opportunity to retaliate upon the colonel for some of the numerous sells he had inflicted upon them. Accordingly, one of them immediately wrote to the grocer in New Orleans with whom the sutler had been in the habit of trading, explained the whole matter to him, and requested his co-operation in carrying out the joke.

He entered into the plot willingly, melted some beeswax, which he poured into two bottles, and, covering them with dust and cobwebs, set them aside, and awaited the arrival of the sutler, who in due course of time made his appearance, and, after completing other purchases, inquired where such an article as bottled beeswax could be had.

The grocer informed him that fortunately he himself happened to have just two bottles left of the identical article he was in search of, which was probably all at that time in the market; but he added, for his information, that this was the last of a choice lot of great age, and of such value that he should be compelled to charge twenty dollars a bottle for it. Indeed, he said, he was by no means anxious to part with it at that price. The sutler at once closed the purchase, and willingly paid the amount demanded.

On his return to the fort he met a group of officers, who, in accordance with their usual custom, had collected around the landing to get the mail and learn the most recent news; and, after a little preliminary conversation, he informed the colonel that he had been so fortunate as to secure for him the last two bottles of beeswax in New Orleans.

"Beeswax! beeswax! what do you mean by beeswax?" said the astonished colonel. (It seemed he had for the instant forgotten the order.)

The outburst of laughter from the bevy of officers standing near, all of whom were in the secret, disclosed to the colonel the fact that the joke had recoiled upon himself, and also showed the sutler that there had been an attempt to sell him. He was not, therefore, in the most amiable mood when he replied,

"Why, sir, you know perfectly what I mean. I

mean the bottled beeswax you ordered, and which I paid forty dollars for, and which must be returned, sir."

The colonel did not, in the slightest degree, seem to appreciate the pith of the joke. On the contrary, he became highly incensed, and, although he said but little, looked daggers at the delighted group of officers around, not one of whom manifested the least sympathy for him, but kept up continual peals of laughter, each one of which was more uproarious than the preceding, until at length the colonel, unable to endure it longer, walked rapidly away in the direction of his quarters, gesticulating wrathfully, and muttering to himself expressions of displeasure, the few syllables that were caught indicating a not very complimentary application to the tormentors he was leaving behind. He, however, with a very bad grace, reimbursed the sutler; but it was quite severe upon him, as he was rather penurious in his disposition. The officers subsequently, when the colonel was not about, enjoyed many a hearty laugh over the joke; but it was never afterward considered safe to give utterance to the word "beeswax" in his presence, unless the offender wished to be ordered into exile at "Botany Bay" (the most disagreeable post occupied by the regiment).

Notwithstanding this, however, the not very euphonious sobriquet of "*Old Beeswax*," by universal acclamation, soon attached to the colonel, and it was a long time before it was forgotten.

CAPTAIN F. BRITTON.

Upon another occasion the colonel was inspecting the quartermaster's affairs at his post, and in passing through the store-houses and shops he observed two or three old horse-shoes lying around, which he picked up and handed to the quartermaster, Captain F. Britton, remarking that they should be carefully preserved for future use; and, at the same time, he added that a great deal might be saved to the government if quartermasters would take pains to collect all the old bits of iron, pieces of leather, rope, and even old broken axe, spade, and shovel handles, all of which might, at some time or other, be applied to useful purposes; and in this connection he endeavored to impress upon the captain the importance of exercising the most rigid economy in all his expenditures, never allowing public property of the slightest value to be misapplied, wasted, or lost. This, he informed him, was a duty he owed to his country, and he trusted that he would not again have occasion to call his attention to the subject.

Captain Britton was one of the most irrepressible wags in the army, and I verily believe he never allowed an opportunity to escape for the indulgence of his besetting propensity. The colonel, in this particular instance, may have been actuated by an honest zeal for the good of the service; very likely he was; but the captain was by no means certain of this; on the contrary, his incredulity led him to suspect that there might be under all this a deliberate covert design to "*sell*" him, and he had too high an estimate of his powers of discernment to be "*sold*" on such easy terms.

He believed he had as much regard as most officers for economy and the best interests of the service, but he most decidedly objected to being made a scavenger of. Accordingly, he listened patiently to all that was said upon the subject, and informed the colonel that the advice had made a deep impression upon his mind, and assuring him at the same time that he should endeavor to profit by his wise counsels. He then added that, if the colonel would pardon the liberty, he should like to ask a special favor of him touching the very subject in question, to which the officer replied, "Certainly, sir; as you seem so ready to adopt my suggestions, it will give me pleasure to grant you any favor in my power."

Not being exactly certain of his ground yet, and being fully resolved not to commit himself, he continued: "I trust, colonel, that you will not be offended or consider me disrespectful if I ask this semi-official favor?"

"Most assuredly not, sir. I have already said I was willing to do any thing in my power to serve you; so speak out frankly, and let me know what you want."

"Very well, then," said the captain, with the most solemn expression of countenance, and apparently moved almost to tears; "very well; my heart is bursting with devotion to our good Uncle Samuel; and if you, my dear colonel, will only oblige me by singing a few staves of 'Hail Columbia,' the 'Star-spangled Banner,' or some other patriotic song, I shall be forever indebted to you."

The colonel seemed quite indignant at the proposition, and exclaimed,

"What do you mean, sir? You know perfectly well I don't sing. Moreover, I regard your conduct as disrespectful—as disrespectful to your commanding officer, sir, and a violation of the ninety-ninth Article of War; and I'll have you to know that I'll take notice of it, sir."

To this the captain replied, "You will remember,

sir, that you expressly assured me you would not regard my request as disrespectful, and I disclaim any such intention. But really, colonel, if you would be so very kind as to sing a stave or two of some national air, I will cheerfully pitch the tune for you."

This touching appeal was in vain, however; the old gentleman didn't sing.

"*TALLY-HO.*"

Another very ludicrous incident occurred in my presence, wherein Captain Britton, and Captain Martin Scott, of coon notoriety, figured.

Captain Scott usually kept a pack of hounds, and would, as a special favor, occasionally take out his friends to participate in a deer or fox drive, but, upon these occasions, he invariably insisted that every one should conform strictly with the most approved rules of the chase. He was himself thoroughly posted in all the technicalities of sporting lore, and lost all respect for those persons who misapplied or ridiculed the proper use of sporting nomenclature. Thus he never failed to correct a man who called a line of geese "*a flock of geese,*" a bevy of quails "*a brood of quails,*" a herd of elk "*a gang of elk,*" etc. He was an uncompromising stickler for the correct and literal application of sporting language upon all occasions, but more especially when in the field.

This peculiarity of his was forcibly illustrated while our army of observation was lying at Corpus Christi in 1846. He proposed one morning that we should take his hounds, go out into a place called the Rincon, where the large jackass rabbits were abundant, and have a drive. Quite a number of officers joined the party, and we started out under the guidance of Captain Scott, who was the acknowledged master of the hunt.

On arriving upon the ground near where the game was supposed to be, the captain stationed the gentlemen around upon the skirts of an extensive chaparral thicket, and prepared to send in the dogs to drive out the rabbits. He gave his last instructions, and specially enjoined upon every one, on the instant a rabbit should make its appearance, to give the view halloo of *Tally-ho*." Now it so happened that among the officers engaged in the hunt was Captain F. Britton.

The hounds were unleashed and taken into the chaparral, and in a very few minutes they gave tongue most vociferously. All were waiting upon their posts with eager anxiety to catch the first glimpse of the game as it broke cover, when suddenly, near the position of Captain Britton, bounded out a mule, with some twenty dogs in full cry at her heels. At this instant of excitement we heard a prolonged cry from the stentorian lungs of Captain Britton of "*Sally whoa! Sally whoa! Sally whoa!*"

The appearance of the terrified mule, and the ludicrous metamorphosis of Captain Scott's "view halloo," turned the whole thing into a farce, which brought forth irresistible peals of laughter from every one in the party excepting Captain Scott. He did not smile; on the contrary, his face flushed, and assumed a most indignant expression. He called off his dogs, and, looking daggers at Captain Britton, went back to camp. Immediately after this he sent a challenge to Captain Britton, and it was with great difficulty that their friends could adjust the matter to his satisfaction without an exchange of shots.

PERFECT POLICE.

Colonel ———, before alluded to, was one of the best garrison commanders in service. His troops were well disciplined; the quarters, barracks, and grounds around the posts he commanded were at all times in perfect order; and he invariably held every one to a rigid accountability for any negligence in carrying out his police regulations. He required all public buildings to be frequently cleansed and whitewashed inside and out; and, as a hygienic measure, liberal use of chloride of lime and other disinfectants was enforced. He took especial pains to keep the parade-grounds well policed, and if he saw a quid of tobacco or the stump of a cigar lying in the walks, he has often been known to call out a police party of several men, with a hand-cart and shovels, to carry them off.

But if there was any one thing that was more repulsive to him than all others, it was a bedbug, and this was so great an abomination that he made ceaseless efforts to annihilate them from every fort that came under his command; and if by chance one of these "couch-pirates" ever invaded his dormitory, it disturbed his slumbers for a good while.

His extraordinary sensitiveness in this regard was well understood by our waggish friend Captain Britton, who at one post, which was regarded by the colonel as a model of police excellence, caused to be collected from some outside source a quantity of bedbugs sufficient to fill a seidlitz-powder box, which he covered and laid aside for a future purpose that will soon be disclosed.

Shortly after this, in discoursing upon his hobby, the colonel took occasion to remark that, for once in his life, he had succeeded in getting a military post into perfect order; that every part was in capital police, and all vermin had been eradicated.

Captain Britton heard the statement, and observed that it was very true the post was clean enough, but he thought there was a slight mistake in regard to the extermination of the vermin, as only a short time before he had seen, as he verily believed, at least a thousand bedbugs in his own quarters.

The colonel looked aghast at this startling assertion, and replied, "I really think you must be in error, captain, for I am quite confident there are but very few, if any, of those disgusting insects in the fort."

The officer assured him that he could not by any possibility be mistaken, as he had seen them with his own eyes.

The colonel then, in a highly excited and positive manner, again expressed his incredulity upon the subject, to which the captain responded:

"Very well, sir; if you doubt my words, perhaps you are willing to sustain your rather uncourteously expressed opinions by risking a little wine upon an investigation of the facts. I myself am so confident of the truth of what I have stated, that I will bet you a basket of Champagne I will capture and bring to this room a seidlitz-powder box full of bedbugs within fifteen minutes' time."

The wager was instantly accepted, and away went the captain to his quarters, returning within the time with his box, which he uncovered and abruptly placed upon the table directly under the colonel's face, while he was engaged in writing, remarking, as he did so, "I've caught them; there they are; and I've won the Champagne."

The violent shock that the old gentleman's high-strung nervous system received as an army of bugs, suddenly released from confinement, poured out over the sides of the box, and extended like skirmishers all over the table, may be more easily imagined than described.

The first effect was like that of a terrific nightmare, paralyzing him to such an extent that he was unable to move hand or foot; but as soon as he obtained a realizing sense of the situation, his powers of locomotion returned, and he jumped like lightning from his seat, upsetting the table in the sudden effort to escape, and scattering his tormentors all over the floor, which only served to increase his perturbation; and, as he bolted for the door, he called out in the most imploring tone, "Take them away! take them away! I'll pay the wine."

CHEAP WINE.

The parsimonious proclivities of this officer were exhibited in a rather unenviable light upon a certain occasion when he gave a dinner-party to Colonel Morgan, who, by-the-by, was probably one of the most absent-minded and "distrait" men that ever lived.

The colonel was not much addicted to giving dinners, and when he did, the "carte" was so meagre, and the wine of such inferior quality, that his entertainments were by no means popular with the officers. The dinner in compliment to Colonel Morgan, above alluded to, was prolonged to an unusual hour, and a good deal of the colonel's cheap wine was consumed during the protracted sitting.

On the following morning, Colonel Morgan, after a very restless night, during which the little sleep he was enabled to get was continually disturbed by semi-somnolent glimpses of his ancestors and other spectral concomitants of indigestion and nightmare, found himself suffering from an excruciating headache, which continued all the morning, making him feel generally miserable and out of humor. While in this condition he happened to meet his host of the previous evening, who very blandly passed the salutations of the morning with him, and anxiously inquired as to the state of his health.

It did not, it seems, for the instant occur to him where or by whom he had been entertained, and in the most ingenuous manner imaginable he replied, "The fact is, my dear sir, that I dined out somewhere yesterday, and they gave me some villainous trash which they called wine, and it has played the very devil with me, sir. My head feels like a mountain with the fires of a volcano raging within."

Notwithstanding his oblivious proclivities, Colonel Morgan was a most conscientious, excellent officer, and a high-toned, honorable gentleman, whom all his acquaintances held in the highest admiration.

So far as his own history was concerned very little was known upon the subject, as he always maintained an absolute silence in regard to his early life. Indeed, it was generally understood that he himself was totally ignorant of every thing relating to his origin. He only knew that from his earliest recollection he had been carefully watched over and abundantly provided for through the agency of some mysterious source, which he was unable to discover to the day of his death. The prevailing opinion among his brother officers was that he, at some period before he entered the service, had been crossed in an *affaire du cœur.* However this may have been, he remained a bachelor all his days, and never seemed particularly fond of ladies' society.

These circumstances may have operated so powerfully upon his proud, sensitive nature as to have exercised a controlling influence in producing the idiosyncrasies in his character. His mental ramblings were sometimes much more devious than at others, although they never amounted to any thing like monomania.

He was a strict disciplinarian and a capital drill officer; yet occasionally, when one of his "distrait" fits would strike him, he made some most ludicrous mistakes. For example: while he was drilling, one afternoon, he became so much absorbed in a deep-brown study that he continued to march the battalion back and forth until after dark, without the slightest apparent conception of what he was about, until the adjutant asked him if he should not send for some lanterns to enable him to post the markers properly. He looked up in bewilderment, exclaiming, "Tut! tut! tut! well, now, I declare, it is dark, sure enough. Dismiss the battalion, Mr. Adjutant;" and away he went toward his quarters, muttering to himself, "Tut! tut! tut!"

The colonel was an enthusiastic sportsman, and prided himself on his shooting.

Once, while he was standing in front of his regiment in command of a dress-parade, and at the time when the band was "beating off," a *line* of wild geese flying unusually low passed directly over him. Under the impulse of the moment, he instantly raised his sword to his shoulder and aimed at them, as if he had a gun in hand; but, discovering the mistake, he dropped the sword, remarking as he did so, "I've lost a splendid shot. If I had my gun I believe I could bag two of those birds—I do, indeed; and possibly I could have killed three."

Hearing some smothered laughing among the men, he instantly recovered his composure, and called out, "Silence in the ranks! Did you never see a flock of wild geese before?"

He could never remember the names of his soldiers, but acquired the habit of identifying and designating them by certain significant acts or incidents connected with their service. As, for instance, in aligning the battalion on parade, he would often call out from the right to men on the extreme left, "Dress up there, you man that drove team on Rum River. Dress back a little, you man that deserted from Prairie du Chien. Steady there, you man who stole the powder and shot from the sutler."

At one time, while he was staying at the old

American Hotel in New York, he went to his room (as he supposed) to dress for dinner, but by some blunder he managed to get into another man's apartment, and, opening the wardrobe, took out a pair of pantaloons of a different color from any he possessed, put them on, and started for the dining-room.

As he was a very tall man, while the proprietor of the pants he had dressed himself in was an uncommonly short individual, he was *sans culotte* from about the region of the knees downward, so that, as the reader may imagine, in parading with his erect, dignified carriage across the large dining-hall, filled with ladies and gentlemen, his singular appearance excited no little amusement for the assembled guests, and it was not until the host sent a waiter to notify him of the outré exhibition he was making that he had the least idea of the cause of the merriment. Then casting his eyes down to his legs, he indignantly remarked, "Tut! tut! tut! that rascally tailor has made my pants too short, or else they have shrunk most confoundedly;" and, turning round, he marched rapidly off, soliloquizing anathemas at New York tailors.

Upon another occasion, while at Fort ———, he dressed himself in full uniform, and had his horse completely caparisoned and brought out to ride at a review and inspection of his command.

Previous to his getting into the saddle, however, by some accident the stirrups had become disarranged in such a manner that one of them was drawn up and buckled near the saddle-skirt, and the other was let down to the extremity of the strap. Not observing the incongruity, he at once mounted, and placed the right foot in the short stirrup, with the leg elevated and bent so as to form an acute angle, with the knee at the apex, while the left leg was extended to its full length in order to reach the depressed position of the stirrup on the opposite side.

In this unsymmetrical posture he galloped out in front of the battalion, and, after acknowledging the salute of the troops, rode around the line, his excessively comical appearance causing much suppressed merriment among the men. But the most ludicrous part of the performance occurred after the review had ended and the battalion was wheeled into column of companies for inspection.

The colonel then rode to the head of the column, called an orderly to hold his horse, and dismounted. But, as strange as it may appear, instead of straightening out his right leg when he reached the ground, the limb, as if in a cataleptic state, continued at about the same deflection from a right line that it had assumed while upon the horse; and, what is still more surprising, when the colonel commenced to walk, his leg remained rigidly doubled up, so that he was obliged to dip his head very low every time he put his right foot to the ground.

The officers and men tried their best to preserve gravity and order, but it was no easy matter. At the first step he took irresistible smiles gathered upon the faces of the officers, and suppressed titterings ran along the entire column; but as the old veteran began to move faster, with his head bobbing up and down at every step, and crying out, at the top of his voice, "*Silence in the ranks!*" the ludicrous effect preponderated over every other consideration. It was more than the best disciplined troops on earth could endure with gravity, and, as might have been anticipated, a simultaneous thundering peal of uproarious laughter burst from the whole command like an avalanche upon the ears of the astounded colonel, who, in absolute unconsciousness of the cause of the insubordinate proceedings, became intensely exasperated, furiously swinging his sword around, and vociferously screaming "*Silence! silence! silence!*"

At the same time, his pace along the column be-

"SILENCE IN THE RANKS!"

came more and more accelerated, and the dipping of his head correspondingly more rapid, which of course only served to augment the drollery of the spectacle, and increase the merriment and disorder in the ranks, until it finally reached such a pitch that the adjutant, in the midst of convulsions of laughter, informed him what had occasioned it.

The colonel, notwithstanding he was something of a martinet, could appreciate a good joke as well as most men, even when he was himself the subject of it. And when he cast his eyes down toward his nether appendages, and comprehended the comical figure he had been cutting, he at once straightened up and joined in the laugh, exclaiming, "Tut! tut! tut! Well, now, I declare, that was funny—very funny indeed! Ha! ha! ha!"

COLONEL BEN. BELL.

Colonel Bell, when I first met him, had nearly reached the patriarchal longevity of threescore and ten, yet he was then one of the best preserved and most genial and convivial spirits I ever encountered.

His well-proportioned, lithe, and muscular frame had been fully developed and matured by many years' active service on the distant Indian frontier, where the healthful and invigorating atmosphere of the mountains and plains served to perpetuate and augment his natural buoyancy of temperament to a degree that seemed to set at defiance the sedative and enervating influences of age.

Many and many a time, after marching all day

in severe storms, had he bivouacked upon the wet ground, without any shelter save his poncho and blanket; and I have, upon more than one occasion, known him, after riding sixty or seventy miles on horseback, to dance all night at a "fandango," and appear as fresh the next morning as if nothing unusual had occurred.

He was by no means a debauchee or tippler, but, at the same time, he was fond of good wine, and did not object to an occasional glass of grog; and, after imbibing a moderate quantity with a good dinner, he possessed an inexhaustible fund of racy anecdotes, which he could relate with better effect than any man I ever knew.

His entire military life had been passed on the border, and only at rare intervals of time had he been able to visit the Eastern cities, so that it could not, of course, be expected that he should be well posted in the capricious and vacillating absurdities of fashion, or the equally mutable conventionalities of dinner-table etiquette.

He was so fortunate upon one occasion as to obtain a leave of absence, and, while making a short sojourn in one of the cities in New England, where the most inflexible rules of propriety were strictly enforced in all social intercourse, and where it was looked upon as rude and unbecoming at dinner-table to laugh aloud or speak above a certain modulated tone of voice, and an unpardonable breach of decorum to perpetrate a bon-mot or take more than two or three glasses of wine—while in this somewhat puritanical city he was honored with an invitation to dine with several gentlemen at the mansion of the nabob of the place.

At the appointed hour he was ushered into the magnificent dining-room, which was brilliantly illumined with numerous jets of gas evolved from gorgeous French chandeliers, and the huge mahogany table was groaning under the weight of a costly service of Sèvres china, embellished with sparkling Bohemian cut-glasses of the most exquisite design and finish, while soup, vegetable, and sundry other dishes, of massive embossed silver and gold, showed that every thing which money could contribute to give brilliancy and effect to the banquet had been unsparingly bestowed by the liberal host.

But this munificent display of luxury and wealth did not seem to be appreciated by the borderer, or to create much more impression upon him than his pine camp-table, garnished with tin plates and cups, would have done.

When the dinner was announced, the colonel seated himself *sans ceremonie* among the other guests, as perfectly self-possessed and as much without *mauvaise honte* as a professional diner-out would have been. It is to be remarked, however, that he would have preferred, before sitting down, in accordance with his usual custom, to have taken an "appetizer" in the form of a whisky cocktail; but as no one set him the example, he reluctantly dispensed with this preliminary, and took his raw oysters on the half-shell, after which the host passed the sherry to him, and he eagerly swallowed a few drops of it from a miniature glass.

The soup and fish courses were then introduced, and disposed of with all due ceremony; but, greatly to the colonel's disgust, the wine remained stationary, and the company, with the exception of a few subdued whispers, was as mute and grave as a Quaker meeting.

After this followed the meat course, and the most piquant *entrées*, all of which passed off strictly *en règle;* but still the bottle did not circulate.

Then came the choicest game, served in the most approved style, unaccompanied, however, with an intimation that another glass of wine would give more zest to its flavor, and the spirits of the party seemed, if possible, to wax more lugubrious and heavy than before, until at length the colonel, having exhausted all his powers in curbing his patience, took the liberty of asking the host if he had ever heard of the ghost that once appeared to some of the army officers in New Mexico.

He replied that he had never heard of the circumstance before, and begged the colonel to relate it. Others of the party expressed their total disbelief in such spiritual manifestations, but all united in urging the colonel to tell the story, which he did in the following language:

"During the Mexican War, as you will doubtless remember, gentlemen, our government sent out troops to take possession of the Territory of New Mexico. The detachment was composed of volunteers and regulars, to the latter contingent of which I had the honor to belong.

"We marched from Fort Leavenworth, on the Missouri River, and our track crossed the Plains, where there was but little to interest or divert our minds from the monotonous and toilsome duties which necessarily devolved upon us.

"Nevertheless, many of the officers were jolly, convivial spirits, whose effervescent flow of good-humor could not be dampened by the most disheartening combination of adverse influences, and they resorted to various ingenious expedients to while away their few leisure hours. Some of them stalked the buffalo or antelope, and amused themselves in innocent field-sports, while others became addicted to the more demoralizing pastime of cards; and while the sutler's supply of liquor held out, this customary concomitant stimulus of gaming was freely imbibed; but long before the march terminated it was seldom that an officer could get any liquor for love or money, and when he did, it came in the form of a prescription from the medical officers, the most of whom had seen service, and were not easily humbugged by 'old soldiers.'

"In spite of this restriction, however, they kept up their spirits wonderfully, the gaming *coterie* especially, which continued to hold its nightly meetings without a drop of whisky.

"They were not, it must be acknowledged, quite as merry as when the 'flowing bowl' circulated freely, as they were all good 'trenchermen;' but the stimulus of betting served to divert their minds from disagreeable duties, and they played on night after night. One dark and dismal night, when their sitting had been prolonged into the small hours of morning, a death-like silence pervaded the entire camp, and all were becoming sleepy and wearied, when suddenly they were startled by the loud explosion of a terrific clap of thunder which burst directly over their heads, and reverberated through the sky like the salvo from a huge park of heavy ordnance, and immediately great drops of rain, driven before a violent tempest, came pattering like buckshot against the tent. The lightning flashed vividly from every point in the heavens, the rain poured down in torrents, and all the elements seemed in an angry mood to conspire in producing the greatest possible chaos.

"The cards were instantly dropped upon the table, and the astounded votaries of gaming sat gazing upon each other in consternation and terror, until, during a brief interval in the lightning flashes, the canvas door of the tent, as if by a magic hand, was slowly and noiselessly raised, and a tall, wan, and cadaverous figure, draped from head to foot in a flowing white robe, seemed to rise out of the earth and fill the opening, and, slowly raising his bloodless and corpse-like arm, he deliberately pointed his long, bony forefinger at the cards upon the table. Revolving his glassy eyes within their cavernous orbits, and directing them reproachfully upon each one of the trembling gamesters in succession, while the tears coursed down the deep furrows of his pale and emaciated visage, he in a most sepulchral and lugubrious intonation of voice gave utterance to speech—yes, gentlemen, this frightful spectre spoke."

Then, appearing to be so much paralyzed by the effect of his own narration that he could proceed no further, he wiped his eyes, and was silent. After the gloom cast over his auditors had become partially dispelled, one of them ventured to inquire if it was really true that the apparition spoke.

"Certainly," replied the colonel; "his utterance was as distinct and emphatic as mine at this moment."

Another inquisitive gentleman asked if he had preserved a distinct remembrance of the purport of the language that issued from the mouth of the phantom.

"Ah! yes," answered he, with a most solemn expression of countenance, "I recollect it but too well—ay, too well, gentlemen; and if I were permitted to live a thousand years I should not be able to eradicate it from my memory."

"Pray, then," said they all (their curiosity now wrought up to the highest point), "tell us what the ghost said."

Thus importuned, the colonel, with the greatest apparent reluctance, replied, "Very well, gentlemen,

A LONG TIME BETWEEN DRINKS.

if you will insist upon my repeating the words that were uttered upon that solemn occasion, you must be responsible for the consequences."

Then, with the deepest intonation of his naturally heavy bass voice, he added, "The ghost said, gentlemen, the ghost said, '*It's a monstrous long time between drinks!*'"

A simultaneous burst of uproarious laughter followed the ludicrous termination of the facetious colonel's story, and it is needless to add that the wine circulated much more freely afterward.

On the arrival of the Army of Occupation in New Mexico our hero was assigned to the command of the garrison at Sante Fé, in which capacity he was required to exercise both civil and military functions. This necessarily brought him in frequent contact with the native Mexicans, whose Spanish dialect he had no more knowledge of than they had of the idiom of the Anglo-Saxon, and all official intercourse had to be conducted through the medium of interpreters.

It so happened upon one occasion, when the interpreter was absent, that a Mexican woman called to see the "*Commandante*" on business, and on entering the office she, with a very graceful obeisance, politely accosted him with the customary salutation of "*Comment esta usted, signor?*" (How are you to-day, sir?) which, as near as the colonel could make out, signified, "I've come to stay, sir."

He was not a little astonished at the unceremonious manner in which the signora declared her intentions, and was very considerably embarrassed at first; but, after a moment's reflection, he concluded

NO INTENDE, SEÑOR.

to let her remain until the interpreter returned. Accordingly, putting the best face he could upon it, he said, "Come to stay, have you, old lady? Very well, then, sit down, and make yourself at home."

Then he added, soliloquizing, "Devil of a fix I'm getting into now, sure enough."

The woman, not having the remotest conception as to the import of what the colonel was talking about, remarked, "*No intende, señor*" (I don't understand you, sir).

"Very well," replied the colonel. "If you *no intended* to stay, what in the devil did you come here for?"

CHAPTER III.

Lieutenant Derby.—General Up-to-snuff.—Reciprocating Hospitalities.—Ball at Detroit.—Mess-banquet at London.—An English Officer's Opinion of the American Army.—Martial Wooing.—Antidote for Inebriation.

LIEUTENANT DERBY.

ALAS! poor Derby. Verily it must be admitted that he was one of the most clever, genial, and amusing spirits of his day.

Overflowing with a redundancy of original, pungent wit, and effervescent, spicy humor, and possessing a prurient, constantly teasing, and insatiable penchant for the perpetration of keen, incisive raillery, at the risk even of incurring the displeasure of his best friends, it is not surprising that the memory of this incorrigible humorist should often be revived in the minds of those who entertain a lively appreciation for vivacious burlesque and sparkling bonmots.

Many of Derby's droll stories have been told by himself, with inimitable gusto, in Phenixiana and in other publications, but some of his happiest hits are only known to his associates.

If the following has ever before appeared in print, I have not seen it:

Some years previous to his death, this officer was engaged in improving the navigation of the Mississippi River, with his head-quarters at New Orleans.

Shortly after this he visited Nahant for his health, and took lodgings at the principal hotel of that fashionable watering-place, where he encountered a large number of pleasure and health seekers from various parts of the country, all of whom were strangers to him. It was in vain that he searched the register for familiar names—not a single one could he discover among them all.

He wandered about over the grounds by himself during the entire day, and, although crowds of people met him at every turn, yet he did not recognize a face.

Among the guests at the hotel was a convocation of dentists, who had assembled there for the purpose of discussing and deliberating upon matters pertaining to the general interests of their profession.

Some of these people, observing Derby continually alone, and apparently without acquaintances, imagined that possibly he might be a brother dentist, but nothing positive was known concerning him until one individual took the responsibility of addressing him, and begged to inquire if he had the honor of speaking to a member of the dental fraternity; to which Derby, with the most bland politeness, replied that, although he might not be regarded as having been regularly inducted into the profession according to the ordinary acceptation of the term, yet he ventured to assert most emphatically, and without the slightest fear of contradiction, that he had but a short time before, with a steam-engine, performed a dental exploit of greater magnitude than had ever before been achieved. This astounding declaration, announced with so much confidence, was soon bruited about among the members of the convention, and intense curiosity was manifested by them to learn who the distinguished stranger was, as well as to ascertain the character and details of the great operation he had performed. The application of steam to purposes of their art was novel in the extreme, and the subject produced an animated discussion among themselves, during which various random conjectures were hazarded regarding Derby's identity, nationality, etc. Some surmised that he might be Dr. Evans, the great Parisian operator, while others thought he looked more like an eminent London dental surgeon; but nothing satisfactory was arrived at, and they finally resolved to appoint a committee to wait upon him and offer him a seat in the convention, hoping that he might thereby be induced to give an account of the wonderful achievement he had alluded to. Accordingly, the invitation was extended to him, to which he responded that he entertained a lively appreciation of the honor they had conferred upon him, but, as he was on the eve of departure, it would be impossible to avail himself of it; if, however, as they stated, the convention deemed it important to the interests of science and for the relief of suffering humanity that he should disclose to them what he had accomplished in the dental line, he should no longer feel at liberty to hesitate in complying with their request. They assured him that the gentlemen present were unanimous in the opinion that the value to the dentistic art of such a contribution as he had indicated could not well be overestimated, and they were quite confident the convention would appreciate it accordingly; whereupon he authorized them to communicate to the association they represented the assurances of his most distinguished consideration, with the announcement of the fact "that he had but a short time before accomplished the exceedingly difficult operation of extracting the huge snags from the mouth of the great Mississippi."

GENERAL UP-TO-SNUFF.

It was while Derby remained in New Orleans that Walker and other filibusters were recruiting men for the Nicaragua War.

As the former was walking through Canal Street, one day, in "undress" uniform, he was accosted by a stranger, evidently from the country, who inquired if he was enlisting soldiers for the Nicaragua campaign. He replied that he was not just then engaged upon that service, but added (pointing to a portly lieutenant of the regular army who happened to be passing in full uniform), "Do you see that officer across the street?" "Yes," replied he. "Very well," said the irrepressible wag; "that man you see over there is the distinguished General Up-to-snuff. *He* is recruiting for Nicaragua."

The lieutenant's name was not Up-to-snuff, but U******ff, which really sounded something like the ludicrous metamorphosis that Derby had applied to it, and with those who knew the peculiarities of the man, the application might be regarded as appropriate. He was quite a ponderous individual, with an erect and somewhat dignified bearing, but excessively inflated and pompous in his deportment. Moreover, he had an inexhaustible stock of "modest as-

GENERAL UP-TO-SNUFF.

surance," and seemed to be fully persuaded that he possessed about all the information that was of any value; at all events, if there was any thing he did not understand, he was never known to admit it. Moreover, he was eminently sensitive upon the subject of practical jokes when there was a personal application to himself, all of which was fully understood and appreciated by Derby. Upon the occasion referred to, U******ff's coat was buttoned up so close around his short neck that it was with difficulty he could turn his head; his belt was drawn so tight around the waist that the adipose tissue was forced out until it almost united outside; and his huge sabre, dangling from the extremities of the straps, thumped and clattered upon the sidewalk as he, with head erect and eyes directed square to the front, strutted along, so that a stranger might easily have mistaken him for a man of some consequence.

As may be imagined, he was not only greatly amazed, but immensely enraged, when the aspiring tyro who had followed him addressed him as "*General Up-to-snuff*," and at the same time expressed a desire to enlist for the Nicaragua War; and he turned suddenly round upon the innocent victim with a most diabolical expression of countenance, and in a thundering tone of voice said, "What do you mean, you scoundrel, by calling me General Up-to-snuff? What do you mean, I say, sir?" Not receiving any answer, he continued, "I believe you have been put up to this thing. Who told you I was General Up-to-snuff, I'd like to know, sir?"

The young man, trembling with apprehension at the infuriated manner of the lieutenant, very timidly replied, "That man over there told me so, sir," pointing at the same time to Derby, who was still in sight, and very likely waiting to witness the result of the interview.

"He did, did he, sir? Very well, sir; you can give my compliments to 'that man *over there*,' and inform him from me, sir, that he is laboring under a slight hallucination; that I am not General *Up-to-snuff;* no, sir, not by a devilish sight, sir! And you can tell him, furthermore, sir, that my opinion of him is that he had better attend to his own business, a devilish sight, sir! Tell him that, sir!" And away he stalked, soliloquizing and gesticulating most vehemently.

RECIPROCATING HOSPITALITIES.

It will be remembered that the threatened invasion of Canada in 1838, by lawless denizens of the United States calling themselves "Patriots," excited, for a time, great commotion among her majesty's loyal subjects along the boundary-line, and that quite a large force of regular troops was dispatched from England to suppress the émeute.

During these troubles my regiment was ordered to the Canadian border, and the head-quarters located at Detroit. At this time there was a regiment of foot and a battalion of artillery posted at London, Canada West, besides several detachments of English troops at other places near us.

Frequent interchanges of visits between our officers and those of the English garrisons, together with the proverbially kind and generous hospitality of the citizens of Detroit, rendered our brief sojourn in this delightful city most agreeable, after having roughed it for many previous years in the wilds of the remote West.

We found many of the British officers intelligent, educated, and companionable, and totally devoid of that arrogant superciliousness and affectation of indifference or contempt for every thing not English which so pre-eminently characterizes some of their compatriots who are occasionally met with in the United States.

The hospitalities we extended to these gentlemen were reciprocated most cordially, and the intercourse seemed to afford them fully as much pleasure as it did ourselves.

BALL AT DETROIT.

In these latter days of festal conviviality, before the humanitarian disciples of temperance had effected any appreciable abatement in the aggregate of alcoholic and vinous fluids consumed, and at a period when it was looked upon as rather creditable than otherwise to bear the reputation of a "valiant trencherman," it is not surprising that gentlemen should occasionally have overstepped the bounds of discretion, and imbibed more than they could discreetly carry. Upon a certain occasion (at Christmas, I think it was) we gave a large ball at the Michigan Exchange Hotel, and sent invitations to the officers at London, several of whom honored us with their presence, and seemed to enjoy vastly the society of the beautiful and accomplished ladies of Detroit, and the dancing was continued until a late hour.

The following day we entertained our English guests with a sumptuous dinner, and during the repast plied them bountifully with Champagne and other choice wines, which that prince of landlords, Mr. Dibble, knew so well how to provide, while the piquant entrées, extending through many different courses, served to protract our sitting into the "small hours" of morning, when our somewhat bacchanalian banquet was concluded over a huge bowl of smoking-hot whisky-punch.

Our guests did ample justice to the good cheer we set before them, and the majority of them were not perceptibly damaged by it, but it must be admitted that a few were not quite as firm upon their "pins" when they rose from the table as before they sat down. Indeed, if my memory serves me correctly, I am under the impression that I saw the servants carrying off two or three who were too weak in the joints to stand without assistance.

I have retained a most vivid recollection of one scarred, veteran old major, who was wounded at Waterloo, and who, if he possessed no other assets, might doubtless have bequeathed to his heirs a long catalogue of sanguinary battles in which he had figured, besides supplementing a codicil embracing numerous severely-contested bacchanalian bouts over the mess-table.

This officer appeared to think the reputation of the service he represented would be seriously damaged if any of our officers drank deeper or more frequently than he, therefore he never declined taking wine with any one at table who nodded to him.

The result was, the ceremony, repeated so often, began to produce a perceptible effect upon him; nevertheless the old warrior continued to stand up valiantly for the maintenance of his convivial nationality, and drank off bumper after bumper, remarking, every time he was asked to "renew the assurances," "Certainly, certainly, sir, with the greatest pleasure," when he swallowed the wine in a twinkling, and invariably added, in semi-soliloquy, instantly afterward, "I'm none of your one-bottle men; I can carry under my jacket three bottles any day."

For several hours, during which the wines circulated freely, the major held his own tolerably well; but when the strong whisky-punch came on, he partook of it so bountifully that it completely deranged his powers of articulation. He then held his glass very unsteadily, occasionally sipping from it, but spilling more than he drank, while he kept up a maudlin soliloquy something like the following:

"I'm—ah—three-bottle man; I'm none of yer (hic) one-bottle men, sir. I've no r'gard for a (hic) one-bottle man. *Blaarst* a (hic) one-bottle man, say I."

He seemed fully sensible of the fact that Captain "*Barleycorn*" was the victor in this engagement, and, turning toward the presiding officer, magnanimously acknowledged his defeat in the following rather ambiguous language:

"Miss'r Pres'dent—I say, Miss'r Pres'dent [loud cries of 'hear! hear!! hear!!!'], that blaarsted Yankee (hic) punch has got into my head a li-li-lil-bit, and I b'lieve, Miss'r (hic) Pres'dent, that I'm sli-sli-sli'ly ex-tos-ificated. I mean to remark (hic), Miss'r Pres'dent, that Major ———, of her majesty's ro-o-y-al —th foot, is most ro-o-o-yally drunk. But, Miss'r Pres'dent, if you Yankee os-si-fers 'll hon-er-er-er us with a (hic) visit at Lon-ern, we'll 'cip-er-cate. We'll make ye all-ze drunk-ze-ze lords, Miss'r Pres'dent."

MESS-BANQUET AT LONDON.

Our gayeties terminated that night. The English officers returned home on the following day, and in the course of a few weeks we were all invited to attend a grand banquet to be given by the mess of her majesty's —th foot at London.

As it was impossible for us all to leave, we sent a delegation of three officers to represent us. These were Captain H**e, and Lieutenants D**s and S*******n, who were convivial men, fond of good dinners, and who gladly availed themselves of this opportunity for a pleasant excursion.

En route they discussed the probable order of the

programme in which they would be expected to enact a part, and delegated Captain H**e (the ranking officer) to respond to any sentiment that might be proposed during the dinner complimentary to our nation or army.

In accordance therewith, the captain set his wits at work, and in a short time concocted quite a clever and appropriate little speech, wherein he exhibited the symbolic types of the two nationalities (the lion and eagle) affiliating and associating together in perfect harmony and good will, and showed by the most conclusive reasoning the great benefits that would mutually ensue from such friendship and alliance.

It was really a very creditable effort, and would doubtless have produced a happy effect had it been delivered intact; but, unfortunately for the captain's elocutionary fame, before the time arrived for him to respond at the fête, his brain had become so much obfuscated by the numerous potations which civility had obliged him to take, that he had forgotten nearly every word of his speech. He only retained a vague remembrance that the lion and eagle occupied prominent positions in it, and, when called upon, he with difficulty rose from his seat, and, supporting himself against the table, thus addressed the assembly:

"Miss'r Pres'dent, and gentl'men, and ladies [of course there were no ladies present], I give you the Bri'sh lion and the 'Mer'can eagle [great applause, with cries of 'hear! hear!! hear!!!']. I give you, fell'r citz-z-z-ns, the 'Mer'can eagle and the Bri'sh lion. May this monarchal quad-er-ped and this republican bird all'rs be good friends [renewed applause]. May they never get into a muss, fell'r citz-z-z-ns; but, Mis-s'r Pres'dent, should this roar-in' quad-er-ped ever elevate his ror-r-yal paw or wag his regal tail at this republican fowl—which we don't antiserpate—but should he dare to do it, Miss'r Pres'dent, may the 'Mer'can eagle scratch out the Bri'sh lion's eyes, by ——."

There was considerable sensation caused by the peroration of this speech, and angry cries of "what! what!! what!!!" uttered with sharp rapidity, were heard from all sides. Very soon, however, some one observed, "Never mind the Yankee—he's tight;" when they turned the whole thing into a good hearty laugh, and gave tremendous applause.

AN ENGLISH OFFICER'S OPINION OF THE AMERICAN ARMY.

Many years ago, before General Scott and Sir John Hervey had adjusted the international complications involved in the settlement of the northeastern boundary question, and when serious apprehensions were entertained of a collision between the local authorities along the border, our government established at Houlton, Maine, some fifteen miles distant from a point on the River St. John where there was an English garrison, a military post subsequently known as "Houlton Barracks." This post at one time was garrisoned by artillery troops under the command of Captain J. B. Magruder, a tall, handsome man of elegant address and courtly presence, whose social congeniality, inherent colloquial tendencies, and sparkling, vivacious bonmots were acknowledged by all his acquaintances.

The following little episode will exhibit his character in a prominent light.

He upon one occasion obtained leave of absence and visited Quebec, carrying letters of introduction to certain English officers, by whom he was received very cordially, and invited to dine at the mess of the —th regiment of ———, which was eminently an aristocratic organization, embracing upon its muster-roll several younger scions of nobility, with other men of large private fortunes, who prided themselves upon their luxurious style of living and entertaining, which in some respects, it was said, excelled that of the household troops.

The mess-hall, upon the occasion referred to, was draped with the colors of the two consanguineous nationalities, exhibiting the Red Cross of St. George, surmounted by the imperial crown, entwined within the graceful folds of the Stars and Stripes; and the mess-table groaned under the weight of a ponderous service of gold and silver plate, which, through an initiatory stipend of a month's pay from all officers who had ever joined the regiment, besides a perennial subsequent tax, had been constantly accumulating for over a century, all of which was exhibited in dazzling splendor upon this occasion.

The carte was printed in gold letters upon white satin, and the numerous French dishes, classified upon it strictly en regle, were of the most recherche and piquant character, while the oldest and most costly wines in the greatest profusion were being reduced to the proper temperature in massive silver coolers all around the table.

In a word, every thing within the power of money, art, and taste seemed to have been exhausted in augmenting and giving brilliancy and éclat to the fête, and it was doubtless imagined that the Yankee officer would be struck with amazement at the blaze of magnificence which flashed upon him as he entered the hall, and *entre-nous* I have no doubt he *was* very much astonished, for he certainly had never before seen any thing like it. But he was very far from exhibiting any surprise; on the contrary, he seemed to look upon the whole thing with as much nonchalance as if it had been an every-day affair; and, with his usual self-confident assurance, he made himself not only entirely at ease, but rather conspicuous in suggesting and leading the conversation, which, among a variety of topics, at length turned upon the subject of the relative pay and emoluments allowed in the English and American armies.

The Englishmen admitted that their pay was small, but said this was a matter of little moment to them, as their private purses enabled them to live as they pleased, independent of their pay; and they appeared to derive especial satisfaction from disclosing the magnitude of their incomes and expenditures.

During the conversation, one of the officers asked Captain Magruder how much pay he received, to which he replied:

"Well, now, my dear fellow, I declare, upon my honor, I have not the most distant conception. It strikes me, however, that I have heard some poor devil of a captain, who was entirely dependent upon his pay, say it was something like two or three hundred dollars a month, but really I'm not positive.

At all events, it's a mere bagatelle, and I never have any thing to do with it myself. I give it to my butler to divide among the servants for pocket-money, and I suppose they know all about it."

With this digression, I now resume my story.

The British garrison upon the River St. John was commanded by Captain Burke, a jolly and facetious son of the Emerald Isle, who bore the reputation of having never been known to decline a very urgent solicitation to join his friends in a social glass, or to have permitted an opportunity to escape for perpetrating a good joke. As may readily be conjectured, two officers of such companionable proclivities did not remain long in close proximity without interchanges of civilities. They and some of their subordinates visited and dined with each other often, and it seems reasonable to suppose that a very considerable quantity of wines, to say nothing of alcoholic stimulants in the more condensed medium of brandy and whisky, may have been consumed upon these occasions.

This amicable condition of things continued for a good while, and the kindest possible relations were maintained between the officers of the two garrisons. At length, however, both commands were relieved by other troops. Captain Magruder was superseded by

Captain Sam Jones, who was an out-and-out "teetotaler," while her Britannic majesty's martial representative, Captain Burke, was replaced by Major ——— (I've forgotten his name), a young sprig of nobility who had seen but little service, and at best was not overstocked with *savoir faire.*

Before Captain Burke left the post, his successor took occasion to ask his opinion regarding the Yankee officers at Houlton Barracks.

He replied that, during his limited acquaintance with them, he had found them social and hospitable enough; "but," added he, "they are the most inveterate tipplers I have ever met with in the whole course of my life, and, what is more, they expect you to drink every time they do. If, however," continued he, "you ply them well with their favorite beverage, *whisky,* you'll find them generally a set of jolly good fellows. Mark this, and you'll get along very nicely; but if, when they visit you, you fail to supply them with *whisky* first, *whisky* last, and *whisky* continually from the moment they open their eyes in the morning until they are carried to bed at night, you'll see no more of them, be assured of that."

The unfledged neophyte, not having the remotest idea that he was being "sold," observed, "That's odd; that's devilish odd, by Jove!" He then thanked the facetious Hibernian for the information, and the latter left for the West Indies.

In due course of time, Captain Sam Jones, with several of his officers who were desirous of perpetuating the friendly relations that had subsisted between their predecessors, rode over to the British fort to pay their respects to the new-comers, and, on their arrival, went directly to the commanding officer's quarters, and were admitted by an orderly, who invited them to sit down while he hastened to notify the major of their presence.

In a few minutes, to their surprise, a side-door was suddenly thrown open, and a tall, slender young man in demi-toilet, with a bottle in each hand, rushed forward, hastily placed them upon a table, flew back and brought in some glasses, then, without the slightest preliminary introduction or other ceremony, rapidly disappeared, saying as he went out, "I—ah—beg pardon, I've no whisky just at this moment, but" (pointing to the table) "there's brandy and gin; help yourselves, and I'll send for some whisky directly."

The officers were greatly astonished at such a unique reception, and discussed its signification until the major (for it was he) came back again with two more bottles filled with whisky, which, with a self-satisfied air, he placed upon the table, and in the most urgent terms pressed them to partake of; and, upon their all declining to drink, he seemed a good deal puzzled, and remarked that he had received from Captain Burke the impression that all American officers, without exception, were in the practice of taking three or four cocktails before getting up in the morning, eight or ten before breakfast, with numerous other drinks during the day, besides wine, whisky-punch, and "that sort o' thing" at dinner.

They assured him he had been misinformed, as none of them ever drank before breakfast, and some of them did not drink at all, not even wine at dinner; whereupon he remarked, "I—ah—beg pardon, but that's very odd. We—ah—never take grog before lunch, ye know, but we drink wine, and all that sort o' thing, at dinner. You don't do things in your service as we do in ours, it seems. We always drink wine at mess; it's regulation, and all that sort o' thing, ye know."

Our officers expressed some curiosity to learn why the queen's regulations should be so much at variance with ours in *requiring* wine to be drank at the mess-table. The major replied, "I—ah—can't really explain why it is, but it's very *dif*-fer-r-rent, ye know."

MARTIAL WOOING.

A second lieutenant by the name of W*****e was once assigned to our regiment, who was born and "raised" in the wilds of Indiana; and although he possessed, naturally, fair intellectual faculties, yet he had received no education save what had been imparted to him in the rudimentary schools of the rural districts along the Wabash Valley.

His vernacular was redundant with the patois of his nativity, and widely divergent from the acceptation of our standard lexicographers.

He did not, however, seem at all conscious of his scholastic deficiencies, and for a good while continued to make use of his anomalous idioms, the oddity of which afforded us no little amusement.

The young man evinced no spirit of segregation, but was disposed to be quite social with his brother officers, and was especially fond of ladies' society. He visited them often, and as his original manner of giving expression to his sentiments diverted them not a little, he was always received kindly, and invited to repeat his calls.

About this time a young lady from New York city, a Miss H——y, visited the family of one of the officers, and remained some months with us. She was highly accomplished, pretty, and exceedingly animated, piquant, and attractive. Moreover, she possessed a most genial, amiable, and kind disposition; but, like many others of the fair sex, her fondness for admiration occasionally carried her so far that her friends very justly charged her with having a dash of coquetry in her composition; besides this, she had a decided penchant for badinage and fun.

No sooner had she been presented to Lieutenant W—— than she comprehended his character at a glance, and at once brought her heaviest metal to bear upon the exceedingly vulnerable citadel of his heart, and in a twinkling made so great a breach therein that the poor fellow surrendered at discretion. For the first time in his life, he found himself most desperately enamored.

He repeated his visits day after day for several weeks, and the young lady, impelled by a spirit of flirtation, encouraged his suit while he was in her presence, but invariably took occasion, as soon as his back was turned, to detail to her young lady companions every thing that transpired during the interviews.

The verdant wooer, not having the faintest conception that he was being made the victim of misplaced affection, persevered in his courtship, and received such encouragement as to call forth from him some very emphatic declarations of admiration. He even went so far, on one occasion, as to exclaim that "*He'd be dog-ond ef he didn't b'lieve she was a ann-gell.*"

This truly frank and sincere, but unique avowal of platonic sentiment, set the waggish young lady nearly frantic with suppressed desire to shout with laughter; yet she controlled her features and preserved a serene cast of countenance, and she even managed to raise the semblance of a blush while casting upon her lover from behind her fan a benignant, coquettish smile of satisfaction as she coyly responded, "Oh! oh! now, my *dear* Mr. W——, how *can* you say so? You make me blush; indeed you do. I can not believe you are sincere—I am afraid you are a gay Lothario, Mr. W——." Then, tapping him very gently upon the shoulder with her fan, and bestowing upon him a most bewitching smile, she added, "*Are you not a gay Lothario, Mr. W——?*"

This question was rather a poser to the enamored "Hoosier," who had never before heard of the person alluded to in her strategic rejoinder. Nevertheless, while pressing his hand upon what he conceived to be the region of the heart, but which, according to the location assigned that organ by anatomists, was a little too low, he replied,

"I don't mind hearin' tell o' that thar individual afore, Miss H——, but I sorter reckon he's no kin o' mine, and you am a *ann*-gell—*I swar you is.*"

Other equally forcible asseverations of his devotion were made during this interview, all of which were received by the young lady in so gracious a manner as to afford him the most encouraging hopes of ultimate success.

Of course the entire conversation was detailed by Miss H—— with much zest to her associates, all of whom she invited to be at her quarters on the following evening. A short time before, Mr. W—— had asked for and been promised a special audience, for the purpose, as she imagined, of making her a formal tender of his heart and hand.

Accordingly, at the appointed hour, they all assembled, and were quietly ensconced in an apartment adjoining the sitting-room, with the communicating door slightly ajar, so that they could distinctly hear every word that was said.

Soon after this the lieutenant made his appearance in full uniform, and was cordially received by his sweetheart, who asked him to take a seat near her, and entered into seemingly a very confidential but rather loud conversation with him, which soon led him to approach the subject of his dearest aspirations.

WOULD YE LIKE FUR TO JINE THE ARMY, MISS H——?

Placing himself upon his knees in front of her, with a most tender, anxious, and beseeching expression of countenance and voice, but with considerable manifestation of diffidence, he said,

"*Would ye like fur to jine th' army, Miss H——?*"

"No," replied she, using his very words, and imitating his peculiar diction, "I don't think I'd like fur to jine th' army, Mr. W——."

At this juncture screams of vociferous laughter burst forth from the mischievous girls in the adjoining apartment, in which the cruel Miss H——, no longer able to control herself, unmercifully joined, which caused the discomfited lover to leap to his feet in great confusion, seize his cap, and rush from the room, and I don't think he ever afterward attempted to pay his addresses to any lady.

ANTIDOTE FOR INEBRIATION.

The moral character of this officer was unimpeachable, and his habits correct and exemplary in every particular. He rarely took a glass of wine even at dinner, and I dare say he never in his life, up to that time, had been intoxicated; but after his grievous disappointment, resulting from the rejection of his matrimonial aspirations by the volatile young lady from New York, together with the cruel ridicule inflicted upon him by her unsympathizing bevy of confederates, it is not so very strange that he should have felt like perpetrating some rash act of desperation.

He then withdrew almost entirely from ladies' society, and transferred his associations to the other sex, and did not now so pertinaciously adhere to his abstemious resolutions. He would now and then indulge in a glass or two, but not more, until upon one occasion the officers were all invited to a supper-party at the house of a hospitable citizen named B****, who lived about five miles from the fort.

Many of them, including the young gentleman from the Wabash, attended the party, and relished the savory game supper amazingly. Lieutenant W—— seemed to be especially happy upon the occasion, and partook rather freely of the Champagne and choice liquors that the gracious host continued to press upon him, until at length he began so sensibly to feel the effects of the unusual number of potations he had imbibed that he directly demurred at taking any more, and, when urged by the host to do so, gave as an excuse that he had already drank as much as he could well sustain without becoming intoxicated, and added that he would not for the world be guilty of committing so scandalous a breach of propriety as that.

Mr. B—— informed him there would not be the least danger of inebriation provided he ate freely of coldslaw, and assured him he had often seen the experiment tried with entire success. Accordingly, he continued to drink, and every glass was followed by a liberal dose of the vegetable antidote, so that before the repast was over he had consumed all the coldslaw, and was filled to nearly the maximum of his bibitory capacity; yet he was able to "navigate" tolerably well, and, after swallowing a stirrûp-cup bumper of stiff hot-whisky punch, he started for the fort, but, just before reaching the sally-port, discovered himself becoming so much intoxicated that he at once resolved to turn back and call Mr. B—— to account for recommending an antidote for inebriation which did not have the desired effect. With this purpose in contemplation, he ordered his driver to turn round, and was carried all the way back to Mr. B——'s house, reaching there about three o'clock in the morning, while the family were in bed and sound asleep.

After knocking several times at the door, and calling in a loud voice, "O-o-o-oh, Miss'r B——! o-o-o-o-oh, Miss'r B——!" he at length aroused the head of the family, who, somewhat startled, leaped from the bed, and, running to the window, called out,

"Who are you, and what do you want at this time o' night?"

Instead of giving a direct answer, the muddled victim continued beating the door and calling out, "O-o-o-oh, Miss'r B——! I say, Miss'r B——!"

Thinking that a serious accident might have happened to some of his guests after leaving the house, B—— hurried to the door, and, on opening it, to his astonishment, confronted the lieutenant holding himself up by the door-post. He anxiously inquired as to the cause of this untimely visit, and invited the officer into the house. He declined, however, exclaiming, in an emphatic and elevated tone of voice, "Miss'r B——! I say, Miss'r B——, *cabbage ain't no 'count, Miss'r B——!*" Then, without uttering another syllable, he staggered back to his sleigh and was driven home.

I am not positive that the trite phrase used in vulgar parlance, "No more account than cabbage," took its origin from the circumstance above related, but it would not surprise me if such was the fact.

CHAPTER IV.

Enlisted Men.—Captain M'Cabe.—Private Orr as a Witness.—Any thing the Cap'n plaizes.—A veteran Drummer.—Improvised Distillery. — Novel Writ of Ejectment. — Cold Weather. — Colonel T*****.—How to make good Bread.—Napton, the Teamster; his Visit to the Moon; what he saw there.—Song of the old Quartermaster's Mule.—Colonel S*********.—Diving for Oysters.—Taking Satisfaction.—Correcting the Parson.

ENLISTED MEN.

THE incidents I propose narrating, wherein certain soldiers enact conspicuous and not very commendable rôles, must by no means be regarded as applicable to the great mass of the rank and file of the old army. There may have been some force in the remark made by an old soldier in extenuation of a not very heinous offense for which he was undergoing trial, that "the court could scarcely expect to find the entire catalogue of cardinal virtues embodied in every individual specimen of a class of men who only received for their services the paltry compensation of six dollars a month." Nevertheless, very many good men were even at that time found in the ranks; and it affords me especial satisfaction in giving my attestation to the fact that I have invariably found the old soldiers possessing the most kind, generous, and disinterested impulses. I am indebted for my existence at this moment to the unparalleled fortitude, endurance, and sufferings of a noble little band of soldiers who nearly sacrificed their own lives to extricate me from the perils of a winter's journey over the snow-clad summits of the Rocky Mountains. It would, therefore, be not only unbecoming, but exceedingly ungrateful in me to attempt any derogation from their many praiseworthy attributes.

CAPTAIN M'CABE.

Of something like forty officers who were attached to the regiment in which I first served, and of whom I can only enumerate five now living, there is none who has left a more indelible impression upon my memory than Captain M'Cabe. This officer entered service from civil life during the War of 1812–14, had proved himself a valiant soldier, and was a disciplinarian of the most exacting and uncompromising type.

The slightest deviations from the literal fulfillment of orders, or an approximation to infractions of regulations, were in his estimation offenses of the most flagitious character, which could be expiated only by the infliction of the severest penalties sanctioned by law and military usage. No such clement word as condonation ever found a place in his vocabulary.

The sturdy old veteran was born and nurtured in the mountains of Pennsylvania, where he received but little education, and that of a rudimental and fragmentary character.

When I met him, however, he had been thrown in contact with men of culture and refinement for so many years that this constant social attrition had worn off some of the more salient asperities developed by his early provincial training, so that, when not under the influence of excitement, he endeavored to deport himself like a gentleman, making use of the politest and most graceful expressions within the scope of his diction; but, whenever the equanimity of his eminently irascible temperament became at all disturbed, he abruptly cast aside his studiously selected forms of expression for the coarse vernacular dictated by his natural impulses.

PRIVATE ORR AS A WITNESS.

He was once president of a court-martial of which I happened to be a member, and before which a soldier was arraigned for drunkenness on duty.

The prisoner pleaded guilty to the charge, but the

ruling of courts-martial then requiring the allegations to be substantiated by evidence, a soldier by the name of Orr was called in behalf of the prosecution, who, it appeared, had been with the accused when the offense was committed, and in all probability was drunk at the same time.

After having been duly sworn, he was asked if he saw the prisoner at the time specified in the charge, to which he gave an affirmative reply.

To the next question, as to whether the accused was drunk, he answered emphatically "No."

This response being so positively at variance with what Captain M'Cabe conceived to be the fact, he, with a stern look of incredulity, turned to the witness, saying, "Did I understand you to affirm, sir, that in your candid judgment you regarded the prisoner as entirely sober upon the occasion alluded to?"

Orr was a little puzzled at this carefully-worded interrogatory, but promptly answered, "I don't pretind to offur-rum that he was intirely sober, yer 'onor, fur we had taken one, an' I don't jist now remimber, but maybe two small horns togither; but he wasn't dhrunk, by no manner of means—I'll take my affidavy of that, yer 'onor."

The captain then asked the witness if in his opinion the accused was, at the time specified, competent to perform all his military duties. He replied, "An' sure, yer 'onor, the pris'ner was not so dhrunk in regard to licker but what he could per-for-rum his duties fust rhate."

The captain, becoming more and more irritated at the perverse tenacity with which the witness adhered to his first asseveration, said to him, "With the kind indulgence of the court, I beg leave to observe to you, *Mister* Orr" (he invariably used this appellative derisively to soldiers when most exasperated), "I take this occasion to remark to *you*, I say, *Mister* Orr, in the most delicate terms, that in my humble judgment you have been laboring under a slight error in this case — a slight error, I say, sir; and allow me to add furthermore, *Mister* Orr, that in my opinion you have perpetrated a deliberate, infernal lie, sir." Then, jumping up, raising his voice to a high pitch, and shaking his fist at the witness, he repeated, "You have told a d—d lie, you know you have."

The old man was called to order by the court, and an admonitory intimation given him that he would not be permitted to intimidate witnesses in that manner, but it was some time before he calmed down and resumed his customary demeanor.

It so happened, after this trial was concluded, that the same man Orr was called as a witness in the next case that came before the court, and previous to his having been sworn, Captain M'Cabe, in view of the scene that had previously occurred, took occasion to ask him, "Will you be so very obliging, *Mister* Orr, as to give me some idea of what you intend to swear to in this case?"

To which the witness, who was perfectly self-possessed, with a bland smile responded, "*I'll sware to any thing the cap'n plaizes.*"

A VETERAN DRUMMER.

There was in our garrison an old drummer by the name of Potter, who had served through several terms of enlistment, and when sober was an obedient, faithful soldier; but, unfortunately for the poor fellow, he was so fond of his grog that he would resort to all manner of expedients, or incur any amount of labor, exposure, or danger, for the sake of gratifying this inveterate propensity. The consequence was that he passed the greater part of his time in the guard-house undergoing the penalty attached to his incorrigible vagaries.

One morning, directly after having been released from confinement, he was ordered by Captain M'Cabe to go to a grindstone standing just without the chain of sentinels, and sharpen an axe which was wanted for immediate use. He took the axe and started out of the fort, but, instead of continuing on to the grindstone, the temptation was too powerful for him to resist, and he turned his steps toward a grog-shop in the vicinity, where he passed the remainder of the day in drinking whisky, and staggered back to the fort after dark in a state of beastly intoxication.

The captain, after waiting some time for the return of the axe, suspected what had occurred, and gave orders for the guard to arrest and bring the truant to him as soon as he returned. Accordingly, on his arrival at the sally-port, he was taken in charge, and escorted, axe in hand, to the captain's quarters, and in reply to the inquiry as to why he had presumed to disobey the order given him in the morning, he, while reeling to and fro, and holding out the axe toward the officer, said, "I say, cap'n, I've been a gr-r-r-rin'in on 'er all day, but that 'ere gr-r-rine-stun she wo-o-on't have no more he-e-expresh'n on this 'ere ha-a-ax nor a toad wants a tail every bit and grain as much." This labored excuse failed, however, to convince the captain that he had complied with the order given him, and instead of being rewarded for his arduous day's labor, he was assigned to quarters for ten days in the dark prison upon an exclusive diet of bread and water.

IMPROVISED DISTILLERY.

The crafty devices and great sacrifices to which men who have become addicted to the inordinate use of ardent spirits will occasionally resort in order to gratify their morbid appetites is forcibly illustrated in the following legend.

One exceedingly severe and protracted winter, somewhere about 1820, shortly after the establishment of Fort Snelling, then called "Fort St. Anthony," it so occurred that every thing at the fort in the form of alcoholic, vinous, and malt liquors was consumed long before spring, and the only place where a drop of spirits could be obtained within a distance of five hundred miles was at the establishment of an Indian trader in the vicinity by the name of Farribeau, who still retained a few gallons of high wines, from which, with a large aqueous component, he was enabled to concoct a nauseous mixture sufficiently stimulating to cause intoxication.

Although the pay of a private soldier at this early period was only six dollars a month, yet some of the most inveterate votaries of inebriation among the enlisted men of the garrison united their slender finances, and, as a special favor, were permitted by the extorsive trader to purchase one gallon of his execrable and well-watered compound for the *modest* price of ninety-six dollars, or the amount of sixteen months' pay of the soldier. What profits were realized from the sale of the remainder of the liquor I did not learn, but was informed that it was all disposed of before spring, after which there was no alcoholic spirits short of Galena, at that season nearly as inaccessible as the hyperborean regions.

The commissary's stock of sugar also gave out during this prolonged winter; and, as there was no possibility of renewing the supply from below until the opening of navigation, a detachment of soldiers, under charge of a corporal, was sent out into the "Big Woods," as soon as the sap began to circulate, for the purpose of manufacturing maple sugar.

Some days after this party had been set at work, the commissary visited their camp to learn what progress they were making, and, on his arrival, to his utter astonishment, found every man in a state of absolute intoxication.

How the party could have got into this condition when there was no liquor within a distance of five hundred miles was incomprehensible to him. That they were all drunk was evident, but by what mysterious process of enchantment this had been brought about was more than he could understand. He at once returned to the fort, and reported the facts to the commanding officer, who did not credit the statement, and sent out other officers to investigate the matter.

They found the party still so stupefied by the influence of liquor that they were unable to obtain from them any clew to the mystery, and it was only after making diligent search in the vicinity of the camp that they finally discovered a diminutive, rude distillery, which an ingenious tinker had improvised by making use of camp-kettles for boilers, and some old trumpets for the still-worm, and, with the aid of an experienced distiller, who also happened to belong to the detachment, they had succeeded in causing the saccharine ingredient of the sap to undergo the vinous fermentation, and the result was a quantity of spirits, which had proved sufficiently potent to reduce them to the condition in which they were found.

NOVEL WRIT OF EJECTMENT.

While Fort Winnebago, now Portage City, was occupied by our troops in 1839, a whisky vender surreptitiously located his establishment upon the military reservation, and for a long time carried on his nefarious traffic with the soldiers, greatly to the annoyance of the officers, who appealed to the United

States District Attorney, and resorted to every other legitimate measure for the purpose of ejecting the intruder, but all was without avail, and the shop remained until Captain M'Cabe devised an expedient which, although not in strict accordance with the literal reading of the statute-books, proved most effectual in this instance. He sent for an old fifer named Curtis, who was an inveterate toper, and had been one of the most constant patrons of the establishment, and asked him if he knew the place. He replied that he had been informed there was an establishment of the kind somewhere in the vicinity, although he was not himself personally acquainted with its precise locality.

The captain was considerably exercised at the cool mendacity of the fellow, and remarked:

"I beg your pardon, *Mister* Curtis, but you will kindly suffer me gently to insinuate, in the most urbane manner, that I find myself unable to resist the force of my own convictions that you must be mistaken in this matter; and I believe furthermore that you are an unmitigated liar, sir. You've been drunk there repeatedly, you know you have; and all I have to say to you now is, that if you and two or three more of your drunken associates should take it into your muddled heads to go to that whisky shop *to-*

night, give the scoundrel a d—d good thrashing, destroy his liquor, burn down his infernal shanty, and bring back three or four camp-kettles full of this vile poison, and remain drunk for a week, I'll play the very devil with every one of you. Do you understand that, *Mister* Curtis?"

The old soldier intimated that he comprehended the signification of the threat, and assured the captain that he need have no fears, as there was not the slightest probability of his ever being guilty of perpetrating such a manifest breach of law and order.

Notwithstanding this, however, the grog-shop, by some mysterious agency, was burned to the ground that same night, and, by an equally astonishing coincidence, Curtis and three of his intimate associates disappeared for several days afterward.

The whisky vender was heard from a few days subsequently making a precipitate retreat in the direction of Mineral Point, and with several patches in his physiognomy exhibiting a deeper tint of crimson than is usually supplied by nature.

I don't think he made his appearance again upon the Reservation.

COLD WEATHER.

One morning during the severe winter of 1830–1,

while Captain M'Cabe was stationed at Fort Snelling, he sent his orderly to the hospital for the purpose of ascertaining the temperature.

Now it so happened, upon the occasion referred to, the atmosphere had become so intensely cold that the mercury in the Fahrenheit thermometer dropped down 40° below zero, and was frozen solid; but the orderly, whose education in meteorology was rather limited, had not the faintest conception that such a result was within the scope of Nature's laws, and when he observed the fact that all the quicksilver had settled from the tube into the bulb of the instrument, he returned in great haste to the captain's quarters, and in an excited manner exclaimed, "Capting! capting! that 'ere thrognomicon she's chock up this mornin'. The marcury won't budge, an' I reckon she's frizzed."

HOW TO MAKE GOOD BREAD.

Colonel T*****, whom I have before alluded to, was a rigid disciplinarian of the old school, who held every one under his command to a strict accountability for all infractions of law, regulations, or orders. This was all very well, so far as it extended; but there are numerous minor offenses not mentioned in the Articles of War or Regulations, which militate against the enforcement of good order and military discipline, that can not be reached by the ordinary correctives resulting from trials by courts-martial.

Colonel T***** was conspicuous for the ingenuity he displayed in conceiving and executing novel and appropriate punishments to meet emergencies of this character.

As an instance, the garrison of Fort Winnebago, commanded by the colonel, was once afflicted with a soldier-baker by the name of M'Mannus, who was a most incorrigible drunkard, and, when in his cups, he was certain to make very bad bread. So well had this become understood, that it was only necessary to examine a loaf of bread to determine whether M'Mannus was drunk or sober. Yet, as the man did not enlist for a baker, and as there was nothing in the Army Regulations whereby a soldier could be tried or punished for making bad bread, there seemed to be no remedy for the evil, and the bread became worse and worse; but, as there was no other baker in the command, M'Mannus could not be relieved or confined without depriving the garrison of this most important item of the ration. He understood this perfectly, and, believing his services indispensable, his debauches multiplied rapidly, and the quality of the bread underwent a corresponding deterioration, until at length it became so intolerable that the colonel resolved to take the matter in hand and apply a remedy.

On the following morning the bread proved worse than it ever had been before. It was compact, heavy, glutinous, not properly baked, and was, in fact, execrable.

As soon as the colonel's attention was called to it, he selected from the batch the worst-looking four-ration loaf he could find, took it to his quarters, and directed his servant to set the breakfast table for two persons, with a large platter in the centre, upon which he placed the loaf, with an enormous cover over it; after which he sent his orderly with his compliments to Private M'Mannus, accompanied by a request that he would favor him with a call at his earliest convenience, as he desired specially to see him.

The baker, who had just finished his breakfast, was a good deal surprised at this mysteriously polite message from the commanding officer; but he buttoned up his coat, brushed his hair, and hastened to comply with the mandate.

Knocking at the door, he was at once admitted by the colonel himself, who, with an air of great civility, thus addressed him:

"Good morning, Mr. M'Mannus; I hope you find

yourself very well this morning, for I wish to have the pleasure of your company at breakfast." Then, pointing to a chair, he added, "Sit down, sir; breakfast is all ready."

The baker, astounded at such unheard-of condescension, and at loss to comprehend the meaning of it, replied that he was greatly obliged to the colonel for his kind invitation, but as he had just risen from the breakfast table he begged to be excused. The colonel assured him that made no difference whatever, and that he must insist upon his taking his breakfast at his table, when he again motioned for him to take his seat in a manner that admitted of no further excuses.

Accordingly, he seated himself at table opposite the colonel, when the servant was directed to remove the solitary cover, which disclosed the huge collapsed five-pound loaf to the eyes of the astonished baker, who now, for the first time, began to get an inkling of the facetious colonel's purpose, who, opening and extending his hands toward him, with a most beseeching smile, said, "Help yourself to bread, Mr. M'Mannus, and don't be afraid of it, for I assure you there is more in the larder."

Seeing no means for escape, M'Mannus reluctantly commenced upon the repulsive-looking loaf, and after eating nearly half of it, informed the colonel that really he should be unable to swallow any more, as he was already suffering great inconvenience from repletion.

"My dear sir," said the colonel, "you certainly must oblige me by eating some more of that delicious bread. Your appetite don't seem very good just at this moment, but it will come after a while, so eat a little more, sir."

He commenced again, and was forced to consume the entire loaf before he was permitted to leave the table. The colonel then said to him, "I hope you have relished your breakfast, sir, as I shall expect you to take your meals at my table whenever you make such excellent bread as that you have been eating."

M'Mannus, who was suffering tortures from the surfeit he had been subjected to, said he hoped the colonel would not have occasion to extend his hospitality to him again very soon, as he should for the future endeavor to make better bread, and he even went so far as to admit that the article produced that morning was not quite as light as he could have desired.

The colonel acquiesced in this opinion, saying, "No, sir, *it is not* quite as light as some bread I have seen in the Parisian cafés, for example, and I think, with all dúe respect for your qualifications as a professional baker, Mr. M'Mannus, I may hazard the assertion that it is any thing but what it should have been; and I might with propriety add that it is a villainous compound unfit for a dog to eat."

Then jumping up and shaking his fist at the man, he said, "How dare you make such bread for my men to eat, sir? How dare you, I say? If you don't get out of my quarters instantly, I'll kick you out, you d—d drunken hound."

M'Mannus made a precipitate exit, and the troops were subsequently supplied with better bread.

NAPTON, THE TEAMSTER.

I have a distinct recollection of an old soldier by the name of Napton, who stammered so badly that it was sometimes almost impossible for him to give utterance to a sentence without prefixing to it an oath. This man, while I knew him, was continually kept upon "extra duty" as teamster, and a very good one he was. For several years he drove oxen, but was subsequently promoted to the command of a mule team, which seemed the attainment of the summit of his aspirations. His attention was so exclusively absorbed in the occupation to which he had been assigned that he paid but little attention to his duties as a soldier.

He was a kind and humane man, and as fond of his mules as a father of his children; besides, he was indefatigable in his attentions to their wants, and applied the most endearing epithets to them. Indeed, he went so far upon one occasion as to give his candid opinion that the mule was the most useful institution in the world excepting whisky.

At one time a professional mesmerist visited our post, and as the mysterious science was then in its incipiency and entirely novel to us, our curiosity was considerably excited. In "prospecting" for subjects to exercise his powers upon after a lecture which this man gave before the officers and enlisted men, he accidentally encountered Napton, who proved a most tractable auxiliary, being so keenly sensitive to the influence of the mesmeric fluid that the professor, when in his presence, obtained absolute control of all his faculties. He was so susceptible a medium that the operator, by simply pointing his finger at him when he was walking, caused him to halt instantly, and go at once into the mesmeric slumber—a cataleptic state in which his own volition seemed absolutely suspended, and every faculty surrendered to the will of the mesmerist.

Once while he was in this condition, with his eyes closed, and apparently unconscious of every thing transpiring round him, we quietly, and without his knowledge, desired the mesmerizer to excite the organ of self-esteem, the medium being totally ignorant of the first principles of phrenology. In compliance with the request, he went behind the man, and, without touching his head, made several passes with his hand over the designated protuberance, after which he said,

"Will you be so kind as to inform us who you are, Mr. Napton?"

Whereupon he straightened up in his chair, folded his arms across his breast, and, throwing one leg over the other in a very stately manner, replied,

"I'm the Gu-Gu-Gu-Guv'ner of the St-t-t-t-t-tate of New York, sir."

After continuing to pour in the current of mesmeric fluid some time longer, the spiritist again asked,

"Who did I understand you to say you were, Mr. Napton?"

Throwing back his head, and assuming a still more consequential air than before, he replied,

"I'm the P-P-P-Pres'dent of the United St-t-t-t-t-tates, sir."

We all laughed heartily at this superlatively farcical response, but Napton maintained a most solemn and dignified expression of countenance, indicating that he really believed himself the important personage whose identity he had assumed.

Among the officers present at our seance was one who was utterly skeptical in regard to all the phenomena exhibited to us, and he endeavored to cast as much ridicule upon the performance as possible.

Although I never saw this officer intoxicated, yet he was far from being a total abstinence man, which fact was well known to the soldiers, with whom he was not popular.

Upon Napton's announcing himself as the chief magistrate of the nation, the lieutenant above mentioned asked him if he would have any objections to giving him the appointment of colonel in the army. After some hesitation, he answered,

"I d-d-d-don't think I can gi-gi-gi-give you that ap-p-p-point-ment, sir."

"If it is not an improper question, may I be permitted to ask why not, Mr. President?"

"Because I d-d-d-*don't* think you're f-f-f-*fit* for it."

"In that case, Mr. President, is there any impropriety in my asking for the appointment of lieutenant colonel?"

"I d-d-d-*don't* think you're f-f-f-*fit* for that either."

"Is there any other position within your gift, Mr. President, which you think I am competent to fill?"

"I think, if you'd keep sober, you'd make a t-t-t-t-tol'ble co-co-co-co-co-*cor*'prul."

This ludicrous response caused a vociferous shout of laughter from every body in the room except the office-seeker, who retired in disgust, remarking as he went out that in his opinion the whole thing was an infernal humbug.

During the seance the professor took his subject upon an imaginary excursion to the moon, and, on their arrival, asked him what he saw peculiar in that planet. After feigning to look around for a moment, he replied,

"I see a f-f-f-f-fust-rate p-p-p-p-pair o' mules, sir."

"What else do you perceive, Mr. Napton?"

To this he replied,

"The g-g-g-gate's shut; I c-c-c-can't get in."

"Why don't you ask the keeper to open the gate, Mr. Napton?"

"I did ask him, b-b-b-b-b-but he wants to know where I c-c-c-c-came from, and I t-t-t-t-t-told him from the U-n-n-n-*ni*ted St-t-t-t-t-tates of 'Meriky."

"Very well, sir; what did he say to that?"

"He said, 'What b-b-b-b-*bis*'ness did you f-f-f-f-foller down there?'"

"You answered that question, I presume, Mr. Napton?"

"Yes'er; I t-t-t-t-told him I was a b-b-b-b-bull driver, by ——."

"Did he admit you then, sir?"

"Ye-e-e-es'er; he opened the g-g-g-gate, and told me to 'd-d-d-d-drive in, you d—d st-t-t-t-tut-terin' vagabond you."

That the mule is the most useful hybrid known is indisputable, but, unfortunately for the poor beast, he seldom receives as kind treatment as Napton bestowed upon his favorites; and, if they could speak, there would doubtless be many a lament fully as heart-rending as that contained in the following stanzas, which were penned by Colonel L—— after having witnessed their cruel usage in Florida:

SONG OF THE OLD QUARTER-MASTER'S MULE.

A Lay from the Land of Flowers.

Know ye the land where the River St. John's
  Rolls on through the palm forest to the salt sea;
Where Sol gilds the mule-yard when morning first dawns,
  And the sheds that give shade to my comrades and me?

Through its hammocks and forests for many a day
  Have I toiled o'er the sands for my pitiful grain,
And sighed at my trough till my tail has grown gray,
  And sweat for my country again and again.

When the war-whoop was heard in the pine-shadowed wood—
  When the drivers all ran, and the fight was a race,
Like a Holy-cross Knight in my harness I stood,
  Calmly smiling at fate, with my leg o'er the trace.

Midst this *donkey brevetment*, oh where's my reward ?
  Ungroomed and unshodden, faint, foundered, and sick,
The first transport that passes will bear me on board,
  Floating down the St. John's to be sold at Black Creek.

Oh! my brothers in toil, yet uncrushed by the chains,
  Be ye warned by my fate; this your doom I foretell:
When the war-clouds have passed, for your service and pains
  You'll be sold at Black Creek by the auctioneer Bell.

DIVING FOR OYSTERS.

I once served under the command of Colonel S*********, who was at that time one of the few surviving veterans of the campaign of 1812.

He was a portly, but fine-looking gentleman of the old school, with an erect and graceful carriage, possessing an exceedingly kind and amiable disposition, and, after a good dinner, was the personification of pleasantry and good-humor.

He took no pleasure in reading, writing, or other intellectual occupations, but was eminently a *bon vivant*, and thoroughly posted in the mysteries of the gastronomic art. He could direct the concoction and cooking of a ragoût, potage à la Juliénne, or other *bonne bouche* with as much artistic skill as the most accomplished professional French *maître de cuisine*, and he probably thought more of his dinner than he did of every other event of his life.

While our Army of Observation was bivouacked at Corpus Christi during the winter of 1845–6, the colonel, having but few military duties to occupy his time, was in the habit of taking out his "pioneer party" to catch fish and oysters for his table.

The men submitted to this cheerfully at first, but after the novelty of the thing had worn off they began to demur at the laborious task which the colonel imposed upon them for his own personal gratification and benefit, and some of them applied to be relieved.

One morning, while lying in my tent just before reveille, I overheard a dialogue between two of the pioneers, one of whom had, as it appeared, just been detailed to serve with the party, and having no knowledge of the character of the duties he would be required to perform, appealed to the old incumbent to enlighten him.

"In the first place," said he, "you'll have to row a boat down the bay every morning, and wade up to your middle for about six hours catching crabs, and you'll have to look out for the 'stingarees,' for they are awful. But what the old man wants you particularly for is to dive for oysters, for he's h—l on oysters."

The other replied, "I'll not do either, for I didn't 'list for a crab-catcher or an oyster-diver, nohow."

"Never mind, you'll have to do it. He'll keep you under water as long as the crabs and oysters hold out, you may depend on that."

How the discussion terminated I am unable to say, as the men soon afterward passed out of hearing.

TAKING SATISFACTION.

Many years before this the colonel obtained a furlough, and went to New England, married a wife, and brought her back to his sequestered frontier station, where there was little society and but few amusements. The newly-married couple were in the practice of walking out a great deal, and it so happened that the bride had brought with her from home a favorite poodle dog, which accompanied them in all their rambles.

The colonel at first did not seem to fancy the attentions that were lavished upon the animal by his mistress, but in time this prejudice was overcome, and at length he was persuaded even to lead the dog about with a ribbon; indeed, he finally seemed to become nearly as much attached to the creature as his wife was.

The old gentleman also had another hobby at this

period that absorbed a good deal of his time when not occupied with his domestic concerns, which was a new and very tall flag-staff that he had taken great pains to have selected with care, and properly dressed, and put up on the parade-ground. He walked around it many times every day, surveying it from every possible direction, and contemplating its graceful proportions with peculiar pleasure and satisfaction.

One morning, as he was taking his customary view of the new military appendage while the flag was being hoisted to its peak, one of the soldiers assisting at the halyards, who happened to be very drunk at the time, made an exclamation which was overheard by the colonel, and was not very complimentary to him, and he ordered the man to the guard-house. The fellow staggered off, but in a very surly mood, remarking, in a suppressed tone, as he passed the officer, that he would have revenge for what he conceived to be an unmerited punishment if he was compelled to wait until he was discharged from the service. He was peremptorily ordered to halt, and asked how he dared to make such a threat against his commanding officer. Instead of prevaricating or denying it, he firmly reiterated his determination. Whereupon the colonel asked, "What kind of revenge do you imagine you can inflict upon me, sir?"

"Be jabers, I'll buy all the oysters in the sutler's store; and, ef that's not enough, I'll cut off your wife's dog's tail; and, ef that's not enough, I'll chop down your ugly old flag-staff, an' so I will."

CORRECTING THE PARSON.

Mr. C****, our post-chaplain, was a highly intelligent and dignified old gentleman, who exercised his ecclesiastic prerogatives with as much stateliness and hauteur as if he had been the veritable sovereign pontiff himself. He entertained us every Sunday with excellent, short, practical discourses, and it is to be presumed that the troops profited by his zealous teachings.

The colonel, although not a member of the Church, set us a good example by regular attendance upon all the services, invariably carrying his prayer-book, and occasionally uniting in the responses.

In order to understand what I am about to relate, however, I should state that the colonel had fallen into the habit of now and then involuntarily soliloquizing, and occasionally his spasmodic exclamations were superlatively laughable.

One Sunday, after the congregation had all assembled, with the colonel occupying a prominent seat near the chaplain, the latter commenced the customary form of service by the following announcement: "*Ninth* day of the month, morning prayer." But, by some oversight, he made a mistake, as it happened to be the tenth day. The colonel, who, with his spectacles mounted, was intently following the parson in his prayer-book, at once noticed the error, and, greatly to the astonishment of every body, in a loud voice uttered the exclamation, "*It's the tenth day, I swear.*"

CHAPTER V.

Volunteers. — Rapidity of Organization and Discipline. — Arkansas Volunteers.—"Let um bile ahead!"—Postage-stamp.—One Hundred and Second Rhode Island.—Rifle-pit.—Cut out of a Ride.—Monterey.—Candidate for the Presidency.

VOLUNTEERS.

THE grave and tragical features of the *Great Rebellion* have been graphically depicted by numerous writers, some of whom have drawn faithful and striking delineations of events during the progress of the sanguinary drama, but as yet I have seen but few representations of the more comical and ludicrous incidents with which the early history of the war abounded.

It is not at all surprising, and indeed might have been anticipated, that thousands of farcical and unmilitary scenes should have been enacted during the incipient stages of the contest, before the troops had received instruction in their duties. Some of these have been published, and are familiar to all; but there are many others only known and retained in the memories of individuals who served in particular organizations and localities, and may soon be forgotten, unless, peradventure, those persons having cognizance of the facts shall take the trouble to preserve them from oblivion by giving the public the benefit of their experiences upon paper.

I do not, therefore, deem it necessary to offer any apology for contributing my mite toward filling this hiatus in the chronicles of the Herculean struggle. It is a subject in which nearly all the world feel a deep and abiding concern.

What I am about narrating will not be altogether devoid of interest to readers generally, but more especially to those genial natures which have the good fortune to be endowed with a love for the humorous, and those who cultivate a healthful *bonhomie* and a cheerful disposition in preference to sombre and lugubrious cogitations, inducing hypochondria, and imaginary or real mental maladies.

No one entertains a higher appreciation and respect for the great achievements of our volunteer troops than myself, and it was a subject of equal astonishment and gratification to me at the commencement of the war to witness the alacrity of our citizens from the Northern and Western States in rushing forward with earnest emulation to the defense of the jeopardized Union cause, and the cheerful acquiescence with which they abandoned the comforts of home, and submitted to the privations and hardships of camp life, and the austerities and restraints incident to military training, as well as the unprecedented celerity with which these men acquired a knowledge of their duties.

The rapidity with which we levied, organized, equipped, and put in the field armies of vast magnitude from the raw material was without a parallel in the history of warfare, and has not only inspired us with confidence in our ability to supplement our military resources to almost any extent, should future exigencies require it, but it has caused our flag to be more respected, and the military power of a great republican government to be more fully comprehended throughout the world than they ever were before. I am constrained to admit, however, that a few exceptions to the facts above stated, so far as they apply to the personnel of our armies, came under my own observation, among the volunteers that were raised in certain remote border-districts of the Southwest; but, unless a person has actually been among those people, and witnessed their anomalous peculiarities, he would hardly be inclined to give credence to some of their idiosyncrasies.

ARKANSAS VOLUNTEERS.

I had occasion, during the summer of 1864, to visit Arkansas and Southwestern Missouri, where I met with several regiments of volunteers which had been recruited in that section of the country.

It is true, some little knowledge of drill and discipline had been hammered into these men when I saw them, but they were still the roughest specimens of soldiers I ever encountered, and I was informed by their officers that, when they were first called into service, it seemed almost impossible to impart to their obtuse comprehensions the faintest idea of the importance of military instruction.

An officer of rank, who was serving with these troops—a man who had passed the meridian of life, was a good soldier, and had seen some previous service in Mexico, gave me a detailed narration of his experience in illustration of the difficulties he had encountered in manipulating native border citizens into soldiers. His description made so forcible an impression upon my mind at the time that I think I can relate it very nearly in his own words; at all events, I will make the effort. As near as my memory serves me, it was as follows:

"My first service in this campaign was with volunteers from Arkansas and Southwestern Missouri. These men were called out upon the spur of the moment, hastily organized, and but partially equipped to meet the sudden and startling exigencies of the momentous occasion, and they consisted of farmers, hunters, and other loyal frontier men, many of whom probably never before saw an organized company of soldiers, and had not the least knowledge even of the rudiments in the art of war. Moreover, many of their officers were elected or appointed on account of their personal popularity, or their liberality in supplying whisky as a lubricator (if I may use the expression) in overcoming the scruples, raising the courage, and elevating the patriotism of the more timid and lukewarm of their 'fellar-citizens,' and generally without any special reference to their knowledge of or qualifications for the profession of arms or the business of war.

"Nevertheless, some of these men applied themselves assiduously to their novel vocation, and subsequently achieved well-merited distinction; but when they were first mustered into service, and assembled at Little Rock and other rendezvous near the theatre of active operations, they were the most crude and unmilitary-looking aspirants for glory it has ever been my fate to encounter.

"Upon their arrival at the rendezvous they were dressed in all varieties of costumes. Some wore uniform coats and butternut-colored pants and vests; others were clad in buckskin coats and uniform pants, while a few appeared in buckskin throughout; and they universally adhered most tenaciously to their native old broad-brimmed hats. Moreover, the greater part of them carried in their hands or on their backs large carpet-bags or sacks, expanded and stuffed out to their utmost capacity with all sorts of traps that were of no possible use in campaigning.

"They were, indeed, a most heterogeneous and motley set, and reminded me more of a crowd of camp-followers who had loaded themselves down with plunder upon the heels of a routed army than of an organized body of soldiers.

"As fast as they reported they were assigned to camps, and immediately put upon a strict course of drill and discipline under the supervision of the best officers that could be found, and it was hoped that ere long they would present a more martial bearing; but their peculiar self-reliant individuality, and the notions of social equality in which they had been nurtured and instructed, were in every respect stubbornly antagonistic to rapid progress in military acquirements; besides, their naturally careless, slouching, and ungainly deportment and habits had become so thoroughly confirmed that it was by no means an easy task to set them up into any thing approximating a respectable soldierly appearance. Their lineage, instincts, and education were all in antagonism to aristocracy in every form. They believed in one common social platform, upon which all humanity stood on precisely the same level. They acknowledged no superiors, and it was probably this independent spirit which, at the commencement of the rebellion, influenced their mistaken estimate of the relative combative powers of men in the two antagonistic geographical sections [a difference of some four or five to one in favor of the South]. In a word, these people relied entirely upon individual courage and skill in the use of fire-arms; they knew nothing of the effects of moral cohesion, or 'esprit du corps,' resulting from proper discipline and long service; on the contrary, they looked upon the entire system of military instruction as not only useless in warfare, but a farce, and treated it accordingly. For example, it was found absolutely impossible, for a time, to prevent their talking and turning around in the ranks at drill and on parade; and no sooner were they posted as sentinels, and their officers out of sight, than they would congregate in groups of three or four, sit down, talk, smoke, play cards, and do almost every thing but attend to their appropriate duties; and, in fact, many of the junior officers appeared to think there was no special impropriety in so doing.

"The officers of the higher grades, who generally had some little knowledge of military matters, were, as may be imagined, supremely disgusted at such gross unsoldierly proceedings, and they resolved to exert all their energies in the enforcement of a more creditable condition of discipline. Accordingly, the most stringent orders were promulgated, requiring frequent drills and other military exercises in strict conformity with the Army Regulations, and the officers of the guards were enjoined to give correct and minute instructions to sentinels, patrols, etc., and to pay vigilant and unremitting attention to the manner in which those orders were executed.

"After a good deal of annoyance and labor we succeeded in inaugurating a uniform system of instruction throughout the camp, which seemed to hold out the encouraging hope of a better state of things, and we congratulated ourselves upon the flattering prospect.

"As I had been instrumental in conducting the details of the new régime, I entertained a laudable ambition to have it carried out properly, and a triumphant issue consummated; and I must confess that I was a good deal encouraged until, one morning, I dressed myself in full uniform, and, mounting my horse completely caparisoned, started out for the purpose of visiting the guards, and ascertaining from personal observation what progress the troops were making under our system of training.

"When I came in sight of the first post, I espied the sentinel seated upon a fence, busily occupied in whittling a stick, with his musket lying upon the ground beside him. As soon as he saw me he jumped down, seized his musket, hurriedly came out to the road, and threw his person into an attitude which he probably considered the position of a soldier, but which was not at all consonant with my understanding of the teachings of Scott, Hardie, or any other tacticians of modern times whose drill-books had come under my observation. His dilapidated, weather-beaten hat, with the broad brim turned up in front, was upon the back of his head; his chin, instead of being '*drawn in*,' was elevated to an angle of something like forty-five degrees with the horizon; his eyes turned up to a still higher inclination, and his head was as fixed and immovable as if it had been held within the jaws of a vice. His concave chest was drawn in, and the natural convexity of his shoulders and back correspondingly augmented and arched, while the abdominal regions were protruded considerably forward, and his legs opened out like a pair of dividers, with his feet exactly parallel to each other and perpendicular to the front.

"It certainly looked as if the man had intentionally reversed the soldierly disposition of every part of his head, body, and limbs; at all events, if he had been turned around, his face placed where the back of his head then was, and the dorsal substituted for the abdominal parts, his attitude, excepting his feet and legs, would not have deviated materially from the correct position of the soldier.

"Before I arrived within a hundred yards of his post, he brought his musket into a position which doubtless he intended for '*present arms*,' with his left hand around the small of the stock, the right hand grasping the barrel near the muzzle, the butt pushed forward, and the bayonet projecting to the rear.

"As I approached, he, without the least perceptible movement of the chin, depressed his eyes toward me, and, with a broad grin upon his countenance, as if he regarded the entire proceeding as something supremely useless and silly, gave his head a short jerking nod as he said, 'How d'do, kurn?'

"I was, of course, most essentially discouraged, but I had no little difficulty in preserving my gravity at this ludicrous exhibition, and yet, as the awkward fellow seemed to be exerting himself to do his best, I took especial pains to instruct him, and kindly informed him that it was not proper for sentinels to talk on post, and that, in presenting arms, he should hold his musket perpendicular.

"He collapsed from his constrained and wearisome attitude into a more careless, easy position at my remark; then coming up to me, and placing his hand upon my horse's neck, replied,

"'Look-a-yere, kurn, I sorter reckon I ain't much fur sogerin nohow, an' I be dog-ond ef I ken git this yere shootin-iron o' mine into shape any way. She won't come "*up-an-dickler*" nohow you can fix 'er.'

"I endeavored to incite the ambition of the willing tyro by the encouraging remark that he would probably be able to execute the manual of arms correctly after he had received a few more lessons; at the same time, I administered a gentle admonition to him for leaving his post and relaxing from the position of a soldier while in the performance of the duties of a sentinel. To which he replied, with the most despondent look and tone of voice,

"'Now look at him! I just like fur to know how

"HALT THAR!"

I'm gwine to do forty things all to once. They want me to haul in my chin, swell out my bussom till she's most busted, cave in my be-owels, squeeze my legs together till you couldn't drive a picayune between um, squar out my feet, and sprawl out my paws to the front like they'd been handlin' something nasty. I tell ye, kurn, this yere can't all be did to once; its no use a talkin'; its on-possible, ole pop, 'sure's yer bornd, an' I'm clean guv out a-tryin'.'

"After giving this man some farther encouragement and information relative to his guard duties, I left, and passed along the line until I encountered another sentinel, who was walking his beat rapidly, and to all appearances keeping a vigilant, sharp lookout in every direction. As soon as he espied me he came to a sudden halt, leaned forward his head, turned his body to the right and left, and, with his eyes contracted, as if he was a good deal puzzled to make me out, scrutinized me from head to foot very closely [I imagine he had never before seen an officer in full-dress uniform], and, as I continued to approach nearer, he came suddenly to a charge, and at the same instant screamed out at the highest pitch of his voice, '*Halt, thar! Whar d'ye come from,* "stranger?"'

"As I did not answer immediately, he, with a most

ferocious cast of countenance, leaped several feet from the ground, and, alighting quite close to me, with his bayonet still pointed directly at my person, exclaimed, in a highly excited manner, 'I'm a *ka-vor-tin kan*-gu-ru! I'm that thing, ole hoss, sartain sure; an' ef yer don't tell me whar yer come from, I'll jab ye with this yere bayonet, by thunder.'

"Not having the faintest conception of what was meant by this rude salutation, and the point of the bayonet being at this juncture in rather closer proximity to my person than was altogether agreeable, I indignantly exclaimed, 'What do you mean? Do you dare to threaten a field-officer in this manner, sir?'

"To which he responded, 'Look-a-yere, Mr. Field Hossifer—ef ye be one—you jist tell me durn'd sudden whether you be one of Uncle Sam's boys or not, *der yer he-ah?*' Then, making another lofty vault into the air, and giving utterance to an exclamation, which sounded, as near as I can express it, like *waugh*, or the suppressed bark of a huge dog, he menacingly awaited my answer.

"I endeavored to calm his impetuosity by explaining to him who I was, and by what authority I called upon him, but it was some time before he was satisfied that it was all right. I finally succeeded, however, in establishing my official identity to his satisfaction, and directed him to give me his orders.

"'Orders!' replied he; 'I don't give nary order to the likes o' you. You'll git 'em from the ole *gin'*ral up thar to head-quarters, I reckon. I'm a private soger man, I is.'

"Perceiving that my meaning was not apprehended, I explained to him that I was not asking orders for my own action, but for those he had received relative to the performance of his duties as a sentinel.

"'Oh ye-as," said he, a gleam of intelligence illuminating his stolid countenance, "I see; you jist want fur to know what I've been drivin at he-ah, don't yer, boss?'

"'Certainly,' said I; 'my object is to ascertain whether you have a knowledge of your guard duties. You will therefore give me *in detail* all the instructions you have received relative to the manner you are to perform those duties.'

"He seemed somewhat puzzled at this, but, after reflecting an instant, replied,

"'Which? *Detail*, did ye say? Why, I toll you I war a private soger; I don't *detail* nobody. The aggetunt up thar to camp—he *detail* every body, I reckon.'

"My patience was nearly exhausted at the perverse stupidity of the fellow, and, almost in despair, I said,

"'Will you, or will you not, tell me what you have been placed here for, and what you have been doing?'

"'Sartain. Why, I've been a-talkin' 'long o' you, hain't I, boss?'

"'Yes, yes; but will you tell me what you have been ordered to do by the non-commissioned officer of the guard who placed you here?'

"'*Az*ackly. Oh ye-as—I see now.' Then, seating himself on a log, he said, 'Now, cap, ef you'll squat yerself 'longside o' me, I'll tell ye all about it.'

"I was not, as may be imagined, in the best humor to receive this familiar invitation in good part, but, for the purpose of learning how far he would carry the farce, I complied with the suggestion, when he placed his hand on my shoulder, looked at me with a most beseeching expression, and, with his mouth close to my ear, said, *sub-voce*,

"'Yer hain't got arry plug o' tobacco 'bout yer clothes, has ye, boss? I've got a powerful hankerin' fur a smoke.'

"I answered in the negative, and directed him to inform me without farther delay what orders he had received.

"'Orders,' said he. 'Oh ye-as, I see; you want them dod-rotted orders. Wall, now, I'll tell yer how it war. Yer see, the surgunt he com'd down he-ah 'long o' me, and says he, "Tom," says he, "you jist stick on this yere post tell somebody—I don't jist now mind who 'twas—comes 'long to take you off."

"'"What *post*, surgunt?" says I. "I don't see nary post 'bout he-ah, an' ef I did, I ain't gwine fur to straddle no post fur nobody. I didn't 'list fur the like o' that."

"'"Ha, ha, ha!" says he. "I don't mean no stake-post; I mean this yere trail right 'long he-ah."

"'"*All-l-l* right, surgunt," says I. "I'll tar-*ry* he-ah tell the cows comes home, you can jist bet your life on that thar, surgunt," says I.'

"I then asked him if the grand rounds had passed his post.

"'Grand which?' replied he.

"'Grand rounds,' I repeated.

"'Nary *round* have com'd this a-way since I war he-ah.'

"'What would you do, then,' I said, 'if the grand rounds were to approach you?'

"'Wall, now, I don't mind hearin' tell o' them fellars afore, but ef they makes sign 'bout he-ah, I'll come a hollar squar on um, sure'—the signification of which I took to be that he would undertake the solution of the somewhat difficult problem of squaring the circle. At the same time he tipped me a significant wink, indicative of his confidence in being able to cope with the formidable unknown.

"After enlightening him in regard to the composition and functions of the grand rounds, I informed him that certain officers were to be saluted with 'present arms,' and others with 'carry arms.' Then, in order to test his memory, I asked how he would salute the commanding officer.

"He very promptly replied, 'I'd come a *pre*-sent on the ole man, an' say, "How do yer find yerself by this time, boss?"'

"I remarked that the general was certainly entitled to a 'present,' but it would be as well to dispense with the verbal part of the salutation.

"The next question I put to him was, 'How would you receive a patrol, should one approach your post?'

"'*Pat*-role?' said he. 'Ef *Pat*-role, or arry other consarned Irishman kicks up a muss 'bout these yere diggins, he'll kotch *par*-tic'lar lightnin'. He'll never eat nary 'nother 'tater, you bet.'

"I explained that the patrol was not, as he seemed to imagine, an individual Hibernian, but an armed body of troops, whose duty it was to pass around the camps for the purpose of ascertaining whether every thing was quiet. He understood this, remarking,

"'Oh ye-as, I see. Them fellars they sorter *rolls* and browses round loose. I'd like monstrous well fur to jine that thar reg-*ment.*'

"As I was about leaving this incorrigible recruit, in absolute despair of being able to teach him his duties, he called out after me, 'Whar do ye stop, cap?'

"'At head-quarters,' replied I.

"'Oh, ye does? Wall, now, mister, I'd like fur ye to tell the ole *gin*'ral, when ye go home, that it's all right up this a-way, an' ef the Rebs is gwine fur to make fight down thar, not to be skeert, fur thar's five or six of us boys from C—— county as has got right smart o' claws, an' ef the ole man will jest let us know when the scrimmage begins, we'll come down an' do some tall scratchin'. We'll go fur um, sartain.'

"After passing entirely around the cordon of outposts, and encountering several other sentinels nearly as intractable as those described, I returned to camp most essentially disheartened.

"Although our efforts were not, for a time, attended with any very favorable results, yet we used our best endeavors to impart instruction to the new levies, and required every thing to be done strictly 'en règle.' Officers of the day, officers of the guards, with contingent details of men from every organization, mounted guard daily.

"The higher grades of officers, as a general rule, applied themselves zealously to their duties, and made commendable progress, but occasionally one appeared who manifested great deficiency in military acquirements, and these sometimes committed most ludicrous blunders."

"LET UM BILE AHEAD!"

"Upon one occasion, at guard mounting, when the new officer of the day was Major ———, who had never before been detailed for the responsible position, he went upon the parade-ground, and took his place beside his predecessor. 'Troop' had 'beat off,' and the adjutant, after bringing the guard to 'present arms,' had faced about, and, with an exceedingly graceful salute, reported, '*Sir, the guard is formed.*'

"At this, to him, rather startling announcement, the major drew his sword, and, imitating the salute of the adjutant, said, in a loud tone of voice, 'Gentlemen, I return your salute.'

"The adjutant repeated, '*Sir, the guard is formed.*'

"The major seemed conscious that something more was expected from him, but what that something was he had no conception of, and, not feeling disposed to display his ignorance by asking information from the outgoing officer of the day, he responded at a venture, 'I'm much obliged to you, Mr. Adjutant. A little more music—let us have a little more music, if you please, sir.'

"The astonished adjutant faced about, and ordered the band to 'beat off' again, then brought the guard to a 'present,' and again reported, '*Sir, the guard is formed.*'

"The major, at this critical juncture, finding himself cornered, and that it was necessary to do something to extricate himself from the difficulty, exclaimed, in despair, 'Yes, yes, Mr. Adjutant, I see they are. *Well, d—n it, let um bile ahead; I'm ready for um.*'"

POSTAGE-STAMPS.

Another amusing incident was related to me by the lieutenant colonel of a Kansas regiment which was recruited at an early period of the war, and commanded by Colonel E——g, who subsequently achieved distinction as a general officer.

This regiment, for the most part, was composed of excellent material, as its war record proved; but a few men were found among its original elements who hailed from the most sequestered districts near the Cherokee line, and these were as difficult to manipulate into soldiers as the wild hunters of Arkansas.

The colonel, however, was a good disciplinarian, and went zealously to work imparting to them rudimental military instruction involving correct notions of discipline, respect for rank, etc., and his efforts were attended with such satisfactory results that, while sitting in his tent one evening conversing with several of his officers upon the great value of strict discipline in a well-organized army, he took occasion to remark that, through their cordial co-operation, his men were now beginning to deport themselves like soldiers, and that it afforded him the highest gratification in observing that the rank and file seemed to appreciate the necessity of paying proper respect to commissioned officers, etc.

While the topic was being discussed the sides of the tent door were slowly drawn apart, and disclosed the tall, lank figure of a backwoods recruit, *sans* hat, coat, or pants, within the opening, and deliberately taking a survey of the occupants.

The colonel was astounded at the cool impertinence of the fellow, and indignantly inquired of him why he presumed to make his appearance before his commanding officer in such scanty attire, and demanded to know what he wanted.

At this brusque salutation the man drew the flaps of the tent together around his neck, only leaving his face exposed, and in the most innocent and ingenuous manner said, "*Thar hain't none of you fellars got arry postage-stomp, has ye?*"

ONE HUNDRED AND SECOND RHODE ISLAND.

The following spicy little episode, which I have never seen published, occurred while the Army of the Potomac confronted the Confederate troops at the siege of Yorktown in 1862.

Our lines at that time extended entirely across the peninsula from York to James Rivers, and the pickets of the two armies were often in such proximity that conversations were occasionally carried on between them.

Upon one occasion, when the Second Rhode Island Infantry (I think it was) was upon outpost duty, one of the vedettes, espying a Confederate soldier within hailing distance, called out to him,

"Heow d'du, Reb?" To which the other replied, "I'ze sort'er middlin'. How's yerself, Yank?"

After the customary salutations had passed, our sentinel inquired what regiment the other was attached to. The man answered, "To the Twenty-third North Carolina."

Now the martial representative from the eminently patriotic little New England State did not for a moment believe it probable that North Carolina had furnished the Confederate Army with any thing like so large a contingent as twenty-three regiments; in other words, he was inclined to believe that his *vis-a-vis* was attempting to sell him. Accordingly he replied,

"'Shaw! You git eout! Yeou don't say you've got twenty-three regiments from North Caroliny, du ye, Reb?"

"We have, Yank, 'sure's yer bornd. Thar's a almighty heap o' sogers in this yere army. You can jist go yer pile on that thar, and weuns low's they ar gwine fur to do some tall fitin' when the scrimmage begins."

He then asked, "What rig-*ment* mought you b'long to, Yank?"

Not feeling inclined to be outgeneraled in what he conceived to be an adroit piece of detective strategy, having for its object the discovery of the strength of our forces, he made the following ambiguous response: "Wall, neou, I kinder guess I b'long tu the Hundred and Second Rhode Island Infantry."

"The *hell* you say, stranger! You don't *pre*-tend fur to say you's got a hundred and twenty-two rig-*ments* from that thar one-hoss, no-'count little state of Rho-dy Island, does ye, Yank?"

"By golly, I guess you'll think so when the fitin' begins, and thur's a darned site more on 'um a comin' every day, I tell *you*, Reb."

The Southerner seemed rather dismayed at this statement, and inquired,

"How many rig-*ments* does you 'low you's got from the State of New York, Yank?"

"Wall, neou, I dun-no fur sar-tain adzackly heou menny; but there's in this 'ere army a all-fired lot on 'um, you bet; I hearn talk abeout a thousand, but mab-by we hain't got mor'n nine hundred and fifty regiments from York State, and e'en a'most as menny from Pennsilvany, I cal-cur-late."

RIFLE-PIT.

Another superlatively ludicrous incident, which actually occurred in the Army of the Potomac, and afforded a good deal of amusement at the time, I have never seen published, but if it has been, I dare say there are many who have not read it. I will, therefore, take the liberty of introducing it here.

During the most severely contested period of the

battle of "Bull Run," General Franklin, in passing from one portion of his command to another, espied a soldier ensconced very securely in a pit where he was completely covered from the missiles of the enemy, which at that particular juncture happened to be flying more densely than he appeared to think consistent with his safety above ground.

As soon as the general saw the man, he called out to him, and asked him what he meant by skulking in that cowardly manner, and in a very peremptory tone ordered him to get out of the pit and join his company instantly. He did not probably recognize the general; at all events, instead of obeying the order, he crouched closer to the ground than before, and, turning his eyes toward the general, placed his thumb to his nose, with his fingers spread out, and slowly moving his head from right to left, replied,

"No yer don't. I know what yer after; ye want this hole yerself, but yer ca-a-a-an't come it, old fellar."

CUT OUT OF A RIDE.

Another superlatively ludicrous episode was related to me as having occurred after this memorable battle, the substance of which was as follows:

After our newly-levied volunteers had been defeat-

NO YER DON'T.

ed, and were endeavoring, by a most precipitate but rather promiscuous retreat, to make their escape to Washington, an officer who had been using his best efforts to rally the dispersed forces encountered a man who, notwithstanding he had thrown away his musket, knapsack, and every thing else that retarded his locomotion, had been unable to keep pace with his comrades, and when the officer approached he was entirely alone, and so much wearied that, in a despairing tone, he said to him,

"I say, Mister Officer, does that ere hoss o' yourn kerry double? Bekase, ef he does, I'd be obleeged to ye ef ye'd let me git up behind and ride a leetle ways, fur I'm e'en a-jest gin out a walkin'."

"No, sir," replied the officer, "my horse will not carry double, and if he would, I should not allow you to ride behind me. Your place is with your company, and, unless you join it very soon, the rebels will be likely to kill or capture you, for they are pressing us very closely just now."

This startling announcement produced so serious an effect upon the nervous system of the young soldier that he seemed to abandon all hopes of escape, and, in absolute despair, dropped upon the ground and burst into a violent paroxysm of crying; whereupon the officer gave him a sharp reprimand, saying, among other things, that he was ashamed to see a soldier behave so much like a child, and that, in his opinion, it would be better for him to go home to his mother.

The only response the poor fellow condescended to make to this observation was, as the officer rode away,

"You g'lang with yer darned ugly ole kickin-up critter. I wouldn't ride behind such a mean cuss as you be, nohow. I don't keer if I be a child—boo-ho-o-o-o-o; I wish I was a baby—an' I wish I was a gal baby tue; an' I wish I was tu hum 'long o' mum-mar, an' so I du—boo-ho-o-o-o-o-o-o!"

MONTEREY.

The foregoing incident reminds me of a circumstance which occurred in front of Monterey during the severely contested battle which resulted in the capture of that place in 1846. In the hottest part of the engagement, when the enemy was pouring down showers of balls and shells upon our brave assaulting columns, General Taylor, while riding around viewing operations upon the north side of the town, espied quite a number of men of the ——— battalion who were quietly lying down in some stone-quarry holes outside the line of defenses.

Taking it for granted they had all fallen in the engagement, the general, with evident manifestation of feeling, remarked, "What terrible slaughter there has been here, Major Bliss!"

Hearing the exclamation, one of the men raised his head and said, "Oh no, general, we ain't dead yet." Whereupon "Old Zack," not in his most amiable mood, responded, "No, sir, I see you are not, and I'll be d—d if I think you intend to be."

CANDIDATE FOR PRESIDENCY.

This allusion to General Taylor reminds me of a laughable circumstance that occurred previous to the battle of Monterey, while the army was en route from Comargo.

It will be remembered that about this time the achievements of General Taylor began to excite attention and interest among the people throughout the United States, and shortly before this his name, for the first time, had been suggested as a most available one for the presidency; but whether this fact had any thing to do with the following episode, I leave it for the reader to judge.

At the time alluded to, General Taylor was riding near the head of the column, in company with several officers of rank, among whom were the veteran

General Belknap, father of our gallant War Secretary, and Colonel Whiting, of the Quartermaster's Department, when they arrived upon the bank of a considerable stream that was not bridged, and which it was necessary to cross.

The water was so turbid that its depth could not be seen from the bank, but it had the appearance of being fordable, and, as the soldiers came up, they at once commenced taking off their foot-gear and rolling up their pants preparatory to entering the stream.

General Taylor, impatient to proceed, took one of the men up behind him and plunged into the water. Colonel Whiting followed with another soldier en croupe; but General Belknap, instead of duplicating the burden of his horse, rode in alone; whereupon Colonel Whiting, turning round in his saddle, and looking at him with an air of some surprise, said, "Why do you not carry one of the volunteers across the river, General Belknap?"

"Because," replied he, "the water is not very deep, the men can not all ride over, and one might as well walk as another. Moreover," added he, while casting a significant glance at General Taylor, who was near him, "*I never expect to be a candidate for the presidency, sir.*"

CHAPTER VI.

PIONEERS OF THE WEST.

Ole Man Sykes.—Bound for Bannock.—Monsieur Maron.—How's your Wife?—New religious Creed.—Black-Hawk War.—A Surrender.—Stampede.—A legal Entanglement.—Visit to Chicago.—Winter in New England.—Stirrup-cup.—Indian Performance.

OLE MAN SYKES.

While journeying through Northern Minnesota in 1858, I had the pleasure of meeting Sir Francis Sykes, an English amateur sporting gentleman, who was returning from an extended hunting expedition upon the head waters of the Saskatchawan and its tributaries, in the Hudson Bay Company's territory. He had several wagons loaded with moose, elk, mountain sheep, and antelope antlers, buffalo heads, panther and grizzly bear skins, and numerous other trophies of his prowess, all of which were kindly exhibited to me, and the manner, locality, and circumstances attending the discovery, capture, and killing of each were minutely described by the distinguished votary of Nimrod.

Sir Francis was eminently dignified and courtly in his deportment, but at the same time there was a high-toned urbanity, mixed with a good share of dry humor, in his composition; and he evinced a keen appreciation for the ludicrous, as the following story, related by himself, will show:

In passing through the unsettled wilds of Minnesota, *en route* to Fort Garry and the hunting-grounds in the Far North, Sir Francis happened to fall in with an old hunter and trapper, who had passed the best part of his life in the mountains, and whose adventures interested him so much that he employed him to act as guide and hunter to his party.

This man was one of those anomalous, self-reliant specimens of humanity only found among the Indians, or in the outer line of frontier settlements, and he regarded himself fully as good, if not a little better, than the President of the United States, or any potentate in the universe. Moreover, he entertained the most supreme contempt for what he considered as the ridiculous conventionalities and customs of civilized society, having no respect whatever for the deference paid by many to rank and titles. He could not be taught to give Sir Francis his proper appellation, but generally called him "Pap," or "Ole man Sykes;" and when he wished to be particularly respectful he would address him as "Cap," "Boss," or "Square." This, however, did not give Sir Francis any uneasiness, as he was a sensible man, and rather enjoyed the thing than otherwise.

The party, augmented by this "Leather-stocking," continued on down Red River to Pembina, and in due course of time arrived at Fort Garry, when the extensive retinue drew up in front of the gate, and Sir Francis directed his guide to go in, find the governor, and say to him that Sir Francis Sykes, just arrived from London, presented his compliments to Governor Mactavish, and begged he would do him the favor of stepping out for a moment, as he desired to speak with him; and, in order to insure that no blunder should be made, he repeated the message to the man, who gave him to understand that he comprehended its purport perfectly, and thereupon entered the fort, quite elated at the importance of his errand, and the confidence reposed in him by his distinguished employer. Having ascertained where the governor's quarters were, he went directly up to the door, and, without ringing or knocking, opened it, entered *sans cérémonie*, and approaching the governor, who was seated at a table busily engaged in writing, administered a hearty slap upon his back with his huge paw, and said, "How are ye by this time, ole hoss?"

Astounded at such audacious familiarity, the dignified governor jumped to his feet, and facing the intruder with a menacing expression of countenance, exclaimed, "What in the devil do you mean, you scoundrel? Get out of my house instantly, or I'll have you kicked out!"

The guide was by no means intimidated or discomposed at this rude reception of his well-meant salutation, but with a significant wink of one eye, as much as to indicate that he knew what he was about, replied, "Hold on, gov; keep cool, and skip the hard words, fur ole man Sykes, out thar to the gate, wants to see ye. He's got some comple-*ments* for ye, I guess. So come along, gov, and don't be skeert; I'll show ye the way!"

BANNOCK OR BUST.

The stoical indifference with which the frontiersman submits to misfortunes of the most disastrous character, as well as his recuperative nature, is strikingly illustrated in the following incident, related by an ex-governor of Montana, who was questioned by some Eastern friends regarding the character and resources of the country over which his official jurisdiction extended.

The governor, who was of sanguine temperament, replied that it was generally regarded as possessing decided advantages over almost any other of our new territories; indeed, he said he had never seen or heard of but one man who was not captivated with it, and that individual did not remain long enough to thoroughly appreciate its merits. The person he alluded to was bound for Bannock, and had met with a good many accidents upon the road, such as losing his cattle, breaking his wagon, and in various other ways, which would have disheartened most men; but he was by no means discouraged, and pushed forward with unabated vigor until he lost all his animals except one ox and a small cow. These, as a dernier resort, he yoked together, and they constituted the only remaining motive power for his wagon. Still he was undaunted in his purpose to accomplish the journey he had undertaken, and, as an evidence of this fact, he had, with a piece of charcoal, written in large characters upon the side of his wagon, "*Bannock or bust.*" At length, however, the severe labor proved too much for the poor cow, and she died; and, as if to complete the catalogue of his disasters, his only remaining animal took it into his head to stampede, and he was then left without any means of transportation. About this time the governor was passing, and observed the man sitting over a small fire in rather a disconsolate mood, but apparently endeavoring to keep up his spirits by whistling "Hail, Columbia!" The inscription upon his wagon, however, had been erased, and a new one substituted in its place, as follows—"*Busted, by thunder!*"

MONSIEUR MARON.

While I was stationed at Fort Winnebago, now Portage City, I encountered, among other unique specimens of humanity, an Indian trader by the name of Maron, who prided himself specially upon his French lineage.

He had, at an early age, enlisted in the service of the Northwest Fur Company, leaving his home in Canada for the Indian country, where he had remained ever since. He had cast aside what he conceived to be the senseless conventionalities of the settlements, and adopted many of the more useful habits and customs of the natives.

When I first met him he was probably over seventy years of age, yet his mental and physical powers were then as active and vigorous as those of most men in the meridian of life; and, strange as it may appear, he had just perpetrated the hazardous experiment of espousing "*à la mode de sauvage*" his fourth wife, who was a vivacious young squaw of about sixteen, and quite an interesting and attractive specimen of her race.

The old man was very much enamored with his new bride, and seemed perfectly happy during the first few days of the *re-re-reiterated* honeymoon; but, possessing a suspicious disposition, and a highly nervous and impulsive temperament, he in a short time took it into his imagination that he was too old to please the fancy of so young a girl, and became furiously jealous of every young man who spoke to his wife, or even came near his house.

Knowing this foible in his character, and being somewhat inclined to practical jokes, I took every opportunity to inquire anxiously after the health of *madame;* but, instead of receiving this in good part, the old man invariably turned away from me manifesting symptoms of great displeasure.

One morning when, as it appeared, the old gentleman happened to be in particularly ill humor, I called at his house, and, after extending to him the customary compliments of the day, I very blandly asked, "Comment se porte la madame ce matin, monsieur?" (How's your wife this morning, sir?)

Instead of giving a direct answer to my courteous interrogatory, his countenance assumed a ferocious expression, and he walked back and forth for some time gesticulating rapidly, and muttering to himself some unintelligible French jargon, the only part of which I comprehended was a frequent guttural roll of the emphatic French adjective "*Sac-r-r-r-ré*," coupled with what I took to be the not very complimentary adjunct of "*Yankee*," most spitefully hissed out from between his teeth.

After giving vent to his indignation in this manner for a while, the expression of his face suddenly changed. Assuming an air of the most triumphant gratification, and walking directly to me, he straightened himself up, placed his arms akimbo, and, looking me in the eyes, said,

"*What for you keep* ax me dat all 'e time, eh? Sac-r-r-r-ré battam. What for, eh? *How's you wife yousef?*"

This superlatively ludicrous retort caused me to explode with an uproarious peal of laughter, which exasperated the old man to such a degree that, coming close to my side, and raising his voice to the highest pitch, he screamed into my ear, "*Mistère Yankee! I like for know how's you wife yousef, eh?*" Then, turning his back upon me in the most contemptuous manner, he rapidly walked away, believing, no doubt, that he had completely demolished me.

Time did not have the effect of assuaging the irritation produced upon his sensitive imagination, or of

HOW'S YOUR WIFE?

reconciling the discords in his household. On the contrary, his jealousy continued to become more and more annoying and vexatious to the young wife, until at length she was unable to endure it longer, and left him for Prairie du Chien, where she found friends that protected her.

The old man took her loss very much to heart, and for days did nothing but walk solitarily around his house with his head cast down, and apparently buried in deep melancholy reflections. Indeed, the poor fellow seemed almost heart-broken.

I chanced to meet him about this time, and, feigning ignorance of what had occurred to him, expressed the earnest hope that madame continued to enjoy her usual good health.

He looked up at me with an expression which indicated any thing but credulity as to the sincerity of my motives, and, with a very indignant scowl upon his face, replied, "Ma femme? you like for find out where he gone, eh? C'est bon, by gar, I tell you! He gone's to ze prairie de sac-r-r-r-ré battam dog, c'est bon, let him gone!"

Maron was of Roman Catholic parentage, and had received his early education under the strictest tenets of that creed; but he had been so long separated from all the influences of Christianity in any form, that he had become rather indifferent to the things that pertained to his spiritual welfare, and consequently gave himself but little anxiety or thought upon the subject; yet, if any one had intimated to him that the course of life he was leading was such as to jeopardize the salvation of his soul, he would have been highly astonished and incensed.

It was seldom, in those days, that we saw a preacher of the Gospel, and the few that visited us were of the itinerant order, whose extended circuits over the sparsely populated district rendered their periodical visits, like those of a higher order of beings, "few and far between."

Father B——, a very zealous ecclesiastic of the Jesuitic order, upon one occasion came to our settlement, and during his sojourn called upon the Frenchman, who received him very kindly, and, after a short preliminary conversation, the priest approached the subject of his mission by inquiring of him if he was a religious man.

With an air of surprise at such a question, the old man answered, "Certainement, monsieur! religious man me, *very mouch.*"

"Pray, Monsieur Maron, will you have the kindness to inform me what denomination of Christians you class yourself with?"

He replied tartly, but with decided emphasis, and rapidly nodding his head at the same time, "*De same as me fader.*"

"Ah yes, yes, I see. Will you permit me, then, to ask you, monsieur, what particular persuasion of religious people your father associated with?"

"Oui, monsieur," replied he, "*wid de same peeps as me grandfader.*"

"Very well, monsieur. Will you also allow me to inquire what name was given to the particular faith that was adopted by your venerated ancestors, and through them transmitted to you?"

He hesitated for a moment, and seemed somewhat puzzled to find an answer to the interrogatory thus reiterated upon him in so many different forms, but he soon rallied and promptly responded, "Oui! oui!! oui!!! *Me religion he de same kind as de bibe.*"

The good "father," in despair at getting any more definite information from him concerning the complexion of his religious sentiments, intimated to him that it was all very well, provided the Bible which he took for his guidance was the version sanctioned by the Romish authorities, but cautioned him against the diabolical influences of the rendering given by the Protestants to the same book.

Some weeks subsequent to this a preacher of the

Methodist persuasion came around, and during his stay among our people he took occasion to call upon the Frenchman, but failed to elicit any more satisfactory information about the old man's religion than the Jesuit had done. He, however, gave him good spiritual counsel, and left a Bible, which he recommended him to peruse daily, and bade him a kind adieu.

He continued on his circuit, and in due course of time returned to the settlement, when he again paid a visit to the Frenchman, hoping that the good seed which he had dropped by the wayside might have germinated during his absence; but, unfortunately for the success of his efforts, the Jesuit had been there in the interim, and had taken the responsibility of throwing the obnoxious Protestant Bible into the fire.

Knowing nothing of this, the preacher inquired of Maron if he had complied with his request in frequently reading the Scriptures during his absence. He answered, "I no reads him mouch now, for ze d—d priest he burns up all de bibe in de fi."

When I next encountered the old man I remarked to him that I had understood the *French* priest had been burning Bibles, and playing the devil generally at his house. He was nettled at the nationality of the allusion, and replied, with considerable irritation, "C'est vrai, zat is so, monsieur. Ze *French* priest he burn ze bibe, but all ze 'Merican peeps he make de dev' too, by gar."

After many years' absence in the mountains about the head waters of the Missouri and Yellowstone, the old man returned to Montreal on a visit to his friends and relatives, but on his arrival he, like Rip Van Winkle after his protracted nap, wandered about the streets, not being able to recognize a single familiar face. All his relatives were either dead or absent, and the friends of his youth had disappeared, so that he soon turned his back in disappointment and sorrow upon the place of his nativity, and resolved to go back to the Indian country and spend the remainder of his days there.

Accordingly, he embarked upon a steamer at Buffalo (the *Uncle Sam*), on which it so happened that General Scott and his staff, who were about making the tour of the Lakes, were passengers. The steamers of that period had no private state-rooms, but there were large dormitory cabins, in which all the passengers slept in berths ranged upon the sides.

On the morning following their departure the general was making his toilet in the cabin, when Maron entered, and omitted to close the door after him.

As it was quite cold at the time, the general looked up at him scowlingly, and, pointing to the open door, said to him, in a very stern and peremptory tone of voice, "*Shut that door, sir.*"

The old man was not accustomed to this dictatorial manner of issuing orders, and, instead of obeying, replied, in an equally brusque manner, "No, General Scott, me no shet e-door. My money good as every peoples, by gar."

The general saw that he had made a mistake, and very graciously begged pardon, but asked the old man very politely if he would be so obliging as to close the door which he had left open.

He answered with a profound bow, "Certainement, General Scott. Me shet e-door for you wid very mouch plaisir."

THE BLACK-HAWK WAR.

The early pioneers of Wisconsin will remember that in the spring of 1831 the government gave notice to the Sac and Fox Indians that, in accordance with a treaty made with a few of their people, they must at once leave the beautiful land of their nativity on Rock River and remove west of the Mississippi. As this treaty, like many others made with the Indians, had been forced upon them by designing agents and rapacious traders, speculators, and interpreters, it was not regarded by them as having the sanction of a majority of the tribe, and they did not, therefore, consider themselves bound to carry out its stipulations. Accordingly, they assembled under the leadership of Black Hawk, established their camp on Rock River, and firmly resolved not to be driven from their homes.

This determination, amounting to a declaration of hostilities, necessitated the calling into the field a considerable force of regulars and volunteers, and among the latter contingent was a battalion of mounted volunteers recruited about the lead mines in Northern Illinois. They rendezvoused at Galena, where they were organized, and elected for their colonel a very respectable lawyer by the name of S——, who doubtless had a thorough knowledge of his legal profession, but was not particularly well versed in the art of war, and evinced no special ambition to immortalize himself by deeds of martial valor. He therefore, at first, positively declined the position; but, as he was an exceedingly popular man, his numerous friends urged him so persistently to take the office, that at length they prevailed upon him to do so.

The battalion was immediately mustered into service, and soon armed, equipped, mounted, and on the way to the theatre of war, from whence it was anticipated that many of them might never return. The continuation of the narrative of the campaign in which this regiment figured was related to me by a friend of Colonel S——, from whom, as he asserted, he received it, and I believe the burden of it to be a correct account of what actually occurred.

After scouting the country for some time in the vicinity of where it was supposed the Indians were waiting an opportunity to make a bold strike, and discovering no recent signs of them, they one evening encamped upon the grassy border of a beautiful stream, and had no sooner unsaddled their horses than a scout came in and reported to the commander that the redoubtable Black Hawk, with his entire band, was then only a few miles distant, and might at any moment be expected to attack them.

This startling intelligence instantly put the camp into a high state of excitement, and some of the bold volunteers, who before this had professed supreme contempt for the savages, now manifested symptoms of decided alarm.

The colonel promptly issued orders for putting every thing in readiness for action. The horses were picketed in close proximity to the bivouac; picket-guards, vedettes, and patrols were sent out on all avenues of approach, and every other precaution was taken to guard against a surprise. The sentinels were instructed to walk their posts continually, and keep a sharp look-out for the enemy in all directions; and special orders were given, in case the Indians were seen, to fire their muskets and give the alarm by crying "*Indians!*"

The colonel, after seeing that his orders for the safety of the camp had been properly enforced, picketed his horse to a black stump with a long lariat, which allowed him to graze within a circle of which the rope was the radius, retired to his bivouac fire, and, without taking off his clothes, laid down for the night. Being much exhausted, he soon fell into a profound slumber, which, however, was constantly disturbed by frightful dreams, in which bloody encounters with the Indians, resulting in the total defeat of his own troops, and followed by the concomitants of tomahawking, scalping, and other barbarities incited by the savage instincts of the enemy, were predominant, so that his imagination became wrought up to as high a pitch of excitement as was possible under the effects of a horrible nightmare.

In the midst of this he was roused from his deep sleep by the sudden discharge of a musket, and the alarming shout of "Indians! Indians! Indians!" in close proximity to his head.

He bounded like lightning to his feet, and in a terrified, semi-somnolent state saw his men running about in all directions, in the greatest possible confusion and terror, and he, for the moment, had but a very faint conception as to who or where he was. Of one fact, however, he felt perfectly confident—which was, that the savages were upon him, and that his only safety consisted in getting away from them as soon as possible.

Accordingly, he instinctively bolted for his horse, leaped upon his back without saddle or bridle, and driving the rowels into his flanks, bounded off at full speed. But one end of the lariat being still fastened to the stump, caused the horse, when he, with tremendous momentum, was brought up at the opposite extremity, to turn heels over head upon the ground, and land his rider some ten or twelve yards in advance, causing him to see more stars than the most powerful telescope ever brought to view in the firmament.

He imagined he had been knocked off by an Indian, but raised himself up again as soon as he recovered sufficiently from the effects of the fall; and his horse, in rising, having turned his head in the oppo-

DISMOUNTED CAVALRY.

site direction, he again leaped upon his back, and, with a vigorous application of the spurs, away he went the second time, until the rope again caused them to turn a somersault, with the colonel sprawling upon the ground. He was, if possible, more stunned by the concussion than before, and regarded it as certain that he had been again knocked down with a war-club or tomahawk, and that he must now be completely surrounded by the savages. This situation seemed to him so perilous that he began to despair of making his escape; but he was a man of great firmness of purpose, and he resolved to make one more effort, and endeavor by a desperate charge to force his way through the hostile cordon. Accordingly, he mounted the third time, and the generous animal he bestrode, in obedience to the will of his master, enforced by a severe punishment with both spurs, again dashed off at full speed, but in a circle around and around the stump, until his feet became entangled in the lariat, and he was thrown down again, this time casting his rider near the black stump, which he, in the darkness of the night, imagined to be an Indian warrior standing knife in hand, ready to take his devoted scalp.

He deliberated for an instant in fear and trembling as to the course he should pursue in this critical position. He was by no means a coward, but was fully conscious of the fact that mercy was not embraced in the catalogue of savage virtues, and that he had little compassion to expect if he fell into their clutches. Yet, as a last resort for escaping a horrible death by torture, he concluded to make a final desperate appeal to the better instincts of the savage heart, and, dropping upon his knees before the stump, he raised his hands in the most suppliant attitude, turned up his eyes with an imploring expression, and exclaimed, in the last accents of despair, "*Mister Indian, I surrender!*"

As the fancied warrior did not respond to this touching appeal, he soon became conscious of his mistake, and, seeing no Indians about, untied his horse, mounted, and set out in pursuit of his stampeded fellow-soldiers, who in the darkness had scattered in the utmost confusion all over the prairies, believing that the relentless chief and his savage band were upon their trail, and even at their heels.

In the obscurity of the night they were unable to distinguish a white man from an Indian, and whenever they separated they seldom came together again. Occasionally one of them, coming in sight of a supposed comrade, would endeavor to overtake him, while the other, believing he was pursued by an Indian, would press his horse vigorously to escape, and in this way some of the fleetest races came off upon that memorable night.

A small squad of the men, who had recognized each other, and united about daylight on the following morning, made a short halt to give their wearied horses a little rest, and were discussing the affair of the previous night, when they saw a negro servant of one of the officers coming on horseback at full speed, and seemingly in great alarm. As he was about passing them without slackening his pace, they ordered him to halt. He screamed out in reply, as he continued to urge his horse forward, "Wha-wha-what ye want? Please don't stop me, gemmen! Do-do-don't do it, I tell ye, fur I'ze the wust demurralized niggar that *pre*haps you ever seed in all yer born'd days!"

They were obliged to point a pistol at him before they succeeded in stopping him. At first he was so much terrified that he could hardly speak. After he had partially recovered they asked him what had induced him to desert his master and run away in the cowardly manner he had done.

He replied, "Wall, now, gemmen, I'll tell ye how it war. Ye see, de boys they thout mabbe mout be Ingines in de camp; but they didn't git very bad

A DEMORALIZED NEGRO.

skeert at fuss, and saddled their hosses; but bime-by dey git sight o' de cunnel, an' he war jist a-gwine it on the most *retreet-in-est* hoss you ever did see; an' they tuck skeert, the boys did, an' they jist broke fur the pur-rar-rees; an' my ole masser he outrun me all to smash, an' my hoss he git used up mighty fass, an' I speck every minute de Ingine he cotch dis chile; but heah I is now, tank de Lor', an' like to git muster out mighty quick."

The result of all this was that the battalion became dispersed over the entire country; some brought up at Fort Winnebago (now Portage City), some at Galena, and others at Prairie du Chien, and it was several weeks before they were assembled again; indeed, it is believed that some of them were never heard of afterward.

An investigation into the affair showed that no Indians had been near the camp when the stampede occurred, and that the alarm was occasioned by a sentinel seeing a large black wolf approaching his post, which he took to be an Indian crawling up to him on "all-fours," and he gave the designated signal of alarm.

A LEGAL DIFFICULTY.

I verily believe that I am one of the most amiable and best-natured men in the world, for I never had a quarrel or serious difficulty with any one, except perhaps at rare intervals with my better half—(but this, dear reader, is emphatically *entre nous*, and is softly whispered in your ear, with the express understanding that she must not be told of it, for the dear old lady might give me a private lecture if she supposed for a moment I disclosed family secrets). But there is one consolation—we always made it up, and were better friends than ever afterward. Moreover, I have never sued any body, and have been so fortunate during my somewhat protracted and diversified career as only once to have become entangled in the meshes of the law.

Upon that memorable occasion it was my misfortune to have been brought before the bar of justice in the wilds of Illinois. This *contretemps* happened during the winter of 1837–38, while I was making a pleasure excursion from Northern Wisconsin to Chicago and back; and as the circumstance was a source of no little amusement to our friends at the time, the narration of it at this distant day may serve to indemnify the reader for the time expended in its perusal.

One lovely morning, when the thermometer ranged many degrees below the freezing-point, and the atmosphere was pure and invigorating, with the snow in the best possible condition for sleighing, I joined a party of ladies and gentlemen, and with four capital horses hitched to a large sleigh well provided with robes, we set out across the prairies for Chicago. Our track led us through Madison, Janesville, Rockford, Belvidere, etc., all of which were then small villages, and the fare we encountered at the primitive inns of the country was not as luxurious then as can be found at the present time; yet we made the best of it, and had a jolly time for about a week, which brought us to our destination.

Entering the city, we drove directly to the "Lake House," which had just been completed, and was regarded by our rural party as about the most magnificent hotel in the universe. Sumptuous apartments were assigned to us, and every thing was done by the obliging proprietor to make us comfortable; and here we ate of the first fresh oysters that were ever introduced into that city (canned oysters were then unknown), and these were brought in sleighs all the way from New Haven, Connecticut, and were, of course, sold at fabulous prices.

This was probably the first time printed bills of fare and napkins had appeared at a Western hotel table, and the comments they elicited from some of the "Hoosiers" and "Suckers" were droll in the extreme. For instance, one verdant individual from the Wabash, after seating himself at the dinner-table, and not having been furnished with those indispensable adjuncts to a modern table, called to the waiter in a loud voice, saying, "Look-a-yere, mister, I don't mind ef I hev one o' them thar catalogues an' towels."

"LOOK-A-YERE, MISTER!"

The bills of fare were gotten up strictly *en règle*, with the different courses, such as soup, fish, etc., etc., duly classified. Even *entrées* were embraced upon the list, but the variety of dishes under this particular heading was usually rather meagre. Indeed, I remember one day to have observed only one dish named in the list, and that read "*Pomme de terre au naturel.*"

After an exceedingly pleasant sojourn of several days in the flourishing new city of the West, we started on our return, with a re-enforcement to our team of two beautiful horses, which I purchased from John Frink, the great pioneer stage-proprietor.

Our first night out was passed in a tavern kept by one P——, at Elgin, on Fox River. If the house is still standing, and has the same landlord (which the Lord forbid), I caution all travelers who may in future have occasion to pass that way to give his establishment a wide berth, for a more unmitigated scamp it has seldom been my misfortune to encounter.

After a night spent in defending ourselves against the incessant attacks of an army, or rather a navy, of "couch pirates," we paid an extortionate bill and gladly left the premises, shaking the dust from our feet as we went out, and, entering our sleigh, drove rapidly away with our six spanking steeds, consoling ourselves that henceforth we were out of the clutches of our rapacious and disobliging Boniface. But in this we were mistaken, and "counted without our host;" for we had not proceeded over about ten miles when we were overtaken by a horseman, apparently much excited, his horse at a gallop, and reeking with sweat.

As he was passing us I remarked to him that he

seemed in a great hurry, and asked if any thing unusual had occurred. Without slackening his pace, he answered, "You'll find out what's the matter when you reach the next tavern." And on he went, leaving us in perplexity as to the cause of his excitement.

A short time after this we arrived at a town in the woods called Sunderland, containing two log houses and a blacksmith's shop. As soon as we had halted at the "Buck-horn" tavern a constable approached and served a writ upon the party, under a charge of petty larceny, with a specification that we had been guilty of purloining a buffalo skin from the house where we had lodged.

Of course we were superlatively exasperated at the impertinent proceeding, and indignantly told the fellow if he took us for thieves he had better search our sleigh, and ascertain for himself whether it contained any thing besides our own luggage.

"That is precisely what I propose to do," coolly replied he; and we all, accompanied by five or six stage-drivers—friends of the man who professed to have lost the robe—went to our vehicle and commenced overhauling our baggage. To our utter astonishment, under one of our own robes was a miserably dirty old buffalo skin which did not belong to us.

The man who had pursued us eagerly seized the article, exclaiming, "That's my property!" and triumphantly held it up to the inspection of the surrounding crowd, who, by significant nods, winks, and smiles, unmistakably indicated that we were regarded by them as very far from being honest travelers.

We afterward ascertained that our host of the Elgin House, in co-operation with the stage-driver, had placed the robe in our sleigh for the express purpose of extorting money from us; and, in accordance with the plot, the driver who had caused our arrest intimated that he was willing to compromise the matter, and quash proceedings upon the payment of five dollars, which we rejected with scorn.

Finding that no levy could be made upon our purses in this manner, he said the law must take its course, and we were taken into the bar-room of the inn, where we found the country justice who had issued the warrant for our arrest, and a ragged old pettifogger, whose bloated visage gave strong presumptive evidence that he would not be likely to decline a pressing invitation "to liquor," together with a motley collection of hangers-on about the tavern, whom curiosity had drawn together upon this interesting occasion.

The magistrate, who was a plain, sensible-looking

old farmer, apparently possessing more knowledge of agriculture than law, was seated before a small pine table, with pen, ink, and paper, and, as soon as the parties were assembled, he intimated that the court was opened and in readiness for business.

The pettifogger then, in a very consequential manner, rose to his feet (he had been seated upon a log of wood near the fire), and, after discharging a huge quid of tobacco from his mouth into the fire, and hemming and hawing, and looking daggers at the prisoners for a while, opened the case with the following exordium:

"May it please the honorable Court and gentlemen, as the attorney for the plaintiff in this important case I remark, *firstly*, that I expect, and I have no doubt I shall have, a fair and impartial hearing and decision from this highly enlightened Court. My client, who is a gentleman of the highest standing in this respectable community, has been feloniously deprived of his lawful property. Yes, may it please yer honor, he has been robbed; he has been robbed! I say; and by whom, yer honor? I'll tell you by whom—by an organized gang of pillagers."

Just at this moment I tapped him on the back and pointed to the bar, indicating that I desired him to drink with me. He asked the Court to excuse him for a moment, went to the bar with me, took a whopper of a drink, and returning to his place, resumed,

"As I said before, yer honor, I think it is a disgrace to the human family that such men as these should be permitted to prowl about our beautiful per-rar-ries and take the property of our honest, hard-working citizens. It's con-*tra*-ry to the principles of the Constitution, con-*tra*-ry to the principles of law, and con-*tra*-ry to good order, and must be stopped; and, may it please yer honor, these men should be made an example of, and heavy damages be given to my client."

At this stage of the harangue one of the other men of our party quietly gave him an invitation to repeat his drink, at which he said to the justice,

"Yer honor will please excuse me for an instant while I take some refreshment, for really my constitution is so delicate that I am unable to speak long without a little suthin' stimulatin'."

Then he went to the bar again and imbibed another glass of whisky. This performance was repeated several times more during his speech, until at length he became considerably affected by the numerous potations he had indulged in; and as the whisky went down his throat, his appreciation of our moral attributes became correspondingly elevated, so that finally he said,

"I don't for a moment suppose, yer honor, that either one of these gentlemen here" (pointing to us) "would be guilty of stealing the paltry amount of an old buffalo hide not worth four bits — by no means, yer honor; but I believe that this gentleman" (pointing to our driver) "committed the theft."

At this accusation our pugnacious Jehu jumped to his feet, and, shaking his fist indignantly in the old fellow's face, said, "You are a drunken old liar, and if you'll come outdoors I'll lick you!"

The magistrate regarded this as indecorous, and entreated the gentlemen to preserve order in court, but it was some time before our driver could be prevailed upon to pay proper respect to the judicial functionary.

The case finally came to a conclusion, and a decision was rendered that the evidence was not sufficient to sustain the charge, and we were released from custody.

Of course the stage-driver was disappointed, and I informed him that I should immediately write to Mr. Frink, his employer, and request his discharge, which seemed to give him considerable uneasiness, and he then acknowledged that our Elgin host was the in-

A SCENE IN COURT.

K 2

stigator of the whole affair. In passing the place several years afterward I learned that the man was dismissed as soon as Mr. Frink received my note.

WINTER IN NEW ENGLAND.

In the course of my devious ramblings for nearly half a century over almost every unfrequented district embraced within the vast expanse of our huge domain, it has been my fortune to encounter a good many hard knocks, as well as a great variety of curious and merry adventures. One of the latter, which amused me vastly at the time, and which I never think of without an inclination for a hearty laugh, I propose to relate; and if my description conveys to the reader's imagination one half of its superlatively ludicrous reality, I am sure he will feel abundantly repaid for the perusal.

I passed the winter of 1840–41 in the very hospitable city of Hartford, Conn., where I was so fortunate as to form an extended circle of agreeable acquaintances, who, by their genial and intelligent social intercourse, contributed greatly to my happiness, and enabled me to while away the monotony of a protracted Northern winter in the most satisfactory manner. In the spring following, as I was about taking my departure, my friends called, and, after wishing me all manner of good fortune, bade me a kind adieu, and all, excepting my particular friend Isaac Stewart, had left. He detained me some time upon the little porch fronting the City Hotel, seeming loth to say good-by; but, as it was nearly time for the arrival of the train, I was forced to tear myself away from him, and was on the point of stepping into the carriage, when he entreated me to come back and take a farewell glass.

I was obliged to decline, remarking, as I closed the carriage door, that we would postpone our drink until my return, and away I went, consoling myself with the fervent anticipation that I might soon be permitted to revisit the excellent friends I was leaving behind. But, alas for the realization of my cherished aspirations, my tortuous trail led me into Texas, Mexico, Arkansas, and Utah, and it was nearly twenty years before I could get back.

The time came at last, however, and I anxiously drove toward the old hotel, where I expected to see a great many changes; but, to my surprise, found all the surroundings looking precisely as when I left, and, to my utter astonishment, there was my old friend Stewart, who was the last to bid me farewell, seated in the same spot upon the little porch, apparently in the same arm-chair, and with his feet raised

"I DON'T CARE IF I DO TAKE A DRINK."

at about the same elevation, and resting against identically the same post as when I declined his invitation to join him in the stirrup-cup.

Getting out of the carriage, I walked directly up to him, gave him a hearty slap on the shoulder, and said, "Well, Stewart, as you are so pressing, I don't care if I do take a drink."

He looked up with astonishment, and did not recognize me at first; but he soon appreciated the joke, and, seizing my hand, replied that his patience was nearly exhausted in waiting for my return, and that, if I had not arrived within the next five or six years, he would have been obliged to drink alone.

INDIAN PERFORMANCE.

Various ingenious expedients were devised to make the time pass off agreeably during my sojourn in Hartford, and one of these, which originated with myself, is the adventure I proposed to relate at the commencement of this paper.

It so happened upon one occasion that I had obtained two complete Sioux Indian warrior costumes, and I suggested to a gentleman (Colonel R. C. Cutts) that we should dress ourselves in them, and try our powers in personating the Indian character. Accordingly, my wife, at our suggestion, accepted an invitation to a tea-party that evening at the hospitable mansion of her friend, Mrs. C——, thus vacating our apartments for us to make our toilets in.

With copper-colored crayon, pulverized and mixed with oil, we besmeared our faces, necks, and hands. We then put on the coats, leggins, moccasins, horse-hair wigs, and feather head-dresses, and, with our tomahawks, pipes, and tobacco-pouches, we were probably the most metamorphosed white men, and the best representatives of the characters we were about to personify that could possibly have been imagined.

In order, however, to enable the reader to get a full appreciation of what I am about to relate, I remark that both of us were very tall, erect, and fully developed, and our dresses fitted our persons admirably, so that when we surveyed ourselves in the large mirror in my parlor our transformation was so perfect that really I could not for my life have told which was which.

I had passed several years among the Chippewas and other Indian tribes, and was familiar with many of their habits, and some of their songs and dances, and could even make myself understood in the Chippewa tongue. And, fortunately for our project, an acquaintance of mine, who was a stranger in the place, and who also could speak some Chippewa, arrived just in time to take the part of interpreter on the occasion.

After the completion of our elaborate toilets, we sent out the interpreter to procure a carriage, and at about seven o'clock in the evening quietly slipped out of the back door, and, entering the carriage, drove around to the front door of our hotel, when the interpreter went in and inquired of the landlord if he could furnish lodgings for two distinguished Seminole chiefs, "Jim Jumper" and "Wild Cat," who had just arrived from Florida *en route* to visit their Great Father at Washington.

This was, it will be remembered, during the protracted Seminole War, when every body had the keenest desire to see two such redoubtable warriors, and the host eagerly responded to the application "that he should be most happy to have the honor of entertaining them." Accordingly, he at once threw open a large private parlor, which he placed at our disposal, and we were ushered into it with all possible ceremony. After locking the door, we seated ourselves upon the carpet near the fire, loaded our huge pipes, and commenced smoking.

Scarcely ten minutes had elapsed before the news of our arrival had circulated over the whole city, and hundreds of curious citizens swarmed about the doors and halls of the hotel, all anxiously awaiting an opportunity to get a peep at the renowned savages. After we had kept them in suspense for some time, and their patience had become pretty well exhausted, the door was unbolted and the crowd rushed in, immediately filling the room to its utmost capacity. They gathered around us, scrutinizing us from head to foot most minutely, and making all sorts of comments upon our dress, accoutrements, and personal appearance, all of which we, of course, were not supposed to understand. They then commenced interrogating the interpreter in regard to our warlike exploits, the number of scalps we had taken, and the number of men we had killed in battle, etc., which were answered to their entire satisfaction.

In the mean time my red brother Cutts, under pretense of talking to me, kept up an incessant jargon, not one syllable of which either he or any body else could understand, and which sounded more like a conglomeration of Dutch, Irish, and hog Latin than any thing else, yet a distinguished philologist present took especial pleasure in listening to him, and pronounced his vernacular a most beautiful specimen of the language of nature; indeed, he gave it as his candid opinion that the dialects of civilized nations might be benefited by the adoption of some of those strikingly illustrative tropes and figures with which James Jumper's (my companion's) conversation seemed to be so exuberantly embellished.

Among the most prominent of the spectators was Judge M——, a distinguished, portly gentleman of the "old school," of highly dignified presence, who prided himself on being able to trace back his lineage directly to the Pilgrims. He manifested the most lively interest in the Red Men, and, after shaking hands with us, said to me in a loud, distinct tone of voice, "Do you speak English, Mr. Wild Cat?"

I gave a negative grunt; then, looking fiercely at him, added, "Whisky, heap," which caused the venerable old gentleman to recoil from me with astonishment, and exclaim,

"What a melancholy fact it is, gentlemen, to see these magnificent specimens of the human race thus bent upon their own destruction! The history of the Red Man shows that when he comes in contact with the pale faces, instead of profiting by their moral teachings, he only learns to imitate their worst vices; and you observe, gentlemen, that almost the only words of English which these poor benighted savages can utter are whisky and tobacco. Alas! the poor Indian! his fate is sealed; he seems to be destined to a speedy extinction. The last of his unfortunate race will soon have disappeared from the face of the earth, and the land of his forefathers will become the heritage of strangers."

Another gentleman present, who had been engaged with my friend Jim Jumper for six months on the northeast boundary, professed to be familiar with the Indian character, and had visited several tribes. His opinions were listened to with profound respect by the assembled tyros. Among other remarks that his observations upon us elicited was "that there had from time to time been many civilized and mixed-blooded Indians who went about the country passing themselves off in public exhibitions as real unadulterated natives, but I assure you, gentlemen," said he, "that I am a good judge of the race, and I pronounce these two men as the first genuine specimens of aborigines that have appeared in this city during my day."

Shortly after this we told the interpreter to inform the landlord that we were so much disturbed by the crowd that we would proceed on our journey that night. Accordingly, we re-entered our carriage, and drove to the house where my wife was taking tea. Our interpreter entered and informed my wife that her husband had sent around two Seminole chiefs, thinking that the ladies might like to see them. They

"EXCELLENT COFFEE!"

were all delighted, and the hostess begged the interpreter to bring them in at once. Accordingly, we were shown into the brilliantly-lighted drawing-room, where the ladies received us most graciously, giving us a hearty squeeze of the hand all around; and when it came my turn to salute Mrs. C——, the hostess, I imprinted a sonorous kiss upon her cheek, which caused her to jump away from me as if she had been shot. She, however, soon recovered her equanimity, and even joined in the laugh which I had produced at her expense, doubtless supposing that my salutation was the customary Indian greeting.

After seating ourselves and smoking our pipes for a moment, we gave an intimation through the interpreter that a drink of whisky would be acceptable. The hostess replied,

"Tell the gentlemen Indians, if you please, Mr. Interpreter, that we are temperance people here, and do not keep ardent spirits; but I'll give them some coffee and cake."

They were set before us, and I emptied the cake into my blanket and swallowed the coffee with a grimace, at the same time saying "*caween nechirchin*" (*not good*), which the interpreter rendered into English as "*excellent coffee*."

From here we went to the house of a particular friend of mine who was not at home himself, but his wife and her mother, an old lady of about seventy, received us with a cordial welcome, and made particular inquiries of the interpreter about our domestic affairs, whether we were married, had children, and whether our families would not be anxious about us in our absence, etc., etc. The interpreter answered that Jumper had thirteen wives, and I six, but that I expected a re-enforcement of three or four more on my return to Florida.

They were, of course, perfectly horrified at such barbarous Mormonism, and seemed almost afraid to look at us after this. My friend's wife became especially nervous, and I told the interpreter that I wanted to hear her play a tune on the piano. She was frightened nearly out of her senses, but dared not refuse the stern look of command I gave her, and, seating herself at the instrument, commenced, in a highly tremulous and nervous manner, to comply with the mandate, frequently casting the most deprecatory glances toward the interpreter, as though she expected every touch of the keys might be the last she would be permitted to make in this world.

The amiable old lady was also very considerably exercised at the same time, and kept as far removed from us as the dimensions of the apartment would permit. Observing her perturbation, I told the interpreter to inform her that we would like very much to see her dance. She replied, "My dear sir, tell them I have not danced a step for over forty years."

I repeated the request in a more peremptory manner, which having been interpreted to her, she imploringly responded, "It is absolutely impossible. I have entirely forgotten the steps; moreover, I have the rheumatism in both legs; and positively the Indians must excuse me."

I then got up, went out upon the floor, and beckoned her to commence, authoritatively intimating to her, by significant gestures, that there was no escape; she must dance.

Not daring to hesitate longer, she rose up with a desperate impulse, exclaiming in a desponding tone, "Oh! oh! my dear Mr. Interpreter, what shall I do?" and in a slow and measured cadence commenced an old-fashioned jig, as an accompaniment to which I beat time with my tomahawk upon the floor; and by encouraging approbatory nods when she quickened the time, and constant threatening mandatory pantomime when it slackened, I gradually induced her to accelerate her steps, until in a short time her feet were moving with a velocity which I venture to say they seldom ever did before, even when she was a girl.

After she had become quite exhausted by the unusual efforts I had imposed upon her, and which elicited much applause from us, I allowed her to resume her seat, and she seemed so much wearied that I was sorry I had compelled her to pass through so cruel an ordeal; and the only excuse I can offer for my indiscretion is, that my uncontrollable love of fun, and my keen appreciation of the ludicrous, preponderated for the moment over all other considerations.

I reproached myself for it afterward, and most penitently entreated the dear old lady's pardon, but I doubt if she ever entirely forgave me, and the only consolation I have under all the circumstances is, that possibly the violent exercise of her "double-quick" minuet may have had a beneficial effect upon her rheumatic malady.

This closed the performance here, and we returned to our hotel, giving as an excuse that the night was so dark we, upon reflection, had determined to come back and stay until morning. The crowd had not yet dispersed, and they entreated us to give them some specimens of our dances, which, after a good deal of persuasion, we with apparent reluctance consented to, and the largest parlor, designated for the occasion, was soon filled with the most prominent citizens of the place, only leaving sufficient room in the centre for us to dance.

Having streaked our faces well with vermilion, and every thing being *comme il faut*, the last act in our ludicrous drama opened by our entrée through a side door, with our tomahawks raised in the right hand, and scalp-locks adorned with little bells jingling in the left hand, our heads thrown back, bodies erect, knees bent, and taking short, jerking steps to the guttural music of a real Chippewa scalp-dance. Around and around the circle we moved, flaunting our war-trophies defiantly over our heads, with an occasional threatening demonstration to the right and left with our tomahawks, and all the time keeping step to the inspiring cadence of the war-song, which at first was in a slow, depressed tone, but gradually rose and accelerated until it became highly animated, and even savagely loud and furious. The perspiration rolled down our cheeks in streams, and we were beginning to be somewhat exhausted, but we determined not to show it, and on we went with a velocity and fervor that would have forced applause from even our illustrious Seminole namesakes themselves.

The appreciative spectators looked on with great satisfaction, and gave us frequent cheers, which, however, were mingled with an occasional demonstration of fear from those in the front rank of the circle, especially when we flourished our tomahawks and gave utterance to the shrill war-whoop. Judge M——, of whom I have already spoken, took especial interest in the spectacle, and occupied a prominent position in the inner circle, and several times, in passing him, I took occasion to flout my tomahawk in rather closer proximity to his head than was altogether agreeable to him, yet he gave no evidence of fear or trepidation except to exclaim, "What ferocious-looking devils they are, sure enough!"

After the dance was concluded we seated ourselves upon the floor, and directed the interpreter to inform the "pale faces" that upon such occasions it was customary among our people to take a big smoke. Accordingly, our pipes were filled, and after a few whiffs, inhaled into the lungs and ejected through the nostrils by way of example, I handed mine to the judge, who, in his anxiety to show all possible respect to our customs, swallowed a large quantity of smoke, and, being unaccustomed to the use of tobacco in any form, he, in his endeavors to expel it through his nose, was taken with such a violent fit of sneezing and coughing that I was obliged to give him some severe slaps upon the back before he recovered. When he had wiped the tears from his eyes I pointed to him and said to the interpreter, "*Ne-che-chin. Che-mo-ko-mon.*" The signification of which the interpreter informed him was, that I regarded him as a very good man, and thought I would like him very much.

The portly gentleman seemed highly delighted at the compliment, and remarked that he would not have expected such refined courtesy from untutored natives like those, and he desired to know why Mr. Wild Cat had taken such an especial liking to him.

My reply through the interpreter was that, if we had him down in the hammocks of Florida, he was so fat that I thought he would make soup enough to feed the whole Seminole tribe, and that I was very fond of soup. The judge shuddered as he raised his hands, and exclaimed, "*The horrible cannibal!*"

Then going up to him and extending my hand, I said, in English, "How are you, judge?" He looked at me in amazement, saying, "Who in the devil are you, sir?" When I told him who I was, he, as well as every one else present, was greatly surprised that we had been able to continue our masquerade so long without recognition.

On the following morning the newspapers teemed with complimentary notices of our dramatic powers, and we were urged to repeat the exhibition, but, after we had made ourselves known, the performance lost its most interesting feature.

It is a remarkable fact that, among all the numerous intimate acquaintances we met with during the entire evening, not one of them had the remotest conception as to our identity, with the single exception of a bright young son of Mrs. C——, who is now an eminent lawyer, and who, after scrutinizing us very closely for a while, whispered to his mother that he believed I was personating Wild Cat. His mother reproved him sharply, and asked him what he supposed my wife would say if she knew that such a horrible-looking savage had been mistaken for her husband. After we had left the house the boy reiterated the expression of his opinion to the company, very much to the chagrin of his mother, who peremptorily ordered him not to repeat it again.

My wife then asked the lady what she would think if she were to assert that one of the Indians was in reality her own husband.

She replied, "*I would not believe you!*"

"Notwithstanding this, my dear madam, I assure you that the person calling himself Wild Cat was nothing more nor less than my veritable lord and master."

Perceiving that she had been "*sold*," and believing that I had gotten up the performance for her especial benefit, she indignantly rejoined that this was by no means the first time I had humbugged her, and that she would yet have satisfaction if she lived long enough.

CHAPTER VII.

PIONEERS OF THE WEST.

A wettin' Beverage.—General Sam Houston.—Duel in Tennessee. —Courting by Proxy.—Houston bothered.—Disciplining Volunteers.—Mrs. L——'s Capture and Escape.

IN passing from the southwestern borders of Kansas into the outer settlements of Missouri and Arkansas a sudden and complete transformation is observed, not only in the habits and customs of the people, but in the appearance of all their surroundings.

For example, in the former state, churches and school-houses have kept pace with the pioneers, and are seen among the remotest hamlets. The children here go to school, newspapers are taken and read, and there is an air of thrift and comfort about the most primitive log tenements that marks the Eastern origin of their occupants; while along the frontiers of the latter states a church or school-house is seldom met with, and it is rare to find a person here who has received the first rudiments of education. The school-master and parson are strangers in those parts, and, if they were to make their appearance, would be regarded as superfluous members of society.

These people are so local and circumscribed in their sphere of life, and so seldom meet with educated persons, that the English language has suffered a very considerable metamorphosis under their vernacular manipulations, so that many of their conventional idioms have become as remote from the teachings of our standard lexicographers as the provincial patois of Southern France is from the pure dialect of Paris.

These anomalous specimens of the genus homo seem to constitute a detached element in our social organization. Their sparsely scattered forest habitations, being far distant from towns or villages, and rarely visited by travelers, almost entirely excludes them from intercourse with the civilized world, and they remain nearly as ignorant of what is transpiring outside their own immediate spheres as the savages themselves. They seldom see a newspaper, and could not read it if it was placed before their eyes; and I honestly believe that some of them, previous to the Rebellion (which has enlightened them a little), could not have told whether General Jackson, General Taylor, or Mr. Buchanan was President of the United States.

Some of the most salient traits in the character of this remarkable type of the Anglo-Saxon race have been exhibited in a conspicuous light among the individuals I have encountered upon the frontier, and it is some of those that I propose introducing to the notice of the reader.

A WETTIN' BEVERAGE.

Upon a hot and sultry summer's day in 1852, as I was journeying on horseback over "Boston Mountain," by the road leading from Arkansas to Missouri, I became wearied and thirsty, and, riding up to the door of a wretched shanty (the intervals between the logs of which might well have entitled it to the appellation of "Oak Openings"), I accosted a haggard-looking old woman who was in possession of the premises, and whose smoky, desiccated visage gave her a striking resemblance to my conception of Scott's Meg Merrilies, and I expressed the hope that she was in the enjoyment of perfect health.

At this salutation she raised her dim, glassy eyes upon me, and in a most doleful tone of voice replied,

"Wa'al, now, *straanger*, I'll tell ye what's the matter: I war middlin' sort o' pert yesterday, but, sure's yer born'd, I'ze powerful weak to-day. Jist about

"'LIGHT, STRAANGER."

sun-up this mornin', maybe a *lee*-tle bit afore, I war tuck with a almighty mizzery in the inards, an' I'ze been *a*-squrmin', an' *a*-kavortin', an' *a*-howlin' ever since" (putting special emphasis upon the italicized letter *a*, and inhaling her breath while she was giving it protracted utterance), "and I'ze swallered cords of apple-jack and tobaccer-juice; but, straanger, 'tain't no sort o' use; it don't begin to knock it; an' it's getten wosser an' wosser all the time." Then spasmodically clasping her long bony fingers around the region of the stomach, and dropping her lank body upon her knees, she belched forth an unearthly screech of agony, but instantly jerked back to an upright position, and in a sharp, authoritative tone said, "'Light, straanger, an' have a char."

I dismounted, accepted the seat, and condoled most sincerely with the poor woman, suggesting to her that possibly the tobacco and liquor might have had the effect of increasing her troubles.

She said no; that when these remedies would not "kill pain," "all the yarbs in Rackinsack (Arkansas) wo'dn't do it."

After the "mizzery" spasm had passed off I inquired where I could find a drink of water. "Thar war plenty water in the spring," she said, but added that "she rec'on'd she had some buttermilk in the spring-house, an' she 'low'd that buttermilk war a heap more wettiner nur water."

In accordance with the suggestion, I drank copiously of the liquid, and felt so much refreshed after it that I cheerfully indorse her opinion in regard to the relative "wettin'" qualities of the two fluids.

SAM HOUSTON.

Speaking of buttermilk reminds me of an anecdote I once heard of General Sam Houston, who was a lover of this lacteal beverage, as many of the good housewives in the Southwest can vouch for.

Before the annexation of Texas to the Union, and when it was an independent republic, with the general at its head as President, the incident I am about to relate occurred.

But, in order to get a proper appreciation of my story, a few observations upon the anomalous condition of society in that then remote and wild region may not be malapropos.

The inducements held out by the Mexican government for the early colonization of Texas brought together men from every state in the Union, and, indeed, from almost every part of the civilized world; and it is perfectly safe to assert that probably no other locality in the universe was ever populated by a community made up of elements more heterogeneous than this. It is very true that there were some highly intelligent and respectable people among them, but the great mass of the early pioneers were of a very different stamp.

Men of desperate fortunes, who had nothing to lose and every thing to gain, went there. Ambitious adventurers, who sought excitement and preferment, here found a rich field for the indulgence of their proclivities. Besides these, an army of refugees from justice, under assumed names, here found a secure retreat from the pale of the law. Such, in short, was the population that declared the independence of the republic, and placed General Houston at the helm of its government.

There never was much unanimity of sentiment among the early politicians of Texas, and even General Houston had a powerful party arrayed against him, which for the most part was made up of highly turbulent and reckless elements—men who gave expression to their opinions regardless of consequences, and frequently enforced them with their bowie-knives and revolvers, in total defiance of law or order.

The non-enforcement of law rather served to encourage this disordered condition of society, and it was seldom a jury was impanneled that dared to convict a man of murder, even when the crime had been perpetrated with the most diabolical malice prepense. These same audacious spirits did not, however, for a moment hesitate to enforce Lynch-law upon a man for stealing a horse, or for putting his brand upon a neighbor's calf or colt.

The consequence of this was that individuals often took the law into their own hands as the only remedy for the redressment of their grievances, so that but few of the early settlers who remained in the country any great length of time escaped a duel or a street encounter, and many lives were sacrificed in this way. It is, therefore, a matter of surprise that General Houston, who continually occupied exalted political positions during a long period, should have escaped entanglement in those broils.

Whatever his enemies may have said of him, his friends regarded him as a man of most indomitable firmness of purpose, and one whose moral and physical courage were beyond question. General Jackson, who was his firm friend through life, pronounced him a brave man and gallant soldier. Indeed, he received a severe wound in the arm while fighting under General Jackson at the battle of the "Horse-shoe." Nevertheless, it is said that, upon several occasions, he declined meeting adversaries in duels upon the ground that it was unbecoming in him to fight "down hill;" in other words, that he did not choose to enter the lists with antagonists who were far beneath him in position; which reminds me of General Putnam's response to a pugnacious individual who sent him a challenge, viz., that "every body knew very well old Put was no coward, and was not obliged to fight every d—d rascal that came along, either."

An incident in the eventful life of General Houston, which occurred in Tennessee before he went to the Cherokee country, affords a cogent argument in refutation of the charge of cowardice which some of his calumniators have brought against him.

At a large political gathering in Nashville about the time he was running for governor, a Mr. I——g sent him a challenge through the hands of the noted John Smith, T.

Now this man Smith, of whose bloody career I shall have occasion to speak more fully at another time, was not looked upon with much favor in that community; and after the general had read the document, he deliberately, and in presence of the whole assembly, while he looked Smith directly in the eyes, tore it into pieces and dashed it upon the ground, at the same time remarking that "he was not in the habit of receiving challenges through the hands of assassins."

The observation was heard by the crowd, and was taken up by General W——e, who, if not a friend of the challenger, did not entertain kindly feelings for Houston, and he said, in a loud tone of voice, "The gentleman seems to be particularly fastidious to-day. I wonder whether he would condescend to accept a meeting with *any* man—for instance, with myself?"

This remark, which was apparently addressed to the people, was of course intended for the ears of Houston. He heard it, and promptly replied, "You had better try me, sir?"

I shall only add that he did try him, and with his life paid the penalty of his indiscretion.

As many are not familiar with the early history of this remarkable individual, I take this occasion to observe that he was a blacksmith by trade, and received but little education during his boyhood, but his eminent natural abilities soon brought him into notice, and the happy faculty which he possessed of ingratiating himself into the favor and confidence of those with whom he came in contact soon gained him many friends, and he was at a very early age sent to Congress from his native state.

His tall, erect, and highly graceful and dignified bearing, united with great suavity of address, and agreeable social qualities, soon made him companions at Washington, and he was regarded as one of the most promising young politicians of that day.

It is said that certain mutual friends were very desirous about this time of bringing about a meeting with the rising young politician and a very beautiful and aristocratic belle of Baltimore, Miss R——y.

To effect this Mr. ——— gave an elegant banquet, to which Houston, the young lady alluded to, and many of the élite of the city were invited, and it was arranged that at an opportune moment during the entertainment Houston's name should be alluded to, and that Mr. M——l, an older member of Congress from Tennessee, should take that as a text for eulogizing his young colleague in such exalted terms as to attract the attention of the ambitious female sprig of aristocracy.

Accordingly, when the proper moment arrived, his old friend, who was from the rural districts himself, and had but little sympathy with aristocracy, said, "Is it Sam Houston you are speaking of? Why, I've known the young rascal ever since he came barefooted over the mountains to work at the blacksmithing business in our county; and when I first met him he had cracks in his heels as wide as your fingers. I tell you he is a self-made man, and he's bound to make his mark."

It may readily be conjectured that this encomium, instead of elevating the youthful hero in the estimation of the haughty belle, only served to render him obnoxious to her. The acquaintance proceeded no farther.

After this the general was Governor of Tennessee, and subsequently he passed a year or two among the Cherokees, and from thence went to Texas, where he founded a republic, and there is no question in my mind about his personal bravery. Moreover, he was an excellent judge of character, and probably no man ever lived who possessed a happier faculty for extricating himself from a critical position than he.

With these somewhat discursive preliminary digressions I proceed with my narrative.

At the period alluded to, the general was in the daily habit of walking out to a farm-house near Austin, where he invariably received a cordial welcome, and never failed to get his favorite buttermilk beverage.

The proprietor of the establishment, Mr. W——d, felt proud of entertaining so distinguished a guest, especially as he regarded him one of his stanchest friends, and he took every pains to induce him to repeat his visits.

Now it so occurred upon a certain occasion, when politics ran high and factious animosities were exceedingly acrimonious, that W——d was nominated for an important office, and, being very desirous to secure the election, he frequently counseled with his old friend Houston in regard to the best method of conducting the canvass.

The old veteran of San Jacinto, with all apparent sincerity, entered most cordially into the views and interests of his friend, and cheerfully gave him the benefit of his matured political experience, and thereby inspired W——d with full confidence in the ultimate success of his election, and every thing progressed satisfactorily, until one day W——d received a letter from a friend, inclosing another written by General Houston to the opposing candidate, in which he expressed the opinion that W——d was utterly unfitted to fill the position, and that every effort should be made to defeat him.

Astounded at such barefaced duplicity, he put the letter into his pocket, and anxiously awaited the general's next visit, firmly resolved to call him to account for it.

He arrived as usual, and seemed in excellent spirits, accosting Mrs. W——d with "Good morning, lady. I hope I find you very well to-day; and, pray, how are the darling little ones this morning, lady? And, my dear old friend W——d, how does it go with you to-day? It seems to me you are not looking as cheerful as usual. I trust nothing has gone amiss."

W——d responded very coldly to this hearty greeting, and, after the general was seated, asked him what he would think of a man who should come to his house every day, profess to be his best friend, partake of his hospitality, and receive numberless other favors, and after all this he should discover that this man was his direst enemy.

"Do you ask me, W——d, what I would think of such a heartless wretch? Why, sir, my candid opinion is that ingratitude is a crime of the deepest turpitude, and I have no hesitation in saying that such a man should be hung. I say he should be hung, sir. Shooting would be too light a punishment for such an infamous traitor."

W——d then produced the letter, and asked his guest if he would do him the favor to read it. After feigning to read it over very carefully, and perceiving that it would be useless to deny its authenticity, he turned up his eyes with a most puzzled and bewildered expression, saying at the same time (in soliloquy), "That handwriting certainly resembles mine, but if I wrote it, how does it happen that I can not remember any thing about it? That's what bothers me."

HOUSTON BOTHERED.

After a moment's reflection, he went up to W——d with the letter open in his left hand, placed it before his eyes, and significantly shaking the index finger of his right hand at the paper, said,

"Who would suppose that I could ever have got so beastly drunk as to write such an absurd letter? You, my dear W——d, know me too well to believe for an instant that this letter expresses my real sentiment. On the contrary, if I was called upon publicly to declare my candid opinion in floral language regarding the relative merits of the two candidates, I should most unhesitatingly and most unqualifiedly exclaim that you were decidedly '*poplar*,' but that your opponent was emphatically a '*lo-cuss*.'"

Almost every page in the early history of Texas is replete with thrilling narrations of Indian barbarities, of desperate personal encounters, and of heroic struggles of Anglo-Saxons to wrest from Mexicans and savages the land of their nativity and graves of their ancestors.

Even after the Spaniards were subdued or driven out of the country and their leader captured, the most populous districts were not exempt from frequent predatory incursions from the warlike and hostile Comanches.

Those ubiquitous freebooters of the Plains, mounted upon fleet and enduring ponies, would, without the slightest previous warning, swoop down upon a settlement with lightning velocity, and before the inhabitants could rally for defense they were away again, leaving fire, desolation, and death in their bloody tracks.

To guard against these sudden raids the people

were forced to remain continually on the alert, with rifles and revolvers by their sides both day and night.

This condition of society brought before the public many bold spirits, who otherwise would probably have remained unknown, and who, by their keen instincts in combating their wily foes, and by their intrepid deeds of personal valor, rendered their names immortal upon the catalogue of border heroes.

Such men as Jack Hays, Ben M'Culloch, Walker, Cook, etc., whose memories are held in the highest veneration by their surviving contemporaries, appeared at this eventful era, and they were intrusted with the command of parties that patroled the outer line of settlements under the appellation of "Rangers."

In the execution of this hazardous duty they had many bloody encounters with the savages, and were often victorious, but occasionally they were overpowered by numbers, and either killed or forced to flee to the settlements for protection or re-enforcements.

Upon a certain occasion, one of these parties, which had been scouting upon the head waters of the Brazos and Trinity, was driven in by the advance of a powerful war-party of Comanches, and the direction from which they were approaching induced the belief among the knowing borderers that they designed striking Nacogdoches, on the Angelina River. To meet the emergency, a large force of militia was hastily called out, with orders to assemble at Nacogdoches, under the command of General Rusk, the then Secretary of War.

They were speedily enrolled, and remained some considerable time *en bivouac* awaiting tidings of the Indians, but no enemy appeared; and at length the President went there himself, and believing the danger over, he at once ordered the disbandment of the troops.

Many of the men who had suffered from Indian depredations were exceedingly anxious for an opportunity to take revenge, and the disbandment was by no means a popular measure with them. Moreover, they did not hesitate to give free expression to their sentiments upon the subject, even to denouncing in the most unqualified terms the action of the chief magistrate.

On the day following the "mustering out," as Generals Houston and Rusk, accompanied by the Adjutant General, M'Cloud, were promenading arm in arm through the streets of the town, which were swarming with the disbanded volunteers, many of them collected in groups discussing the propriety of the President's order, their attention was called to a stalwart young backwoodsman, dressed from head to foot in buckskin, who had evidently taken several drinks of whisky, and was loudly and vehemently expatiating to those around him, and making frequent, and not very complimentary, use of "Sam Houston's" name.

General Houston, who could not avoid hearing some of these allusions, turned to his companions and said, "It appears to me, General Rusk, that you do not preserve very good discipline in your command."

"They have been disbanded, and I have nothing farther to do with them," replied the general. "Moreover," he added, "I am of the opinion that it would not be so easy a matter to stop their talking, even if they were still in service."

"Come along with me, gentlemen, and I'll show you how to quell such disgraceful exhibitions," said Houston.

The others merely observed that "they would like to witness the performance," and followed into the packed crowd, which made way for the distinguished personages, enabling them to penetrate to the side of the noisy orator, who still continued his vociferous harangue, accompanied by the most violent gesticulations and contortions of his arms and body.

Walking deliberately up to him, and laying his hand upon his shoulder, the general, in a mild but emphatic tone, said, "Are you not aware, my young friend, that you are disturbing the peace and quiet of this respectable community, and that too, sir, in presence of the President of the Republic?"

The fellow suddenly ceased speaking at this unexpected interruption, and, turning upon the huge individual who addressed him (he did not know the general, it seemed), he, in a very low but firm tone of voice, while his eyes flashed fire, asked, "Are you Sam Houston, the President?"

"Yes, my young friend, I have the honor to bear that distinguished cognomen."

The young giant then drew back a step or two, and, concentrating all his powerful energies into the effort, sprang like an infuriated tiger upon the astonished general, knocking him down, and at the same time exclaiming, "Well, d—n you, old Houston, you are the very man I wanted to see." He was immediately pulled off by the spectators, and proceeded with his interrupted declamation as if nothing had happened, while the general retired to his lodgings, fully convinced that his friend Rusk was no disciplinarian.

At one time, while Generals Houston and Rusk

were at Austin, it is said that a friend of the latter reported to him that General Houston had, upon more than one occasion, denounced him in the severest terms, and his friends were unanimous in the opinion that his reputation and honor demanded that the insult should be noticed. He did not, however, pay much attention to the matter at first, but at length it became so notorious that he called on Houston and required an explanation.

As soon as the object of his visit was proclaimed General Houston burst into a violent fit of laughter, and going up to Rusk, placed his hand upon his shoulder, saying,

"It seems to me, my dear Rusk, that you are unnecessarily exercised this morning. You must be conscious of the fact that we sometimes chastise our children; and are we not permitted upon certain occasions to inflict upon our wives an affectionate pinch? Yet this does not signify that we love them any the less. I would ask you, then, if a man can't curse his best friend without his taking offense, who in the name of common sense can he curse, I should like to know?"

The general acceded to this paradoxical simile with a questionable grace, and suggested to his friend that in future he would thank him to dispense his anathematical tokens of affection in a little more private manner than he had been in the habit of doing.

STORY OF MRS. L——'S CAPTURE AND ESCAPE.

The verity of the somewhat paradoxical adage that "truth is sometimes stranger than fiction," was never more strikingly presented to my mind than upon an occasion when listening to a detailed account of the capture by the Comanches of a woman upon the Texas border, and the unparalleled achievements, sufferings, and fortitude connected with her captivity and her subsequent escape therefrom.

In order that the reader may get a full understanding and appreciation of the facts as they occurred, a few explanatory observations upon the peculiar features of the country where the scenes were enacted, and the character of its population, seem indispensable.

Before the inhabitants of Texas surrendered the sovereignty of their republic by contributing their rising "lone star" emblem to swell and emblazon the constellation of the glorious Union galaxy, and, indeed, for many years previous to the achievement of their independence from Mexican rule, they were continually subjected to the merciless and bloody incursions of those barbarous freebooters of the plains, the Comanches and Kiowas, who have to this day kept up their outrages upon the border occupants of that state, in absolute defiance of all the efforts of our government to prevent them.

They have repeatedly been informed by our authorities that Texas has become incorporated into the Union, that we are now one and the same nation, and that they would not be allowed to make any discrimination between the people of the two sections. Yet they do not seem to comprehend the existing relations, and the antagonistic attitude assumed by Texas toward the United States during the Rebellion, which the Indians were perfectly cognizant of, only served to confirm their previous impressions that there was no real national unity established between us.

These nomads range over a vast extent of country about the waters of the Arkansas and Red Rivers, hundreds of miles removed from all white settlements, and in this unfrequented district they leave their women and children while absent upon protracted raids into Texas and Mexico.

In the execution of their atrocious ravages they are always well mounted, and pass stealthily along outside of the populated sections of the country, until they learn from their scouts when a favorable opportunity offers for the accomplishment of their purposes, when, like tigers pouncing upon their prey, they swoop in upon their unwary victims, murdering and scalping the men, and making captive the women and children, whom, with their booty, they carry hurriedly away to their distant haunts, where it is impossible to track or pursue them.

The chronicles of the wars between the early colonists of New England and the aborigines abound in thrilling narrations of heroic deeds and sufferings, of miraculous escapes from torture and the stake, as well as of the marvelous fortitude and courage evinced upon many occasions by the women of that eventful era; but I have yet to learn any thing, either from history or romance, that impressed me as being more remarkable or more deserving of commendation than the signal exploit of mental and physical valor and endurance which I am about to relate, and which can substantially be vouched for by several creditable living witnesses.

Beyond the extreme outer line of settlements in Western Texas, near the head waters of the Colorado River, and in one of the remotest and most sequestered sections of that sparsely populated district, there lived, in 1867, an enterprising pioneer by the name of Babb, whose besetting propensity and ambition consisted in pushing his fortunes a little farther toward the setting sun than any of his neighbors, the nearest of whom, at the time specified, was some fifteen miles in his rear.

This proximity did not afford him quite as much "elbow-room" as he would have desired, for he was decidedly averse to human attrition, and the jostling consequent upon closely packed communities; but he was a kind and indulgent husband, and cheerfully suffered this little inconvenience for the gratification of his better half, who was rather more fond of society than himself, and objected to going any farther away from the settlements.

The household of the borderer consisted of his wife, three small children, and a female friend by the name of L——, who, having previously lost her husband, was passing the summer with the family.

As this woman is the heroine of our narrative, and performed a conspicuous *rôle* in the exciting scenes I shall attempt to depict, a brief description of her person and characteristics seems to be apropos in this connection.

She is represented as having been, at the period alluded to, about twenty-five years of age, with an erect and commanding presence, but possessing eminently a graceful feminine person of rather less than medium proportions; yet she was no delicate, ethereal, hot-house exotic, who required constant shelter and protection from every unusual atmospheric asperity. On the contrary, she was a veritable type of our vigorous, self-reliant border women, who encounter danger or the vicissitudes of weather without quailing.

Born and nurtured upon the remotest frontier, she inherited a robust constitution, and her active life in the exhilarating prairie air served to develop and mature into perfect symmetry and beauty a healthy womanly physique, which is rarely met with in the impure and enervating atmosphere of the cities.

The contour of her naturally graceful figure had not been squeezed and warped, by those instruments of torture called corsets, into an outline entirely at variance with the inimitable model designed by the Almighty in his own perfect image, neither had she sacrificed her natural hair to the feverish, steaming ordeal of attaching to the back of her head a fish-net stuffed out with a huge coil of flax or defunct hair cable. She was no slave to such senseless and disgusting mandates of fashion, and suffered her long glossy locks to hang in massive waving curls all over her shoulders.

Her features were regular and classic, and the glances from her jet-black eyes, surmounted by exquisitely penciled brows, were, when she was excited, as vivid and piercing as the dazzling scintillations from calcium lights.

Her complexion did not carry that pallid, sickly hue so characteristic of city women, neither had she been inducted into the mysteries of rouge, cosmetics, or other appliances of the toilet, for her cheeks required no such artificial adornment. By constant impact with the salubrious prairie breezes they had become tinged with a shade of rich brown, and, when under the influence of excitement or exercise, the rapid pulsations of crimson pigment, which flashed from her heart beneath her transparent skin, rendered her complexion more beautiful than any thing within the power of art.

Her costume was designed and made for comfort and use, without regard to the arbitrary dictates of fashion. There were no elaborate puckered frills, flounces, furbelows, or dromedary-like humps to load down or deform her person, nor was the crown of her head surmounted by a Tyrolese doll's hat, yet the *tout ensemble* of her limited wardrobe was comely and appropriate.

Besides her other personal attractions she is said

to have possessed a large element of vivacious, social *bonhomie*—a spontaneous Di Vernon-like abandon, which attracted and fascinated all who came within the sphere of its influence.

She probably seldom, if ever, during the entire course of her life, rode in a carriage; and the only means of locomotion familiar to her, aside from that bestowed upon her by the Creator, was upon horseback.

At an early age she had been taught to ride, and in after-life it had been one of her chief sources of pleasure to mount her horse in the cool of the morning, and gallop away for miles over the verdure-clad expanse of the plains, where the spicy aroma from an ocean of fragrant flowers permeated the entire atmosphere with a pungent and exhilarating perfume, and where her free, independent, and fearless nature had ample scope.

In the saddle she felt perfectly self-confident; and while dashing at full speed over the gentle undulations of the prairie upon her favorite horse, her long locks streaming in unconfined luxuriance in the breeze, and her lithe, supple person yielding in centaur like unison with every movement, pulsation, and breath of the generous animal that shared her enthusiasm, she presented an equestrian model of bewitching beauty and grace.

The cares, perplexities, and luxuries of civilized society were unknown to her, yet she was contented and happy; and here she would probably have passed the remainder of her days had nothing occurred to break in upon the monotony of her career.

But, alas! like the capricious mutations of all other human calculations, the current of her peaceful and innocent avocations and pastimes was destined soon to encounter a most abrupt and unforeseen interruption, the details of which will constitute the burden of the following narrative, which was related to me by the agent of the very Indians concerned, and may therefore be relied upon for truth and accuracy.

Upon one bright and lovely morning in June, 1867, the adventurous borderer before mentioned set out from his home with some cattle for a distant market, leaving his family in possession of the ranch, without any male protectors from Indian marauders.

They did not, however, entertain any serious apprehensions of molestation in his absence, as no hostile Indians had as yet made their appearance in that locality, and every thing passed on quietly for several days, until one morning, while the women were busily occupied with their domestic affairs in the house, the two oldest children, who were playing outside, called to their mother, and informed her that some mounted men were approaching from the prairie. On looking out, she perceived, to her astonishment, that they were Indians coming upon the gallop, and already very near the house. This gave her no time to make arrangements for defense; but she screamed to the children to run in for their lives, as she desired to bar the door, being conscious of the fact that the prairie warriors seldom attack a house that is closed, fearing, doubtless, that it may be occupied by armed men, who might give them an unwelcome reception.

The children did not, however, obey the command of their mother, believing the strangers to be white men, and the door was left open. As soon as the alarm was given Mrs. L—— sprang up a ladder into the loft, and concealed herself in such a position that she could, through cracks in the floor, see all that passed beneath.

Meantime the savages came up, seized and bound the two children outdoors, and, entering the house, rushed toward the young child, which the terror-stricken mother struggled frantically to rescue from their clutches; but they were too much for her, and, tearing the infant from her arms, they dashed it upon the floor; then seizing her by the hair, they wrenched back her head and cut her throat from ear to ear, putting her to death instantaneously.

Mrs. L——, who was anxiously watching their proceedings from the loft, witnessed the fiendish tragedy, and uttered an involuntary shriek of horror, which disclosed her hiding-place to the barbarians, and they instantly vaulted up the ladder, overpowered and tied her; then dragging her rudely down, they placed her, with the two elder children, upon horses, and hurriedly set off to the north, leaving the infant child unharmed, and clasping the mangled corpse of its murdered parent.

In accordance with their usual practice, they traveled as rapidly as their horses could carry them for several consecutive days and nights, only making occasional short halts to graze and rest their animals, and get a little sleep themselves, so that the unfortunate captives necessarily suffered indescribable torture from harsh treatment, fatigue, and want of sleep and food. Yet they were forced by the savages to continue on day after day and night after night for many, many weary miles toward the "Staked Plain," crossing *en route* the Brazos, Wachita, Red, Canadian, and Arkansas Rivers, several of which were at swimming stages.

The warriors guarded their captives very closely

until they had gone so great a distance from the settlements that they imagined it impossible for them to make their escape and find their way home, when they relaxed their vigilance slightly, and they were permitted to walk about a little within short limits from the bivouacs; but they were given to understand by unmistakable pantomime that death would be the certain penalty of the first attempt to escape.

In spite of this, Mrs. L——, who possessed a firmness of purpose truly heroic, resolved to seize the first favorable opportunity to get away; and with this resolution in view, she carefully observed the relative speed and powers of endurance of the different horses in the party, and noted the manner in which they were grazed, guarded, and caught; and upon a dark night, after a long, fatiguing day's ride, and while the Indians were sleeping soundly, she noiselessly and cautiously crawled away from the bed of her young companions, who were also buried in profound slumber, and going to the pasture-ground of the horses, selected the best, leaped upon his back *à la garçon*, with only a lariat around his neck, and, without saddle or bridle, started quietly off at a slow walk in the direction of the north star, believing that this course would lead her to the nearest white habitations. As soon as she had gone out of hearing from the bivouac, without detection or pursuit, she accelerated the speed of the horse into a trot, then to a gallop, and urged him rapidly forward during the entire night.

At dawn of day on the following morning she rose upon the crest of an eminence overlooking a vast area of bald prairie country, where, for the first time since leaving the Indians, she halted, and, turning round, tremblingly cast a rapid glance to the rear, expecting to see the savage blood-hounds in eager pursuit upon her track; but, to her great joy and relief, not a single indication of a living object could be discerned within the extended scope of her vision. She breathed more freely now, but still did not feel safe from pursuit; and the total absence of all knowledge of her whereabouts in the midst of the wide expanse of dreary prairie around her, with the uncertainty of ever again looking upon a friendly face, caused her to realize most vividly her own weakness and entire dependence upon the Almighty, and she raised her thoughts to Heaven in fervent supplication.

The majesty and sublimity of the stupendous works of the great Author and Creator of the universe, when contrasted with the insignificance of the powers and achievements of a vivified atom of earth modeled into human form, are probably under no circumstances more strikingly exhibited and felt than when one becomes bewildered and lost in the almost limitless amplitude of our great North American "pampas," where not a single footmark or other trace of man's presence or action can be discovered, and where the solitary wanderer is startled at the sound even of his own voice.

The sensation of loneliness and despondency resulting from the appalling consciousness of being really and absolutely lost, with the realization of the fact that but two or three of the innumerable different points of direction embraced within the circle of the horizon will serve to extricate the bewildered victim from the awful doom of death by starvation, and in entire ignorance as to which of these particular directions should be followed, without a single road, trail, tree, bush, or other landmark to guide or direct—the effects upon the imagination of this formidable array of disheartening circumstances can be fully appreciated only by those who have been personally subjected to their influence.

A faint perception of the intensity of the mental torture experienced by these unfortunate victims may, however, be conjectured from the fact that their senses at such junctures become so completely absorbed and overpowered by the cheerless prospect before them that they oftentimes wander about in a state of temporary lunacy, without the power of exercising the slightest volition of the reasoning faculties.

Instances of such mental alienation, strange as it may appear, are by no means uncommon; and I have myself seen several persons whose minds for days, after having been lost and found, were greatly deflected from the channels of sanity.

The inflexible spirit of the heroine of this narrative did not, however, succumb in the least to the imminent perils of the situation in which she found herself, and her purposes were carried out with a determination as resolute and unflinching as those of the Israelites in their protracted pilgrimage through the wilderness, and without the guidance of pillars of fire and cloud.

The aid of the sun and the broad leaves of the pilot-plant by day, with the light of Polaris by night, enabled her to pursue her undeviating course to the north with as much accuracy as if she had been guided by the magnetic needle.

She continued to urge forward the generous steed she bestrode, who, in obedience to the will of his rider, coursed swiftly on hour after hour during the greater part of the day without the least apparent labor or exhaustion.

It was a contest for life and liberty that she had undertaken, a struggle in which she resolved to triumph or perish in the effort; and still the brave-hearted woman pushed on, until at length her horse began to show signs of exhaustion, and as the shadows of evening began to appear he became so much jaded that it was difficult to coax or force him into a trot, and the poor woman began to entertain serious apprehensions that he might soon give out altogether and leave her on foot.

At this time she was herself so much wearied and in want of sleep that she would have given all she possessed to have been allowed to dismount and rest; but, unfortunately for her, those piratical quadrupeds of the plains, the wolves, advised by their carnivorous instincts that she and her exhausted horse might soon fall an easy sacrifice to their voracious appetites, followed upon her track, and came howling in great numbers around her, so that she dared not set her feet upon the ground, fearing they would devour her; and her only alternative was to continue urging the poor beast to struggle forward during the dark and gloomy hours of the long night, until at length she became so exhausted that it was only with the utmost effort of her iron will that she was enabled to preserve her balance upon the horse.

Meantime the ravenous pack of wolves, becoming more and more emboldened and impatient as the speed of her horse relaxed, approached nearer and nearer, until, with their eyes flashing fire, they snapped savagely at the heels of the terrified horse, while at the same time they kept up their hideous concert like the howlings of ten thousand fiends from the infernal regions.

Every element in her nature was at this fearful juncture taxed to its greatest tension, and impelled her to concentrate the force of all her remaining energies in urging and coaxing forward the wearied horse, until, finally, he was barely able to reel and stagger along at a slow walk; and when she was about to give up in despair, expecting every instant that the animal would drop down dead under her, the welcome light of day dawned in the eastern horizon, and imparted a more cheerful and encouraging influence over her, and, on looking around, to her great joy, there were no wolves in sight.

She now, for the first time in about thirty-six hours, dismounted; and knowing that sleep would soon overpower her, and that the horse, if not secured, might escape or wander away, and there being no tree or other object to which he could be fastened, she with great presence of mind tied one end of the long lariat to his neck, and with the other end around her waist, dropped down upon the ground into a deep sleep, while the famished horse eagerly cropped the herbage around her.

She was unconscious as to the duration of her slumber, but it must have been very protracted to have compensated the demands of nature for the exhaustion induced by her prodigious ride.

Her sleep was sweet, and she dreamed of happiness and home, losing all consciousness of her actual situation until she was suddenly startled and aroused by the pattering sound of horses' feet beating the earth on every side.

Springing to her feet in the greatest possible alarm, she found herself surrounded by a large band of savages, who commenced dancing around, flouting their war-clubs in frightful proximity to her head while giving utterance to the most diabolical shouts of exultation.

Her exceedingly weak and debilitated condition at this time, resulting from long abstinence from food and unprecedented mental and physical trials, had wrought upon her nervous system to such an extent that she imagined the moment of her death had arrived, and fainted.

The Indians then approached, and, after she revived, placed her again upon a horse and rode away with her to their camp, which fortunately was not far distant. They then turned their prisoner over to the squaws, who gave her food and put her to bed; but it was several days before she was sufficiently recovered to be able to walk about the camp.

She learned that her last captors belonged to "Lone Wolf's" band of Kiowas.

Although these Indians treated her with more kindness than the Comanches had done, yet she did not for an instant entertain the thought that they would ever voluntarily release her from bondage; neither had she the remotest conception of her present locality, or of the direction or distance to any white settlement; but she had no idea of remaining a slave for life, and resolved to make her escape the first practicable moment that offered.

During the time she remained with these Indians a party of men went away to the north, and were absent six days, bringing with them, on their return, some ears of green corn. She knew the prairie tribes never planted a seed of any description, and was therefore confident the party had visited a white settlement, and that it was not over three days' journey distant. This was encouraging intelligence to her, and she anxiously bided her time to depart.

Late one night, after all had become hushed and quiet throughout the camp, and every thing seemed auspicious for the consummation of her purposes, she stole carefully away from her bed, crept softly out to the herd of horses, and, after having caught and saddled one, was in the act of mounting, when a number of dogs rushed out after her, and by their barking created such a disturbance among the Indians that she was forced, for the time, to forego her designs, and crawl hastily back to her lodge.

On a subsequent occasion, however, fortune favored her. She secured an excellent horse, and rode away in the direction from which she had seen the Indians returning to camp with the green corn. Under the certain guidance of the sun and stars, she was enabled to pursue a direct bearing; and after three consecutive days of rapid riding, anxiety, fatigue, and hunger, she arrived upon the border of a large river, flowing directly across her track. The stream was swollen to the top of its banks; the water coursed like a torrent through its channel, and she feared her horse might not be able to stem the powerful current; but, after surmounting the numerous perils and hardships she had already encountered, the dauntless woman was not to be turned aside from her inflexible purpose by this formidable obstacle, and she instantly dashed into the foaming torrent, and by dint of encouragement and punishment forced her horse through the stream, and landed safely upon the opposite bank.

After giving her horse a few moments' rest, she again set forward, and had ridden but a short distance, when, to her inexpressible astonishment and delight, she struck a broad and well-beaten wagon-road, the first and only evidence or trace of civilization she had seen since leaving her home in Texas.

Up to this joyful moment the indomitable inflexibility of purpose of our heroine had not faltered for an instant, neither had she suffered the slightest despondency, in view of the terrible array of disheartening circumstances that had continually confronted her; but when she realized the hopeful prospect before her of a speedy escape from the reach of her barbarous captors, and a reasonable certainty of an early reunion with people of her own sympathizing race, the feminine elements of her nature preponderated, her stoical fortitude yielded to the delightful anticipation, and her joy was intensified and confirmed by seeing at this moment a long train of wagons approaching over the distant prairie.

The spectacle overwhelmed her with ecstasy, and she wept tears of joy while offering up sincere and heartfelt thanks to the Almighty for delivering her from a bondage more dreadful than death.

She then proceeded on until she met the wagons in charge of Mr. Robert Bent, whom she entreated to give her food instantly, as she was in a state bordering upon absolute starvation. He kindly complied with her request, and after the cravings of her appetite had been appeased he desired to gratify his curiosity, which had been not a little excited at the unusual exhibition of a beautiful white woman appearing alone in that wild country, riding upon an Indian saddle, with no covering on her head save her long natural hair, which was hanging loosely and disorderedly about her shoulders, while her attire was sadly in need of repairs. Accordingly, he inquired of her where she lived, to which she replied, "In Texas." Mr. B. gave an incredulous shake of his head at this response, remarking at the same time that he thought she must be mistaken, as Texas happened to be situated some five or six hundred miles distant. She reiterated the assurance of her statement, and described to him briefly the leading incidents attending her capture and escape; but still he was inclined to doubt, believing that she might possibly be insane.

He informed her that the river she had just crossed was the Arkansas, and that she was then on the old Santa Fé road, about fifteen miles west of Big Turkey Creek, where she would find the most remote frontier house. Then, after thanking him for his kindness, she bade him adieu, and started away in a walk toward the settlements, while he continued his journey in the opposite direction; but he still followed the exit of the remarkable apparition with his eyes until she was several hundred yards distant, when he observed her throw one of her feet over the horse's back *à la femme sauvage*, and, casting a graceful kiss toward him with her hand, she set off on a gallop, and soon disappeared over the crest of the prairies.

On the arrival of Mr. Bent at Fort Zara, he called upon the Indian agent, and reported the circumstance of meeting Mrs. L——, and, by a singular coincidence, it so happened that the agent was at that very time holding a council with the chiefs of the identical band of Indians from whom she had last escaped, and they had just given a full history of the entire affair, which seemed so improbable to the agent that he was not disposed to credit it until he received its confirmation through Mr. Bent. He at once dispatched a man to follow the woman and conduct her to Council Grove, where she was kindly received, and remained for some time, hoping through the efforts of the agents to gain intelligence of the two children she had left with the Comanches, as she desired to take them back to their father in Texas; but no tidings were gained for a long while. Meantime she formed the acquaintance of a man at Council Grove whom, as I understood, she married, and, for aught I know, may be there yet. Wherever she is, I most heartily wish her all possible happiness.

The two captive children were, as the agent informed me, ransomed at a subsequent date, and sent home to their father.

It will readily be seen, by a reference to the map of the country over which Mrs. L—— passed, that the distance from the place of her capture to the point where she struck the Arkansas River could not have been short of about five hundred miles, and the greater part of this immense expanse of desert plain she traversed alone, without seeing a single civilized human habitation.

If any other woman, either in ancient or modern times, has performed as signal an equestrian achievement as this, I have yet to learn it.

CHAPTER VIII.

West Point Military Academy.—Cadet Brown's Eccentricities.—Decapitating Professor Z—— K——.—A Conflagration.—Court-martial.—Cadet K——.—Excused from Duty.—Shirt Collars down.—Reporting to the Superintendent.—Wearing the Uniform.—"Touch off Thompson."

WEST POINT MILITARY ACADEMY.

THE pupils of the Military Academy at West Point are appointed from every congressional district in the United States, and from widely separated geographical sections, between the inhabitants of which there was rarely any intercourse at the time I was a member of the corps of cadets, which was before railroads were constructed, and when it required nearly a month of wearisome traveling to make the overland journey from New York to St. Louis or New Orleans. It will readily be understood that a new class arriving at the Academy during that period, with all their diversities of garb, dialects, education, and other local peculiarities, would present a most heterogeneous assemblage, and that it would require a vigorous application of discipline, accompanied by a good deal of discordant social attrition and some hard knocks, before the asperities of these incongruous elements would commingle, and the social amalgamation become blended and harmonized.

Such was the case during my time, and spirited discussions upon the relative merits and peculiarities of the people of the different states and sections were of frequent occurrence among the "plebs," and these sectional controversies were at times so acrimonious as to lead to pugilistic encounters, but which, I am happy to say, rarely resulted in any thing more serious than a black eye or a bloody nose.

It must be admitted, however, that, in the end, this sectional prejudice almost invariably yielded to more just and harmonious relations; and I question if a school could have been found upon the face of the earth wherein the pupils, on receiving their diplomas, entertained for each other a more sincere friendship, or a more ardent *esprit du corps* than did the graduates of West Point; and, as a general rule, they manifested a high regard for law and regulations, as well as a most exalted sense of honor; but here, as every where else, there were, of course, some exceptions to the rule.

The familiar old adage that "boys will be boys" [and sometimes very refractory ones too] has held good ever since the world was created; at all events, evidences of the fact may be traced as far back as the primeval days of that incorrigible youth whom his Maker pronounced a "*mendacious vagabond*," and who might possibly have turned out better had his earthly patriarchal progenitor, who fixed the designation of "*Cain*" to his name, made timely application to his back of that salutary, persuasive instrument entitled "*cane*." Under these circumstances, the opinion is hazarded that, unless the Millennium interposes its regenerating influences to purify the flagitious nature of the human family, there is every reason to believe the maxim above quoted will continue "apropos" to the end of time.

Seriously speaking, I question if a college or school of magnitude can be found in America which does not contain one or more waggish boys whose proclivities for practical joking and the perpetration of frolicsome pranks preponderate over all other wiser considerations.

The most inflexible rules of discipline, even when enforced to the letter, only serve to augment the inveterate proneness of these "*mauvais sujets*" to indulge their besetting propensities; and, as inscrutable as it may appear, neither the apprehension of punishment and disgrace, nor the certainty of encomiums and honors resulting from meritorious conduct and exalted classical attainments, seem to have the least weight in deterring them from the exercise of their ruling eccentricities.

These contumacious spirits unfortunately are, for the most part, endowed by nature with the brightest intellects, and might, by assiduous application to their books, attain high positions in their classes, as well as elevated rank in society; but, instead of choosing this wise part, they are prone to neglect their studies, set at defiance all rules and regulations, and thereby become marked objects of suspicion to professors and tutors, besides inflicting pain and sorrow upon their relatives and friends.

The Military Academy at West Point has probably been less afflicted with unruly pupils than almost any other educational institution in the country, and for the manifest reason that no infraction of the regulations is permitted to pass unnoticed, so that a cadet rarely escapes the penalty attached to an offense. That institution has not, however, been altogether exempt from the rule, and I have known several wild boys, or rather men, as they are usually designated, who so adroitly covered their wayward tracks that they were not discovered for some time, but they were invariably detected in the end, brought to trial, and punished.

A most pernicious hallucination seems to pervade the minds of many of the cadets, or, rather, such was the fact when I was with them, which was, that but little, if any opprobrium should attach to a pupil who is expelled for improper conduct, provided there was nothing dishonorable connected with its perpetration. Indeed, some went so far in those days as to applaud insubordination as rather a bold and creditable thing, while, on the other hand, they entertained serious fears of being dismissed for deficiency in scholastic attainments.

This idea, I take it, was based upon the popular maxim that "it is better to be a knave than a fool;" but I can assure all such young gentlemen as indorse this fallacious notion that the public look upon those who have been expelled for demerit resulting from improper conduct with less favor than they do the other class. Besides, I have my doubts if a man is necessarily a dunce because he happens to be found deficient in one special branch of his education, when perhaps he may excel in others. He may not, for example, be able readily to grasp the more abstruse problems in mathematics, but may be eminently proficient in literary achievements. As an evidence of this, I have known several young men who, after having failed to pass the examinations at the Military Academy, have subsequently attained high honors in civil professions.

CADET BROWN'S ECCENTRICITIES.

Nearly half a century has elapsed since I became a member of the corps of cadets, and numerous changes have taken place within the period, but essentially the existing admirable régime had been inaugurated previous to that time under the efficient superintendence of that courteous gentleman and accomplished officer, Colonel Thayer, aided by the model soldier, Major [afterward General] Worth, and an able corps of professors of eminent scientific attainments, some of whom may still be found at their posts, veterans in the service of their country.

Of all the events that transpired during the period of my academic term, none is more indelibly stamped upon my memory than that which I am about to relate in illustration of what has been asserted.

It was the arrival at the institution of a youth, whom for designation I will call Brown, who was appointed in the class of 182–, and who hailed from the wilds of the then "Far West," where, like most other pioneers, he had become imbued with the popular democratic dogma "*that one man is as good as another*," unless, perchance, he had been "*raised*" on the border, when, I dare say, *he* would have converted the aphorism into a Milesian bovine of the male gender by the adjunct of the words, "*if not a little better*."

In other words, if any appreciable difference existed in the merits of individual specimens of the "genus homo," that difference, in his estimation, might probably have been measured by the relative spaces intervening between the locale of the persons and the more populous districts.

Possessing a pre-eminently bright and vigorous intellect, with a wonderfully keen appreciation of the ludicrous, and a perfectly self-reliant individuality, all his associations and education had been such as to render him thoroughly antagonistic to aristocracy in every form, and especially to that phase conferred by military rank and titles.

As might have been anticipated, he did not remain long at the institution before he began to evince a spirit of insubordination, as well as an aversion for the close application and confinement necessary to insure a respectable standing in his studies. The consequence was, he neglected his books, and passed the greater part of his time in concocting and perpetrating schemes of mischief and frolic. I can not, of course, vouch for the literal authenticity of all the rumors that were current in regard to the young man's doings, and very likely many things may have been attributed to him of which he was absolutely innocent; but, as many of them were credited among his associates, it is presumed that those were substantially true. I merely give them as they were circulated among the cadets, disclaiming all other responsibility.

DECAPITATING PROFESSOR Z—— K——.

Among the escapades of least turpitude which marked the brief career of this froward youth, the following may be mentioned as characteristic examples.

An excellent officer by the name of Z—— K——, who, by the conscientious discharge of his duties, had often been obliged to notice and report the lawless vagaries of unruly cadets, and thereby had rendered himself especially obnoxious to them, was generally known under the familiar but not very euphonious soubriquet of "Old Zeb," and his recognition of a cadet in the act of violating any regulation was usually regarded as equivalent to an entry upon the conduct roll of the amount of demerit involved in the infraction of the regulation.

His appearance was therefore invariably looked for by refractory boys with apprehension and alarm, and his name was a terror to all evil-doers.

One evening, as Brown and his room-mate, in the old "South Barracks," were discussing what they conceived to be the unjustifiable idiosyncrasies in the professor's character, they became considerably exercised, and many epithets, the direct antipodes of blessings, were coupled with his name.

Brown feigned to wax furious upon the occasion, and, seizing a pillow-case and a large butcher-knife, put on his cap, and, in a state of the most intense apparent excitement, rushed out of the door, with the emphatic declaration "that he'd be d—d if he did not bag old Zeb's head before morning, or perish in the attempt."

His companion was certainly a little surprised at his infuriated manner, but did not for a moment entertain the thought that he had the remotest idea of carrying his bloody threat into execution, consequently he gave but little heed to it.

In the course of about an hour, however, the door of their room was thrown violently open, and Brown, in a state of the wildest apparent perturbation, with the butcher-knife in one hand, and the pillow-case containing something about the size and proportions of a man's head in the other, and both covered with blood, rushed into the room, and, throwing them down upon the floor, exclaimed, "I told you I'd have it before morning, and there is his bloody old head, and you'll not be bothered any more with *his* reports, I reckon."

At this startling announcement his room-mate sprang to his feet, bounded like lightning through the door, and, in the utmost consternation and terror, hurried to the room of some of his friends, and reported the horrible intelligence.

Of course, all were intensely shocked at the tidings of the assassination, and it was some time before they became sufficiently collected to reason or deliberate upon the proper course to pursue. They finally resolved, however, to go in mass back to the apartment, and investigate the facts more fully before making a formal report of the murder to the authorities. Accordingly, they cautiously and silently approached the door on tiptoe, and, softly turning the knob, gently opened it, and ventured a timorous peep into the apartment, when, to their great astonishment and delight, instead of beholding the ghastly head of the murdered professor, they espied Brown with his coat off, his sleeves turned up, and busily occupied in basting a huge goose which was suspended by a string, and roasting before the fire.

The sudden transformation of what they conceived to be a solemn tragedy into the most superlatively ludicrous farce was too laughable not to be appreciated by the assembled spectators, and they all participated in the savory supper which followed the young man's successful but not very sanguinary raid.

A CONFLAGRATION.

The most of Brown's pranks were harmless in their character, but one that I am about to notice assumed a more serious type.

As the sequel of his last misadventure terminated his brief academical career, and created no little excitement at the time, I will relate it as a warning to those young gentlemen whose martial aspirations may hereafter incline them to embark in the laborious undertaking of contending for a diploma at our national military school.

After a few feeble efforts to attain a respectable position in his studies, the incorrigible youth at length arrived at the conclusion that his friends had made a mistake in his calling, as his prospects for achieving distinction in the profession of arms were becoming every day more and more precarious, and, at the same time, his whimsical vagaries multiplied in a corresponding ratio.

About this time an old outbuilding (an appurtenance to the barracks) became so much of a nuisance that a universal desire was manifested in the corps of cadets to have it removed, but no legitimate means were within the scope of their powers for accomplishing the result, and it remained an eyesore to every body until, upon one dark and stormy night, the alarm of fire was heard, and the obnoxious building was discovered to be in flames. All available means were put in requisition to extinguish it, but the boys' hearts were not in the success of the effort, and the structure was burned to the ground. How or through whose agency the fire originated was at first a mystery to the authorities as well as to almost every body else.

It was perfectly well understood that some one had set the fire, and various conjectures were afloat in regard to the identity of the incendiary.

Although no one, excepting those directly concerned, knew positively who was the author of it, yet many believed that Brown and his associates had something to do with it.

As the turpitude of the offense was considered so great, and its effects so likely to prove derogatory to good order and military discipline, the authorities resolved to probe the matter to the bottom, and hold the guilty parties to a severe account. Accordingly, a court of inquiry was convened, with Captain ——— as president, before which the entire corps of cadets were summoned to appear, and their testimony taken under oath.

The evidence adduced before Brown was called elicited facts which went to show that he was committed in the matter. He was, however, put upon the stand, and, after having been duly sworn, was asked to state to the court what he knew concerning the burning of the building. In response to which he, with the utmost assumed ingenuousness and gravity, after considerable deliberation, said:

"I do not know that I shall be able from personal knowledge to add any thing to the information which the court has already received upon the subject. There are numerous random rumors circulating among the cadets; whether they are true or false, I take it that no persons, excepting those directly implicated, can determine. Moreover, I presume, the court do not care about listening to 'hearsay' evidence."

The court, at the suggestion of one of the members, was "cleared," and after a brief consultation the doors were reopened, and the recorder asked the witness if he would please inform the court what some of the rumors were that he had heard.

He replied, "I can not, as I remarked before, vouch for the authenticity of these irresponsible reports, and, indeed, I have not charged my memory with many of them. I have, however, a distinct recollection of one, which implicates some of the leading functionaries of the institution, and, unless the court should insist upon my repeating it, I would prefer remaining silent."

He was informed that the court could not consume time in listening to irrelevant remarks regarding his opinions or scruples, and he was directed to give a prompt categorical answer to the question; to which, with apparent reluctance and a most solemn cast of countenance, he responded,

"They do say, may it please the gentlemen of the court—they do say that Colonel ——— brought the shavings, and that Captain ——— set the old thing on fire" [the superintendent and the president of the court being the officers alluded to].

At this most astounding announcement a smile was observed to flit over the face of every member of the court except that of the president, who maintained his customary dignified and imperturbable gravity, merely remarking that he was decidedly opposed to the introduction of any more "hearsay" testimony.

Abundant evidence was evoked during the progress of the investigation to convict Brown of the offense; charges were at once preferred against him, a court-martial convened, before which he was arraigned, and an emphatic plea of "*Not guilty*" was placed upon the record of proceedings.

After the witnesses for the prosecution had been examined, the prisoner, in accordance with the usual formula, was asked if he had any evidence to adduce or defense to make. The evidence at this stage of the proceedings was of so conclusive a character that he felt assured there was no prospect of his acquittal, and, his waggish propensities predominating to the last, he resolved, as the sporting fraternity would express it, "to die game;" and, as a characteristic prelude to a graceful drop of the curtain upon the finale of the last act in the ludicrous military drama wherein he had played so conspicuous a rôle, he responded to the interrogatory in the following words:

"I'm not altogether satisfied that it will be of much service to my cause if I call witnesses in behalf of the defense, or that it will avail much for me to make a formal defense, provided the vote upon the verdict is to be taken in the manner I have understood it usually has been."

The members of the court manifested no little surprise at this mysterious insinuation, and the judge advocate asked him "in what way he supposed the vote would be taken."

"I am not positive," replied he, "that my information upon the subject is correct, but it has been quietly whispered around among the boys that the practice heretofore has been, when cadets have been tried for offenses involving the penalty of dismissal, for the judge advocate, after the court is cleared, to put the question in the following manner: 'All those in favor of finding the accused guilty of the charges and specifications alleged against him will keep their seats; those in favor of acquittal will forthwith jump out of the window;' and as a man can seldom be found who feels inclined to break his neck by leaping out of a window three stories from the ground, the verdict is generally unanimous for conviction, and the unfortunate victim is dismissed."

It is hardly necessary to add that this young gentleman took up the line of march for his border home very soon after this, and I was informed that he subsequently figured as a lawyer of very considerable eminence in his native state.

CADET K——.

Another contemporary of mine, by the name of K——, from one of the New England States, was fully as much given to practical joking as the youth from the more rural districts of the West.

Upon one occasion, when he was upon the sick-list, and had been excused from duty by the surgeon, he happened to pass Major Worth, and failed to raise his cap to him as required by the Regulations.

The major's keen eyes detected the omission, and, being a good deal of a martinet, he called to the young man, remarking, in his habitually prompt and emphatic manner, "You did not salute me, *sir!* Are you not aware, *sir*, that it's your duty to salute all commissioned officers whom you pass, *sir-r-r?*"

"Certainly," replied K——, "certainly, sir, I'm fully conscious of that requirement, but I am excused from *all duty* to-day by Doctor Wheaton."

SHIRT COLLARS DOWN.

At one time an order was issued requiring cadets at dress-parades to have their shirt collars *turned down.* The evening following the promulgation of the order, the corps appeared on parade with their shirt collars neatly turned over their stocks, the single exception being our eccentric hero, who exhibited a superlatively ridiculous contrast to all the others.

His interpretation of the language of the order, although literal, was very remote from the signification intended to be conveyed by the authority from whence it emanated. He had managed, by the ripping of seams or some other means, to get his shirt on upside down, and made his appearance on parade with something like a foot of the skirt turned over his coat collar, and hanging in numerous folds loosely about his shoulders.

Amid the universal titter that passed along the entire line of the battalion at this unique spectacle, K—— remained as solemn and motionless as a statue; and as he cast an inquiring glance around, his countenance seemed to indicate a total unconsciousness of any cause for the unusual merriment.

He was at once ordered to his quarters in arrest; but he rendered an excuse the following morning, wherein he professed great indignation at the injustice of the treatment he had received, and contended that he had complied with the order to the letter, his collar having been *turned down* more than that of any other man in the corps. Whereupon he was released from arrest, a correct interpretation of the order given to him, with an admonitory caution against a repetition of the offense. But in a short time after this the young gentleman retired to private life.

REPORTING TO THE SUPERINTENDENT.

Among the pupils at the Military Academy are frequently seen young men from the frontier districts, who, on entering the institution, are exceedingly untutored and unsophisticated, but who subsequently attain high scholastic honors, and become accomplished officers and gentlemen.

A characteristic specimen of this class of tyros is alluded to in a book of mine called "Army Life on the Border," but as many may not have seen this description, I take the liberty of repeating the substance of it in this connection.

I have a distinct remembrance of the arrival at the Academy of the young man alluded to, as his manners, garb, and language were such as to render unmistakable his remote border origin. He was from one of the frontier states, and had never before been but a short distance from home.

Before leaving home his father had furnished him with a horse, saddle, and bridle, and, with his scanty wardrobe packed in a capacious pair of saddle-bags, he set out on his long journey for West Point.

After many days' hard riding he at length arrived at Jersey City, where, after selling his horse, he took his saddle-bags on his arm, and, crossing the ferry, entered New York, with the intention of "putting up" at the first respectable tavern he could find.

He passed up Courtlandt Street and Broadway, with his eyes continually searching for the sign-post and swinging sign which he supposed to be the universal evidence of a tavern throughout the civilized world, but his search was in vain. He found nothing but one vast conglomeration of stores, shops, and private houses; not a single inn did he meet with. Finally, after becoming considerably fatigued in wandering about the streets, he discovered the sign of an oyster saloon; and as he had never before had an opportunity of testing the merits of the bivalves, he entered the establishment, and, putting down his saddle-bags, informed the waiter that "he didn't mind ef he tuck a small chance of them thar oysteers hisself;" and in answer to the inquiry of how many he desired, said, "He reckon'd about half a peck." Accordingly, they were set before him raw, "on the half shell."

He did not at all fancy their appearance; yet, as he observed persons all around him devouring them with much apparent relish, he selected one of the largest, raised it with his fork, and, after scrutinizing it very attentively for a moment, put it in his mouth; but no sooner had it come in contact with his palate than it was ejected, with intense disgust, half way across the room; at the same time he called out to the waiter, "Look a yere, mister, you jest take away these yere nasty varmints, and bring me some bacon and eggs."

Soon after this he delivered a letter of introduction with which he had been provided to a gentleman in the city, who kindly showed him to a hotel, and assisted him in purchasing a trunk with a suitable wardrobe. On the following morning he took the steamer for his destination, and in due time landed upon the wharf at West Point.

His letter of appointment required him to report in person to the superintendent, Colonel Thayer, who, although a very refined, courteous, and kind gentleman, was exceedingly rigid in enforcing the strictest discipline and the highest respect for military authority.

My young friend, after ascertaining where the colonel's quarters were situated, shouldered his large trunk (he was then about six feet high, and correspondingly developed), and staggered under its weight up the steep hill to the superintendent's quarters, put down his trunk upon the steps, knocked at the door, and was at once admitted into the colonel's presence.

Unlike most cadets on their first introduction to this dignitary, he was not in the slightest degree abashed, but felt entirely self-possessed, and, without an invitation, taking a chair close to the colonel, and looking him directly in the eyes, said, "Ole man, are you Colonel, or Captain, or What-you-call-um Thayer?" To which the old gentleman very gravely replied, "I am Colonel Thayer, sir."

"Wa'al, now, look a yere, kurn," said the youth, "this yere hill o' yourn *am* a breather; ef it ain't, d—n me."

The colonel comprehended at once what kind of a specimen of humanity he had before him, and directed his orderly to show him to the barracks, where he was soon inducted into the mysteries of wholesome discipline.

As some may have a curiosity to know what success this untutored youth of the forest met with in his academical career, I add for their information that he applied himself zealously to his studies, attained a good standing in his class, and, on graduating, was an accomplished gentleman and scholar, who reflected credit upon the institution, and was afterward favorably known as the author of a History of Texas.

WEARING THE UNIFORM.

It does not strike me as at all wonderful that pupils of the West Point Military Academy, after undergoing four long years of close application to a rigid course of study, relentless discipline, and total seclusion from society (which was the policy in my time), should have been rejoiced when their academic career terminated, and they were permitted to throw off the dingy gray livery of their initiatory martial servitude, and put on the uniforms of commissioned officers.

Whatever may have been the experience of others, I, for one, am forced to acknowledge that I have been unable to detect the slightest tint of the rose in my recollections of school life at West Point.

The necessary requirements of guard and police duties, drills, parades, and other hard work incidental to rudimental training, with unremitting study, mental anxiety, and constant apprehension as to what might have been the result of our annual examinations, wherein a large percentage of the young men were invariably dismissed for deficiency in acquirements, all combined to render this the least happy period of my existence.

So indelibly were the impressions of these school-days stamped upon my mind, that for twenty years afterward, whenever I was tortured with a visitation of nightmare, my imagination generally carried me back into that dreaded examination-hall, where, in presence of an assembled "board of visitors," I was forthwith summoned to the blackboard by some professor; and when the hallucination assumed its worst type, after indulging in an indigestible supper, it was sure to be that one who was considered the most exacting and uncompromising, and whom I have never since been able to look upon without a retrospective sentiment of trepidation and horror; for this man, when in his least amiable mood, usually assumed a most benignant smile, and was pre-eminently polite and courteous in his demeanor, but was regarded then as most dangerous.

So well was this peculiarity of the professor understood in the corps of cadets that the boys became terrified just in proportion to the politeness and urbanity of his manner toward them during the course of their examinations.

I never for a moment flattered myself that the old gentleman entertained any special regard for me while I was at school, but I am positive that, whenever I encountered his image during my nocturnal visitations subsequently, I was so unfortunate as to see the spectre with a broad and eminently diabolic smile upon his countenance, while he in the politest terms desired me to elucidate some very abstruse and knotty problem about which I had not the faintest conception. Of course I was obliged to acknowledge my inability to perform the task, or to "*'fess*," as the cadets have it, and I suffered all the mental torture that I would if the circumstance had actually occurred.

As may be imagined, I found but little romance in cadet life at the Military Academy, and I can give direct and unqualified attestation to the fact that the happiest day of my life was that on which, with several classmates, I made my entrée into New York City after graduating.

We were at that time dressed in full spang-new uniforms from top to toe, and, as we promenaded up and down Broadway, we probably entertained about as elevated notions of our own individual consequence as any boys ever did. I distinctly remember that I was fully of the opinion that every man, woman, and child we passed regarded us with admiration and envy.

The truth is, we felt like prisoners just released from confinement, and we certainly enjoyed our freedom to the fullest extent, yet I dare say this has been the experience of nearly every young man who has passed through the severe ordeal at the West Point institution.

Young officers are generally fond of appearing in uniform even among citizens, which is all right enough. I see no impropriety in it; nevertheless, I have observed, after an officer has seen a few years' service with troops, where he is obliged to wear his uniform constantly, he is glad of the opportunity, when he goes into the cities, to put on the garb of a citizen, and for the reason that he does not care about attracting special observation. Besides, there are, at the present time, many classes of people in civil occupations whose clothing is something like, and perhaps may have been copied from the army uniform; such, for instance, as railroad employés, policemen, letter-carriers, etc., so that an army officer in uniform might readily be mistaken for one of those useful and most worthy members of society. This might not, however, be in exact accord with what the former conceived to be due to the importance of his position, and this is another reason why old officers prefer citizen's attire when off duty.

General S****** related to me quite a ludicrous little episode which occurred to him shortly after leaving West Point, and as it serves to illustrate what I have said above, it may not be considered out of place in this connection.

During the general's early military career, while he was a brevet second lieutenant, stationed at Fort Morgan, in Mobile Bay, he and a friend, Lieutenant T*****, obtained leave of absence for the purpose of visiting Mobile, and wishing to make as respectable an appearance as possible, they dressed in full uniform, and, embarking upon a passing steamer, went up to the city.

While waiting upon the levee for their luggage to be landed, several inquisitive boys were attracted by their rather flashy uniforms, and especially by the broad red stripes upon their pants, and the general's capacious military cloak, which he had, "à la espagnol," arranged in graceful folds around his person, with one side thrown over his shoulder something in the style of the Roman toga, and in such a manner as to exhibit to the best advantage the bright scarlet lining. At the same time he had put himself into a very consequential attitude, with his arms folded across his breast, and his jaunty little forage-cap resting upon the front of his head, and turned saucily just a trifle to one side. While in this dignified and graceful posture, one of the boys timidly approached him, and said, "Please, mister, when is your circus a comin'?"

They were most essentially disgusted at the stupidity of the youth, who was unable to perceive the difference between a commissioned officer of the regular army (a West Pointer at that) and a circus-rider, and of course they scorned to answer so absurd a question, but walked away up the street toward the Battle House, with several of the pertinacious lads, whose curiosity was now considerably excited, following in their wake. I should remark, however, that the two lieutenants were attached to the Third Artillery, each having the designation of that regiment (figure 3) upon the front of his cap.

As they proceeded on the crowd of boys increased, and various random conjectures were hazarded as to who the strangers could be, but no satisfactory conclusion seemed to be arrived at until one of the urchins exclaimed, "I have it, boys! I have it! Them fellars belong to number three fire-engine company." And he at once ran up to them, saying, "I say, fellars, when is your machine goin' to squirt?"

The general says they hurried on to the hotel, changed their dress, and thenceforth appeared in citizen's attire while in the unappreciative city of Mobile.

"TOUCH OFF THOMPSON."

Among the most anomalous specimens of juvenility that have figured in the annals of the Military Academy at West Point was one whom, for designation, I will call Thompson, which will serve the purposes of our legend as well as any other, and, if his vagaries were half as whimsical as they have been represented, he certainly was a most original character.

As near as I remember, this youth commenced his military career somewhere about 1840, and from the date of his first appearance at West Point until he left he evinced the most eccentric tendencies. For example, he was in the habit of wandering about the grounds alone at a rapid pace, with his eyes turned up toward the sky, seemingly absorbed in the contemplation of some very important astronomical question, and manifested no disposition to enter into conversation or associate with his fellow cadets; indeed, when directly addressed, he often failed to reply, and would generally pass his most intimate acquaintances without the slightest token of recognition.

In a word, he was probably one of the most unsocial, *distrait*, and peculiar individuals that ever lived.

When his name was called upon parade he was generally so absorbed in a "brown study" that he paid no heed to it, and consequently was reported absent when he was actually present in the ranks.

This became so common an occurrence, and his demerit marks augmented so rapidly, that he was at length obliged to request the file adjoining him to jog him at the instant his name was called by the orderly sergeant; but his neighbor usually administered this jog in so vigorous a manner that it startled the young man so much that it caused him to leap several feet from the ground, and jerk out the required response in a sudden spasmodic tone, which sounded more like *hap* than here. It was not unlike the sound produced by the expulsion of a close-fitting wad from a pop-gun, and at first created no little merriment in the company.

So long as Thompson was touched at the proper instant it was all right, and he escaped being reported absent; but whenever his prompter neglected or forgot to administer the required punch, he rarely answered to his name; and, as singular as it may appear, he never failed to give utterance to the sharp monosyllable *hap* whenever he was jogged in the ribs, whether his name was called or not, even if the admonitory thrust was applied several times during one roll-call. The response followed the touch of the adjoining file with as much certainty and celerity as the report of a gun succeeds the explosion of the fulminating powder.

This peculiarity of Thompson's soon became so well understood throughout the corps of cadets that unscrupulous members of his company, who were desirous of playing truant, would sometimes engage Thompson's prompter to give him the signal when their names were called.

They would say, "I wish you would touch Thompson for me at tattoo or réveille," and, if the proposition was acceded to, the innocent victim prevented them from being reported absent.

The application of the finger to the young gentleman's side, with the consequent explosive ejaculation, was so similar to touching a lighted port-fire to the fuse of a cannon, that the expression "Touch off Thompson for me at parade," etc., soon became understood by all except the most prominent actor in the farce, who soon acquired the sobriquet of "Touch off Thompson," which tenaciously adhered to him until he left the school.

CHAPTER IX.

PRAIRIE INDIANS.

Indians as Prisoners.—Winnebago Dandy.—Push-met-te-haw.—Treatment of Prisoners.—Indian Diplomacy.—A Comanche's Opinion of the Pale Faces.—A civilized Indian's Opinion of the Government.—Black Beaver.—A facetious Indian.—Aboriginal Precocity.—Aborigines as they are.

THE Prairie Indians, who are probably as expert equestrians as the Bedouin Arabs, always go into battle well mounted, and, when properly armed, are most formidable enemies. Formerly, when these people possessed no fire-arms, but were solely dependent on the bow and arrow, which has a very limited effective range, they were far inferior to the white man in action; but, now that they are well provided with rifles and revolvers, this difference has greatly diminished, if not entirely disappeared. And why should not this be the case? The prairie warrior has sufficient courage, and is an adept in the art of war as taught and practiced in the school of his ancestors. He has made this his study from childhood, and has learned all the arts, manœuvres, and subterfuges necessary to prosecute successful partisan warfare;

and although his strategy may not in all respects coincide with the teachings of Vauban or Mahan, yet, when we are forced to make war upon him, we are compelled to adopt a portion of his tactics or make failures.

One of the reasons why the Indians fight so desperately when hard pressed may be attributed to the fact that they have the utmost horror of being taken prisoners and held in captivity. They themselves make slaves of their captives, and they have no other conception of the condition of a prisoner of war save that of the most abject and degrading bondage, which to them is more repulsive than death.

Some years ago our troops in Western Texas captured a party of Indians belonging to a band that had stolen government animals, and among them was a chief, who, with his wife and two children, were detained as hostages, while the others were sent out and required to bring back the depredators with the stolen stock.

The chief and his family were put into a tent guarded by two sentinels, who were instructed to keep a vigilant watch over them and prevent their escape.

One dark night, after every thing about the camp had become hushed and quiet, and the squaw and her children were fast asleep, the chief took his knife, and, noiselessly crawling to their bedside, drove it to the hilt in the breast of each in rapid succession; after which he jumped to his feet like lightning, leaped through the door, lighting upon the astounded sentinel, whom he thrust to the heart with his knife, and, giving a terrific war-whoop, bounded away into the darkness; but, before he was out of range, the other sentinel fired, and finished the bloody tragedy by dropping the murderer dead in his tracks.

The savage instincts of the Indian of the Plains, and the wonderful control and mastery he acquires over the horse, were strikingly evinced during a bloody engagement between our troops and a party of Cheyennes, near Fort Wallace, in 1867.

In the heat of the battle a cavalry soldier was wounded, and fell from his horse out of reach of his comrades, when one of the savages rode up at full speed, reached down from his horse, seized the soldier by the hair of the head, and, without slacking his gait in the least, drew him up to his saddle-bow, and with his tomahawk beat out his brains; then tearing all the clothing from the mangled body, he dashed it upon the ground again, and giving a fiendish howl of exultation, rejoined his companions.

WINNEBAGO DANDY.

The Indians, as a general rule, are eminently an imitative people, and when thrown in contact with white men, especially those high in rank and authority, they are prone to copy their manners and customs.

There still lives among the Winnebagoes an old Indian called "Dandy," who was a member of the first delegation from that tribe that ever visited Washington City. While *en route* to the national capital, the party was detained at Galena some time waiting for a steamer to descend the Mississippi, and as they were strolling about the town one day, they came near a Methodist church where service was being held during the season of a revival. Greatly astonished at the first glance of this strange novelty, they hastily drew up around the windows, and saw the house crowded with people, many of them, under the influence of the preaching, becoming intensely excited—some clapping their hands, others stamping, jumping, and making mysterious gestures and contortions of limbs and body, while at the same time the entire congregation were shouting at the highest pitch of their voices, all of which was perfectly incomprehensible to the Indians, who looked on the spectacle with wonder and amazement, and made various random conjectures as to the meaning of these unusual proceedings.

One of them suggested that the "Big Medicine man" (the preacher) might be exerting his powers of incantation to exorcise and drive away bad spirits which had got possession of the people. Another one surmised that possibly this was a big pale-face war-dance. And one even went so far as to pronounce the whole company stark raving mad. But none of their opinions seemed to meet the concurrence of the majority of the party until Dandy, who had looked on with great interest for some time, at length assumed an air of importance, and exclaimed, "I have it—I have it; I'll tell you what's the matter!" Then, pointing his finger to his head, he added, "*Whisky too much! whisky too much!*" And they all walked off in disgust, verily believing that the good disciples of Wesley were on a terrible spree.

On their return home after visiting their "Great Father," at the urgent entreaty of the people of Albany, they were prevailed upon to give an exhibition of their songs, dances, etc. A room was procured, and at the proper hour Dandy stationed himself at the door, and received twenty-five cents from each person admitted. A good house was secured, and the performance passed off to the satisfaction of every body, until the appreciative audience was about to disperse, when Dandy again took possession of the door, and demanded another quarter from each one before giving them egress, and it was with difficulty that the interpreter could convince him that this was not allowable.

PUSH-MET-TE-HAW.

It is said of a distinguished former chief of the Choctaws, "Push-met-te-haw," who was probably one of the most talented Indians of whose history we have any knowledge, that upon an occasion after our authorities in Washington had used all their efforts to induce him to sign the "Dancing Rabbit Creek" treaty, by which they ceded to the United States all their lands east of the Mississippi River, and which he had persistently declined, that General Jackson, then President, called him to the White House, and, after exhausting all arguments without avail, placed himself before the chief, and in a highly excited manner thus addressed him:

"I'll have you to know, sir, that I am Andrew Jackson, President of the United States, sir; and, by the Eternal, you *shall* sign that treaty."

Push-met-te-haw was not in the least intimidated, but sprang to his feet, and, in imitation of the President's emphatic manner, replied,

"I know perfectly well who you are, sir; and I'll have *you* to know, sir, that I am Push-met-te-haw, head chief of the great Choctaw nation; and, by the Eternal, I'll *not* sign that treaty, sir."

This Indian was not of royal parentage, but had risen from obscure origin to his lofty position in the nation solely upon his own merits; and being a proud, dignified man, he was somewhat sensitive on the subject of his lineage. On the occasion of his first visit to Washington his reputation preceded him, and he received marked attention from the principal dignitaries, and was even invited to dine at the White House. He accepted the invitation; and during the repast, Mrs. Madison, the mistress of the presidential mansion at that time, manifested a lively interest in him, making particular inquiries about his family; and she was especially desirous of knowing whether he was able to trace back his ancestry for many generations through a lineage of distinguished chiefs. His countenance clouded, and assumed a stern expression of displeasure at these interrogatories, and for some time he made no reply; but at length he said,

"Push-met-te-haw was not born like common mortals, and he never knew father or mother; but on one bright and beautiful summer's night, when all nature was hushed in profound and silent repose, suddenly a deep sound was heard approaching, like the rumbling of distant thunder; soon the sky became dark and lowering; heavy clouds, driven by a furious tempest, piled upon each other in the loftiest vaults of the heavens, and poured down rain and hail in torrents; ponderous peals of thunder exploded and reverberated, like continuous salvos of gigantic artillery, throughout the entire canopy of the sky; the lightning flashed in angular scintillations vivid streaks of fire; and every element of nature seemed in a mad frenzy to contribute toward the sublime and fearful chaos — in the midst of which a huge thunderbolt, directed by the hand of the Great Spirit, was sent down from heaven and struck a gnarled oak, shivering its gigantic trunk into ten thousand atoms, and from out of its heart bounded forth a full-grown Indian brave in complete war costume, with his rifle upon his shoulder. Thus entered the world, and such is the pedigree, of the warrior who now stands before the Great Chief's squaw."

TREATMENT OF PRISONERS.

During the existence of the "Lone-star" republic of Texas a white man was captured on the Brazos by the Comanches, who carried him away to their camp, and, in accordance with their custom, subjected him to all the menial offices of a slave. While in camp he was kicked about most unmercifully, forced to cut and carry wood, herd horses, pitch lodges, etc., etc., and on marches they compelled him to pack enormous loads of kettles, frying-pans, and other rubbish, until his back and feet became terribly lacerated; and he was so much worn out by hard work, starvation, and cruel treatment, that at length he abandoned all hope of bettering his condition, and in agonizing despair wished himself dead.

About this time some of the chiefs of the band returned from a visit to Austin, where they had been kindly received by General Houston, the president, and were shown all the novelties of the capital, and, among other places, they were taken into the State-house while the Congress was in session, and the mysteries of legislation explained to them. They were highly delighted with what they saw, and took especial pride in displaying their new acquirements to their people at home. And they even went so far as to propose that, in future, when any important tribal business was pending before the council of the nation, they should, like the pale-faced law-makers, put it to vote and decide it by the majority.

This proposition was acceded to by all; but it so happened at the first meeting of their deliberative council that they had forgotten some of the details of the forms they had witnessed at Austin, and they were obliged to call upon the white captive to enlighten them. He consented to instruct them provided they would make him a member of the council, and permit him to introduce the first resolution. The request was acceded to, and a presiding chief was appointed, who informed the white member that his resolution was then in order; whereupon he took the floor, or rather the ground, and said, "Mr. President, I propose to the great council of the Comanche nation—the greatest nation on earth—[cheers, with prolonged guttural how's! how's! how's! all over the lodge]—I propose, I say, Mr. President, that hereafter every gentleman Indian, in accordance with the customs of the pale faces, be required, on marches, to pack his own kettles and herd his own horses."

The resolution was received with applause, and carried unanimously, and thenceforth the captive was relieved of his burdens.

INDIAN DIPLOMACY.

It is generally believed by those who are not familiar with the character of the aborigines of the West, that they, like the African race, are inferior in intellect to the Caucasian, and that their powers of mind are so limited that crafty and designing white men can cheat and cajole them without their being aware of the fact. This, however, is very far from being true, as can easily be shown. The fact is, the intellectual and reasoning powers of the natives are in the highest degree active and bright, and they possess as correct an appreciation of right and justice, and as vivid a conception of wrong and fraud, as any other people.

Nearly all the trouble we have encountered, in our dealings with the Indian tribes for the last fifty years, has resulted from the non-compliance on our part with treaty stipulations, together with the injustice and fraud practiced upon them by dishonest agents; and this is as well understood and appreciated by them as it would be by white men.

A few apposite examples which I am about to relate will illustrate this most conclusively.

A chief of one of the bands of Sioux told the commissioners who were making a treaty with them that his people did not want any more agents who had fathers and brothers-in-law to support from their annuities. That the one present (pointing to an ex-agent) came among them with all his worldly effects contained in a carpet bag, but accompanied by a considerable retinue of relatives, all of whom occupied positions about the agency for four years, and when they went away it took several wagons to carry their effects. They were all rich.

A chief of another prairie tribe, in a council with General H——, told him that their agent, who was present, had stolen half their goods, and buried the balance.

Along the western slope of the Rocky Mountains, near the base of the snow-clad and elevated peaks of the Sierra de la Plata, upon the head waters of the Colorado of California, and in one of the most picturesque, but remote and unfrequented sections within the limits of our entire possessions, are found two nomadic bands of Indians, called "*Ca-po-ta*" and "*Woman-o-che*"—*Utes*—who are yet uncontaminated by contact with the Anglo-Saxon.

That ubiquitous and all-pervading cosmopolite, the gold-hunter, who has "*prospected*" almost every other "*gulch*" and crevice in our vast mountain ranges, has not as yet penetrated into the heart of this particular locality, so that the natives of this section may be said to retain to this day very nearly their normal condition.

I visited the country alluded to but a short time since, and came in contact with many of the Indians who roam over it, and upon one occasion the principal chief of the *Woman-o-ches*, "Pe-as-te-cho-pa," with twenty of his braves, paid a visit to my camp. The chief was a man of highly dignified bearing, about sixty years of age, and a magnificent specimen of his race. Possessing a commanding and well-proportioned figure of the "*Apollo Belvidere*" type, which was tall, erect, and lithe, with an open, intelligent, and kindly expression of countenance, all his movements and gestures were eminently dignified and graceful.

He bore the reputation of being a great warrior, and had performed many daring and signal feats of valor; but it was said of him that, during the excitement of battle, the lineaments of his features underwent such an entire metamorphosis, that the calm repose of his usually benignant countenance then assumed an expression of the most savage and diabolical ferocity.

After going through the customary Indian greeting of hugging and rubbing faces together, they seated themselves upon the grass, and informed their white brothers that a big smoke was the next important feature on the programme. This preliminary having been disposed of with all due ceremony, the chief said he would like to be informed as to the object of this visit of the pale faces into his country; and he was particularly desirous to know if this was a prelude to the advent of gold-hunters, to which he and his people were firmly opposed, as he said they were fully aware of the fact that this would lead to their speedy demoralization and extinction.

He was assured that this was not the object of the visit, but that it was one merely of curiosity and pleasure. He was satisfied, and a long talk ensued, during which the chief inquired if any of the party ever communicated, either orally or by letter, with their "great-grandfather," the President of the United States; and on being informed that my chief, General Sherman, was in constant communication with his venerable relative, he said it would be agreeable to him if the general would make known to the head chief of the whites that the Utes, from time to time, had had a number of agents sent to them, some of whom had proved good and others bad. For example, he was of opinion that Kit Carson and three others whom he named were honest men, and that when presents were sent out for his people by the President these agents had always brought them directly to the tribe, where they fairly distributed them; but he was sorry to say that he had not so much confidence in three other men whose names he mentioned, and who also had been their agents. He added, It is a very long road from Washington to our hunting-grounds, and when our great-grandfather starts out a train of wagons loaded with presents for his red children in the mountains, under charge of such agents as those last mentioned, they do not, as a general rule, go far before they come to a road leaving the main trail and turning to the right. One wagon takes this road, and gets lost. In a little while another wagon takes a road to the left, and is heard of no more. And thus they continue to depart from the train, until at length, when its destination is reached, only two or three of the original outfit remain. All the others have disappeared, and it was impossible to tell what became of them; but he had been informed that those agents suddenly and mysteriously became rich.

As a new agent had just been appointed for these Indians, it was suggested to the chief that perhaps he had better suspend judgment in regard to him until they had given him a fair trial, and that possibly he might prove as honest and true a friend to them as Carson had been.

He did not seem inclined to discuss the merits of the new agent, but continued to detail his grievances, saying that his people were very destitute of all the necessaries of life; that they had put on their very best attire to pay this visit of ceremony, and that it was plain to be seen they were then nearly naked; moreover, he said, they had nothing to eat, except a few wild berries that grew in the mountains. That when Kit Carson was their agent he often gave them provisions, and occasionally he even presented them with sugar and coffee, which they did not like at first, but soon became very fond of, and now they preferred it to any thing else; so that, if the party had any thing to spare, he would be mighty glad to get it.

I sympathized with them most sincerely, gave them some provisions, and reiterated the expression of earnest hope that their new agent would do more for them than any others had done; and that, when he undertook to conduct a train of wagons containing presents for them from Washington, he would keep them in the broad, straight road, and allow none to wander away and get lost on side trails.

The chief, who had seemed averse to saying much

about their new agent, when pressed in this manner, remarked that it was true he did not know much about the man, but they would prefer an agent like Kit Carson, whom they knew well.

A COMANCHE'S OPINION OF THE PALE FACES.

The limited intercourse that has existed between the prairie tribes and the whites does not appear to have prepossessed the former much in our favor, as the following incident, which was related to me by Mr. Israel Folsom, a very intelligent and educated Chickasaw, goes to show. Upon a certain occasion, while he was visiting the Comanches, he remarked to a chief that it was only a few years since the people of his own nation were equally as uncivilized as the Comanches, but that, through the instrumentality of the white missionaries, they had been induced to abandon their precarious hunting habits, and had learned to read and write, and cultivate the soil, so that they were at that time enabled to live in the same manner as the white people, and were always supplied with abundance of food.

The chief replied that he had no doubt there were some advantages to be derived from education, and that he had often given the subject his serious consideration, but that the pale faces were all such arrant rascals that he was afraid to let them take up their abode with his people. Whereupon Mr. Folsom suggested to him that probably he had met with only the bad specimens of the white race, and that he himself had known very many good men among them who had conferred important benefits upon the Red Man.

The Comanche admitted that possibly such might be the case, but he had always been under the impression that there were but few, if any honest white men. He said farther, that if the Chickasaws would send out one of their educated men to teach their children to read and write, they would have no objections.

A CIVILIZED INDIAN'S OPINION OF THE UNITED STATES GOVERNMENT.

The Prairie and Rocky Mountain tribes are by no means the only exponents of the aboriginal race who have exhibited a lack of faith in the honor and probity of the pale faces.

The facts I am about to narrate go to show that instances are not wanting to prove that their more civilized brethren have occasionally evinced equal caution in placing implicit reliance upon the promises of our authorities. In 1849 I received orders to escort a large number of emigrants across the Plains en route for California; and, as my instructions required me to traverse an unexplored section, I was desirous of securing the services of the best guide that could be found. Accordingly, after making diligent inquiries among the border white people near the point of my departure, I came to the conclusion that a Delaware Indian, called Black Beaver, was probably the best man for my purposes, as, in addition to his being familiar with a good deal of the country over which I was to pass, he had the reputation of being an honest, reliable man, and a good interpreter for intercourse with the Prairie Indians.

Accordingly, when we reached his cabin, which happened to be near our track, I called upon him, and proposed to employ him for the expedition, which I supposed would occupy several months; at the same time I informed him that I was a government officer, taking it for granted that this would give him confidence in the truth of my statements, and be regarded by him as a guarantee for the faithful performance of any contract I might make with him. He listened attentively to all I had to say, and, after deliberating for a while, said it would be impossible for him to go with me, as his private affairs were just then in such a state that he could not possibly leave home for so long a period.

I then suggested that he might employ some friend to transact his private business in his absence, and that I would reimburse him for any loss or damage he might sustain by accompanying us.

After a good deal of hesitation, and with considerable seeming reluctance, he replied that, in the event of his determining to accept my proposition, he did not think it at all likely he would ever receive any compensation, as he was firmly impressed with the conviction that the United States government was not honest, and rarely, if ever, paid its debts.

I was, of course, greatly astonished at such an affirmation as this, and desired him to inform me what had induced him to arrive at so unjust a conclusion.

He replied that, during the Mexican War, at the earnest solicitation of our authorities, he had levied a company of Delawares, and that they served as scouts and guides under General Harney while General Wool's column was marching into Mexico from San Antonio, and that, previous to their being called out, a positive assurance was given them that they were to receive the same pay and allowances as the white volunteers. After having served faithfully for several months, they were disbanded a long distance from home, and, instead of being paid for their services, certain discharge papers were furnished them, which they were told to forward to Washington, when the money would at once be remitted to them.

As soon as they reached home the vouchers were transmitted according to directions, but in a short time they were returned with a statement that they were irregular, and directions given for the substitution of new papers in a different form. A good deal of time was consumed in sending to the proper officers to have the corrections made. At length, however, this was executed, and the new vouchers forwarded to Washington, where they remained a good while before they were reached in the regular order of succession; but they finally came back to the Delawares with the indorsement that certain other minor irregularities had been detected, which required correction before they could be liquidated.

At this stage of the proceedings the Indians began to think their claim was a hopeless one, but still they persevered, and, after having the papers corrected a third time according to instructions, sent them to Washington, hoping they might possibly get the money this time; but they were doomed to disappointment, and, after waiting month after month, and hearing nothing further from them, they ultimately abandoned all hope of ever receiving their pay.

Beaver very naturally felt indignant at what he conceived to be a direct violation of good faith on the part of the government, and closed his comments upon the subject with this emphatic declaration: "I 'spect, captain, that government he tell plenty lies —maybe so cheat um heap. I no want go with you."

As I could not well dispense with his services, I assured him that if he would accompany us I would myself be personally responsible that he should receive every cent of his dues, and, if he desired it, I would give him his money every night. This assurance quieted his apprehensions, and he consented to accept my proposition.

We were absent over six months, during which time Beaver rendered very important services as guide and interpreter, and, as he did not insist on the daily payments, there was due him, on his return, something like four hundred dollars.

I discharged him at Fort Washita, and immediately afterward he saddled his mule, came to my tent, and said he was about starting for home, and was ready to receive his pay.

The money had been counted out for him, but, for the purpose of seeing how it would affect him, I said, "All ready, are you? Very well, Beaver, you have served the government faithfully, and deserve to be well paid, so I'll just sit down and write a paper, which you can send to Washington when you get home, and no doubt they will forward you the money in a few months."

His countenance fell instantly, and he indignantly replied, "You goin' give me paper, captain? What for you give me that paper? 'Spose you give me one d—d paper I throw him in the fire."

"Very well, then, Beaver," said I, "if you don't like papers I'll pay you the money," and he was paid in silver, which was very acceptable to him.

A few weeks afterward I met Beaver again, and asked him if he had appropriated his money to a good purpose. He replied yes; that on his arrival at home he had given his friends a "*big feast*," which lasted several days, and consumed all his money. He added, "I'ze big Injun now, captain."

Upon my asking him how he found his family on his return, he replied, "I'ze had mighty bad luck since I went away."

"Indeed," said I. "What has happened, pray?"

"Both my wife he make dead since I been gone."

I expressed sincere condolence for him in his duplicate affliction. "Yes," he said, "I feel mighty bad, captain; I like better lose three my best hosses." But soon he seemed to recover his spirits, and observed, as he left me, "Maybe so ketch um nodder one wife some time."

A FACETIOUS INDIAN.

The Indian warrior, when in the presence of strangers, never allows himself to relax the stern dignity of his demeanor by a smile or any other exhibition of joy or hilarity, neither does he manifest the least curiosity or surprise at the exhibition of the most astounding novelties, but prides himself upon his power of maintaining the most imperturbable gravity upon all occasions and under all circumstances.

This marked peculiarity in his character has given rise to the impression that the Red Man is a cold, phlegmatic, and unimpressible creature, who is totally incapable of conceiving or appreciating any thing like pleasantry or gayety; but this is entirely fallacious, as there are no more gossiping and jocular people in the world than the Prairie Indians when assembled around their camp-fires in the evening, after a successful day's hunt, with their larders well stocked with meat; and the continual outbursts of laughter and merriment that always proceed from these social gatherings show conclusively that they are as gay and mirthful as any other class of people. That they are also addicted to practical jokes will be evident after reading what I am about to relate.

In the summer of 1866 a marauding party of Apache freebooters came into the vicinity of one of our military posts in New Mexico, and, after reconnoitering the surrounding country, concealed themselves in the adjacent mountains overlooking the fort, and laid in wait for several days watching for a favorable opportunity to make a descent upon the government animals.

Selecting an occasion when the guards were weak and not particularly on the alert, they in broad daylight crawled up under cover of a hill, and, mounting their horses, dashed out with the most unearthly yells, and swooped down upon the herd of horses that were quietly grazing in close proximity to the fort, which terrified them so much that they broke away from the herders, and started off at full speed toward the mountains, closely pursued by the savages.

The astonished soldiers used every endeavor to prevent the "stampede," and numerous shots were exchanged in the running mêlée, but the Indians were too strong for them, and they were forced to abandon the pursuit.

Among the herding party was a bugler-boy, who was conspicuous for his bravery in the fight, and for the persistent efforts he made to turn the animals back toward the fort; but all was without avail; on they went, with the savages close to their heels, giving forth vociferous shouts of exultation, and directing the most obscene and insulting gesticulations to the pursuing party.

While this exciting contest for the animals was going on, an old Apache brave dashed up in rear of the bold bugler-boy, and could, without doubt, easily have killed him; but, instead of doing this, his propensity for a joke preponderated over his bloodthirsty instincts, and with his hand he knocked the boy's hat from his head, and at the same time encouragingly patted him on the back, as much as to say "Good boy!" and rode away without doing him any harm.

ABORIGINAL PRECOCITY.

Numerous instances have come under the observation of the writer going to show that the early development of intellect and reasoning power is more premature and rapid among the natives than with the white race.

This may perhaps, in some degree, be attributed to the fact that the Indian women are unable to bestow much time or care upon their offspring, and their children are often left to shift for themselves, which must, of course, make them more independent and self-reliant than they otherwise would be.

Any one who has visited a camp of wild Indians, and witnessed the sports of the young boys, with their bright, speaking countenances, and their keen apprehension of every thing that is said or done, will be fully convinced of the fact. The following incident is a forcible illustration of it:

In the spring of 1867 a party of Apache marauders made a raid upon one of our most remote military posts, situated near the summit of the Sierra de la Madre, and succeeded in stampeding and driving off a number of animals, and a party of soldiers and citizens was immediately collected and started in pursuit.

The trace led them over precipitous and lofty mountain passes and through deep and difficult defiles for many long miles, extending even into the heart of Arizona, where it terminated in a rancherio, or village, where the families of the depredators were located. Here the pursuing party overtook the Indians, and a battle ensued, which resulted in several of the savages being killed, and a number wounded and captured.

Among the latter was a little girl about nine years old, who at first was as much terrified and as wild as a young antelope would have been; but, by a little coaxing and kind treatment, she soon became reconciled to her situation, and was taken back to the fort, where she was adopted into the household of the Mexican guide who accompanied the expedition. She was very kindly received by the family, and new clothing and blanket substituted for the few filthy rags that hung around her person; and, to all appearances, the young savage was contented and happy in her new home.

After a few weeks had elapsed, as the officers of the fort were sitting out in front of their quarters one evening, they heard (as was supposed) frequent howlings of wolves near the guide's house; but this was not an unusual occurrence, and did not attract special attention.

On the following morning, however, the guide made his appearance at the fort with a most doleful countenance, and informed the officers that his adopted child had disappeared during the night;

and an investigation of the affair disclosed the fact that the wolves which were heard the evening before were nothing more or less than two Apache braves, who had followed the trail of the soldiers all the way in from their remote rancherio in the mountains, and, by concealing themselves in the vicinity, had ascertained where the captive child was, and resorted to this novel method of communicating to her a knowledge of their proximity; and the little creature, with an instinctive, or, rather, with an acute reasoning perception which seems almost marvelous in so young a child, had at once recognized the call of her friends, and set about making preparations for escape.

The guide's house was built of boulder rocks laid up in mud mortar, not very tenacious, and the girl very adroitly and noiselessly managed to loosen and pull out one of these rocks, making an aperture of sufficient size to permit her egress, with her new wardrobe, into the open air. The family were all asleep while this was going on, and knew nothing of it until they found the child missing in the morning, when her tracks were followed to where she met two Indians, from whence the trace of the three led into the mountains, where it was lost and could be found no more.

ABORIGINES AS THEY ARE.

The distinctive ethnological traits which mark the character of the aborigines of this continent have been delineated in various conflicting aspects by different writers, whose observations have led them upon courses widely divergent, and their conclusions have been drawn from stand-points very remote.

By some the natives have been invested with the liveliest sentiments of generosity, hospitality, gratitude, and other attributes which we have been taught to eulogize as moral excellencies adorning the human character; while others, unable to discover any such commendable traits, have described them as addicted to all the crimes and vices known to the legal and biblical calendars, and as utterly devoid of every attribute that tends to elevate humanity in the scale of civilization and moral progress.

Neither of these conclusions is, in my judgment, absolutely correct or incontrovertible; but one fact which affords a preponderating bias in favor of the advocates of the opinion last mentioned is, that those persons who have come in contact with the Indians, and thereby had the most favorable opportunities for studying their habits and character, have, almost without exception, entertained unfavorable sentiments toward the race.

There is unquestionably some truth on both sides of the controversy, for it is undeniable that the natives have occasionally manifested good as well as evil tendencies; but of one fact, I imagine, there can be no dispute—namely, that the history of the colonization of this continent affords conclusive proof that, with a few notable exceptions, whenever the Indians have come in juxtaposition with the "pale faces," from that moment dates their moral deterioration and diminution in numbers. There seems to be a radical antagonism in the characteristics of the two races which renders their contiguous coexistence impossible.

Numerous examples might be adduced where tribe after tribe, through the baneful influences of "fire-water," and the vices which have been introduced and inculcated among them by avaricious and unscrupulous white men, have degenerated into the very decrepitude and decay of barbarism, and rapidly wasted away and ultimately vanished from the face of the earth.

My friend Colonel L**, who is familiar with the Indian character in all its phases, does not, if we may judge from the sentiments so feelingly depicted in the following lines, appear to be in exact accord with Mr. Fenimore Cooper in his exalted estimate of the poetical and romantic elements in the nature of the savage.

INDIANS AS THEY ARE.

Sanico old is a warrior bold,
  And his head has grown gray from years—
You'd swear on the book, at the very first look,
  That it never grew gray from fears.

A besom of wrath o'er the wild war-path
  He swept in his manhood's prime;
But his pace is now slow, for he's "crankie" below,
  And his *physique* has served out its time.

He's cousin by blood of Prince "Buffalo-cud,"
  And grandsire of "Buffalo-hump;"
His wife's a Tonk'way, with the soft *sobriquet*
  Of "The lizard that sleeps on the stump."

He enjoys the free air when the weather is fair,
  And creeps into his lodge when it rains;
He's fond of dog-stew, but he dotes on *ragoût*
  Of mule-meat, *garni* with warrior's brains.

He'd a virtue most rare in the dark of his hair—
  That is, ere his locks had grown white—
For, from rag-tail to chief, so accomplished a thief
  Never emptied a halter at night.

Alas! his high fame and his heroic name
  Are eclipsed in these heroic times:
There are robbers more bold, if the truth were but told,
  But their names must be nameless in rhymes.

THE WAR-CHIEF.

He leaned against a prairie oak,
  A dark-browned forest child,
As tall a chief as ever broke
Hard-bread beneath a wigwam's smoke
  When storms without blew wild.

Chief of his tribe, but not *the last:*
  He had six dusky boys
From six feet two to two feet six;
And four were death on carrying "*bricks,*"
  And two upon a noise.

Besides, he had two loving wives,
  And might have had a score;
Perhaps with one he'd been content,
As many a far more loving gent
  With *none* has been before.

But I'm digressing—to my song;
  Where was I? let me see—
A native warrior, tall and strong,
I left him, if I am not wrong,
  Leaning against a tree.

He was a beauty to behold
  For seekers after sights,
With moccasins untied and old,
And bloodshot eyes, that plainly told
  He had been drunk for nights.

Since then I've wandered more or less
  'Mong Indians tame and wild,
And that's about as fine a spec-
imen of nature's nobleness
As I have found, I must confess,
  In any "*forest child.*"

CHAPTER X.

Rapid Settlement of the Northwest.—Enterprise of the English and American People contrasted.—Benefits of Co-operation.—The Sterile Region.—Texas Pacific Railroad.—Route of the Thirty-fifth Parallel.—North Pacific Railroad.—Union and Central Pacific Railroad.

THE wonderful improvements and magical transformations that within the brief period of four decades have been evolved from the rapid settlement of the great Northwest, and the unprecedentedly speedy and expanded development of the varied and limitless resources of that most fertile and attractive section of our magnificent domain, seem marvelous indeed.

A glance at the history of the colonization of the Eastern States from the advent of the Pilgrims at Plymouth two hundred and fifty years ago to the beginning of the present century exhibits the march of civilization struggling tardily but manfully onward from the shores of the Atlantic to the West.

The progress of the heroic little band of pioneers through the wilderness east of Lake Erie and the Ohio River, which was infested with numerous tribes of hostile savages, who interposed a stubborn resistance at every inch of their advance, was difficult, slow, and sanguinary; nevertheless, the incipient wave of migration, swelling as it progressed, rolled steadily forward, forcing back, step by step, the original occupants of the land, until many of them were dispersed or annihilated in the futile effort to subvert the consummation of the inevitable destiny of the pale faces upon this continent.

When the tidal volume of inland migration approached the boundaries of Indiana and Michigan, a sudden and vigorous re-enforcement of power was imparted to it. Then it began to receive that great aggregation of numbers, vitality, and strength which carried it with immense velocity, and with a momentum as ponderous and irresistible as that of the Gulf Stream, entirely over the continent, destroying or driving before it the hordes of opposing natives who stood in its track, and disseminating its elements of human enterprise and development throughout every habitable fraction of the country; and suddenly, as if by the wave of a magician's wand, or by the fiat of the Creator, that solitary wilderness, throughout all its vast amplitude, was made to blossom like the rose. The wild but fertile virgin prairies were at once metamorphosed into beautiful plantations, yielding bountiful returns to the husbandman, and places which, from the creation of the world, had known no human habitation other than the Indian lodge, were speedily transformed into populous cities and towns, where abodes of industry, wealth, and luxury abound. The aboriginal tribes, like snow under the fervid rays of a meridian sun, are so rapidly vanishing from the face of the earth, that the time is not far distant when the hunting-grounds of their forefathers will be trodden by the race no more forever. In short, the omnipotent power of American civilization has possession of this continent, and under its colossal domination a new world of culture, refinement, and progression has come suddenly into existence in place of a state of absolute barbarism.

As an evidence of the supremacy and progress of this transition, it is necessary to mention the fact that as late as in 1832 it required a month of toilsome traveling to make the overland journey from the city of New York to the remote hamlet of Chicago, which then contained only about two hundred inhabitants, and was not as well known to the American public as Sitka in Alaska is at the present time.

The contrast between this and the existing condition of the country seems almost incredible. The same journey can be accomplished now with perfect ease and comfort in thirty hours; and Chicago to-day, claiming a population of over three hundred thousand souls, is the largest grain and lumber mart, besides being one of the best built and most enterprising and flourishing cities of its magnitude in the world.

Appreciation in the value of real estate in the Western cities has been commensurate with their rapidly augmenting populations. For example, land in the suburbs of Chicago which in 1833 could have been bought at one dollar and a quarter an acre, can readily be sold now at five thousand dollars per acre. In other words, this property has doubled in value every three years for thirty-nine years, and I dare say similar results might be cited of the rise of property in other Western towns.

Wisconsin, at the time alluded to, was a wilderness, unpeopled save by savages. There was at that time but one house between Green Bay and Chicago, that of my friend Solomon Juneau, an Indian trader, upon the spot where the beautiful city of Milwaukee now stands, and only one log cabin upon the road leading from Chicago to Galena, which was at Dixon's Ferry, on Rock River. Not a single white man lived at Fond du lac or Madison, and, with the exception of a few miners and half-breeds in the neighborhood of Mineral Point, Prairie du Chien and Green Bay, I believe, there was not then a farmer in Wisconsin. Even as late as 1838 no civilized tenement had been erected between Madison and Janesville, and but three upon that portion of the Mississippi River lying between Prairie du Chien and Fort Snelling.

Minnesota at that period was *terra incognita*, and was looked upon by the army of officers who had been stationed there as possessing too cold a climate ever to become available for agriculture.

But what do we behold now? Almost the entire area of Wisconsin, Illinois, Iowa, and Minnesota is absorbed, and a great part of it cultivated by enterprising, industrious, and thrifty planters, who annually derive many millions of dollars from the products of their labor, and the numerous railways intersecting the country in all directions afford convenient, rapid, and cheap access to home markets; while the Creator, in his benignant economy, has placed at our disposal that continental arterial trunk, the mighty Mississippi, with its numerous confluents, issuing from the heart of the most lovely and attractive region beneath the canopy of heaven, and embracing an aggregate of many thousand miles of navigable waters, that afford a gratuitous, illimitable, and ceaseless motive power for transmitting to the ocean, over a broad and accessible highway, the produce of half our possessions. These vast advantages are destined ultimately to impart an immeasurable increase of proportion, vigor, and solidity to the commerce of the world.

In a word, the expansion of our settlements during the last half century is without a parallel in the history of the human race; and, in my humble judgment, no one, whose perceptions have not been deflected from reason by prejudice or interest, can fail to realize the logic of the conclusion that, if the government and people of Great Britain were disposed to co-operate in developing and combining the resources of British America with those of the United States, the international affinity and moral cohesion that would follow such community of interest and action would be so firmly cemented and consolidated by mutual benefits of a social, commercial, and political character as to exercise a controlling influence over the commercial destinies of the world. Moreover, it does not require the premonition of a soothsayer to foretell that such reciprocity of purpose and execution would inevitably prove the harbinger of more kind and neighborly relations than at present exist.

But, as I have before had occasion to remark, the sluggish apathy and morbid caution of our venerable transatlantic progenitors, when contrasted with the fearless, dashing spirit of enterprise and prompt execution which has signalized the achievements of their descendants, released from the shackles of monarchical domination, receives a forcible illustration in the glaring reality that for two centuries the government of Great Britain has possessed a tract of territory adjacent to our own, lying upon the waters that flow from the West into Lake Winnipeg, and equal in extent to four times the area of the great State of Ohio, all of which is rich and productive, and admirably adapted to the requirements of the husbandman, and which has been allowed to remain up to this moment an undeveloped wilderness. As mysterious as it may appear to those not familiar with the facts, although there is a difference of ten degrees in the latitude of this section and that of the most desirable grain-growing districts of the United States, yet the climatic combinations in the more northern locality are of such peculiar character as to carry the isothermal belt of Central Illinois directly through the heart of the country alluded to.

If this part of the British dominions possesses the

great natural advantages ascribed to it, the question arises why it has not before now been occupied and developed.

The only solution of this mystery that occurs to my comprehension lies in the fact that it has been wanted for perpetuating the tenure of the franchise of a powerful oligarchical monopoly (the Hudson's Bay Company), and this "penny wise and pound foolish" policy has set the authorities to bar up against immigrants all avenues of approach to this vast tract of fertile territory.

That the drowsy optics of our cousin John Bull, after his protracted slumber, are at last beginning slowly to open upon the gravity of the impending crisis, the following quotation from a sensible pamphlet, published at London in 1866 by Thomas Rawlins, F.R.G.S., author of "America from the Atlantic to the Pacific," most pointedly indicates. He says:

"To the directors and stockholders of the Hudson's Bay Company we would say the emigrant is even now thundering at your doors; he demands a passage; he asks by what right you exclude him. Why have you not borrowed a lesson from the progress of the country adjoining? Are you blind to your own interest? for if you continue to pursue your present policy you assuredly will be.

"Brother Jonathan possesses a *capacious maw. He is snuffing the savory morsel of the Fertile Belt* (the Saskatchawan country); but once let him get a few *squatters' rights*, and there will soon be no necessity for any action on the part of the board of directors. Their power will have slipped from their grasp, and the road to the Pacific be shut out to us forever. We must not, we can not permit such suicidal lethargy to continue. We are all interested that unless something is done soon, the connection between the Atlantic and Pacific coasts in English interests is irretrievably severed, and the supremacy of British power in North America will be greatly endangered."

The somewhat equivocal compliment paid us in the gastronomic figure above quoted is eminently characteristic of the nationality of the writer, and exhibits the true measure of John Bull courtesy and amenity; yet it contains an admission regarding the relative enterprise of the two nations which I should hardly have expected from an Englishman.

Verily, it must be conceded that the dismal picture of the future which he so earnestly exhibits to the serious contemplation of his countrymen seems almost prescient; indeed, it may truly be added that it has already been partially verified, for, notwithstanding the "suicidal lethargy" of our English neighbors, our people, with the alert, wide-awake spirit of enterprise and *élan* which characterizes all their achievements, have been expending their capital and labor, their bone and muscle, in the very direction foreshadowed above, and they have already spanned the broad continent from ocean to ocean with one grand trunk railway, which traverses fifty-five degrees of longitude, uniting the most easterly and the most westerly cities of our territory, besides having several other transcontinental trunk roads in rapid progress of construction, with numerous tributary branches, all accompanied by the universal adjunct of the magnetic telegraph (the conception and production of American genius), which, by the continual interchanges of thought and language that flash over its wires, not only brings our remotest hamlets into hourly communion with almost every city in the universe, but renders man throughout the civilized world nearly as ubiquitous as his Creator. Moreover, the fact is indisputable that "Brother Jonathan," in his voracious absorption of domain, has proved himself to be something of a gourmand. That he has been blessed by Providence with a "maw" of respectable proportions, an excellent appetite, and capital powers of digestion, is beyond question; besides, his keen olfactories certainly *do* enable him to "snuff" from afar the savory aroma of a choice "*bonne bouche*" in the form of rich auriferous or agricultural acquisitions; and although he has of late been a little clogged with racy viands of this description, still no dyspeptic symptoms have as yet appeared, and I have not the slightest doubt, if the piquant "morsel" so graphically and temptingly depicted above were properly served up and placed in his mouth, he would manage to "worry it down."

In view of the fact that many thousands of our enterprising and intelligent citizens have, within the last twenty years, made the toilsome overland journey across the continent, and the still more significant reality that the Union Pacific Railroad transports daily hundreds of passengers from ocean to ocean, it seems strange that the great mass of the inhabitants of the United States should at this late day entertain the erroneous idea that no natural obstacles interpose to the settlement and development of new agricultural states like Missouri, Kansas, and Nebraska, entirely over the continent to the Pacific Ocean.

But this is a fallacy which can easily be dispelled by any one familiar with the physical geography of the country, and its adaptation to the requirements of the husbandman.

As there is every reason to believe that the North and South Pacific Railroads will be vigorously pushed forward to speedy completion, there are, doubtless, many of our citizens who are desirous of investing money in these enterprises, while others, influenced by the hope of improving their condition, may be induced, by the alluring prospects held out to them, to migrate West, for the purpose of opening farms and making new homes for their families upon the lines of the roads, and these people will, of course, desire accurate information regarding the character of the country in which their future destinies may become involved; but, as the chief sources of reliable statistics upon the greater part of the sections through which these roads will pass are contained in the voluminous reports of different explorations and surveys that from time to time have been made across the continent, there are but few who have had the opportunity or time to wade through them.

The task I propose undertaking in the following pages of this chapter is to give a succinct and accurate summary of the agricultural features of the country in such a plain and unmistakable form that no one who takes the trouble to read it with a map before him need be deluded by the misrepresentations of interested or designing parties.

As a general rule, the arable belt within the scope of our domain upon this continent extends from the Atlantic coast to about the 99th meridian of west longitude, when a sudden transformation takes place. The woodland disappears, and the great plains of the West commence, wherein, with the exception of the main trunk streams, which have their sources in the far distant mountains, but few water-courses are found, and these not unfrequently contain unpalatable water.

It is true, the grass upon these elevated pampas is generally abundant and nutritious, and, where water for stock can be found, it may be made available for pasturage; but, in consequence of the almost total absence of summer rains, and the extreme aridity of the thirsty soil, it is only along the immediate borders of the streams, where artificial irrigation may be resorted to, that crops can be produced with any certainty.

The fertile belt varies in width in different latitudes. Commencing at the most southerly point of our territory, where agriculture can be made remunerative, which would be in the vicinity of Corpus

Christi, Texas (as nearly all the country south and west of this is unproductive, except for grass), the southwestern boundary of the fertile belt runs to the northwest, crossing the track of the Southern Pacific Railroad near the 101st meridian of W. longitude, and follows this meridian as high as the 33d parallel of latitude, embracing the beautiful country watered by the San Antonio, Gaudalupe, Brazos, and Trinity Rivers, which is eminently adapted to agriculture.

The line then trends to the northeast, crossing Red River in about latitude 99½°, and the Arkansas, Kanzas, Platte, and Missouri Rivers somewhat farther east. Thence it runs nearly north to the British possessions, when it bears west to the head of the Saskatchawan River, in longitude about 115°, and here the fertile belt extends to within about four hundred miles of the Pacific coast.

West of this somewhat meandering line, up to the foot-hills of the Rocky Mountains, except upon the borders of the streams, farms can not be made.

As many persons are desirous of knowing what the character of the country is along the different lines of transcontinental railroads, and as this will convey a tolerably correct general idea of the entire country, I propose, in this paper, to describe the features of the country upon each route as much in detail as my time and the data at my disposal will permit.

Before commencing my descriptions, it is proper I should remark that my conclusions have, for the most part, been drawn from my own personal observations, having passed over the summit of the Rocky Mountains at five different points, viz., in latitude 32° 55′, and longitude 108° 25′, near Fort Bayard; also in latitude 36° 20′, and longitude about 107°, near the head of the Chama River; also in about latitude 38° 15′, and longitude 107° 20′, through the Cochetope Pass; also in about latitude 41° 30′, and longitude 107° 50′, near where the Union Pacific Railroad passes; and in latitude about 42° 20′, longitude 109°, at the South Pass.

Having also crossed the Plains from the Mississippi River to the Rocky Mountains upon six different routes within the same latitudes, a glance at the map of the country will show that I have seen a good deal of the districts under consideration.

My remarks upon that portion of the country which I have not traversed are deduced from the reports of the different surveys for the Pacific Railroads, and from information obtained of other reliable men who are familiar with it.

It is possible that my observations and conclusions

may not entirely coincide with the opinions of some of the gentlemen who are interested in the Pacific Railroads or the new territories, but, as my statements are intended to be strictly veracious and unprejudiced, I am persuaded the thanks I shall receive from disinterested persons who desire information will more than counterbalance the effects of any obloquy I may sustain from other parties.

I will commence my narrative with a description of the country through which the "Southern Transcontinental or Texas Pacific Railroad" (which has just been chartered by Congress with a subsidiary land provision) is designed to pass.

The general course of this road, after leaving the border settlements of Texas, is to run near the 32d parallel of latitude, and strike the Rio del Norte at or near El Paso del Norte, and is within this section confined exclusively to the domain of Texas, all title to which the United States has yielded to that state.

All the constructed and projected eastern tributary branches of this road traverse fertile districts of country, abounding in excellent timber, grass, and water, and admirably adapted to agricultural purposes, and embracing, besides the country upon the numerous tributaries of the Arkansas and Red Rivers, the confluents of the Trinity, Brazos, and Colorado of Texas, upon all of which there are flourishing farming settlements.

This favorable character of country extends west to the eastern border of the Llano Estacado, or Staked Plain, that great North American desert which, in its extreme dimensions, stretches from north to south about 400 miles, and from east to west some 250 miles, and is 4000 feet above the ocean level. Upon this elevated plateau there is not a tree or bush, and, with rare exceptions, not a drop of water, and no man inhabits or attempts to cross it without transporting water for himself and his animals.

The railroad will probably cross the southern spur of this plateau, where it is only about seventy miles wide. I passed over this spur in 1849 where it was 125 miles in width, and found the greater part of it as firm as a Macadamized highway, and as level and smooth as the ocean in a calm.

The road will descend from this plain to the Pecos River, a narrow, deep, and exceedingly tortuous stream issuing from the Sacramento and Guadalupe Mountains, which have a considerable amount of pine timber on their slopes; its waters bitter and unpalatable, with no wood upon its banks near the crossing; and, in consequence of the depression of the water below the earth's surface, I doubt if it can be made available for irrigation in the vicinity of where the railroad will cross it.

From thence the road will pass over an elevated and arid section, with only three places where water is found after passing the Guadalupe Mountains to the Rio Grande.

From El Paso the track will probably follow up the Rio Grande to Fort Selden, sixty miles, passing through the Mesilla Valley, which has a dense farming population, and is the most productive section of New Mexico, growing luxuriant grain and delicious fruits, but the area of arable land here is confined to the narrow river valley.

Rich silver mines have been worked remuneratively in the Organ Mountains, fifteen miles distant from the Mesilla settlements.

Passing the Rio Grande at Fort Selden, the road rises to a high plateau, which it traverses for seventy-five miles, without a tree or a drop of water save at Cook's Spring, which furnishes a limited supply. The next water is in the Mimbus Creek, a small brook about ten feet wide, which is absorbed by the sand a few miles below the crossing.

Five miles beyond this is an immense boiling spring, as hot as fire can make it, and here an enterprising Virginian had established a ranche, with bathing-rooms for guests, but shortly after I passed he was murdered by the Apaches, as I was informed.

From the Mimbus to the summit of the Sierra Madre, 5200 feet above the sea, the ascent is so gentle and uniform as to be almost imperceptible. This section is a vast undulating plateau, interrupted by irregular, bare, rugged, and isolated mountains, or short ranges through which the railroad may be carried with practicable gradients.

From the Pima villages the road will probably follow the course of the Gila to its confluence with the Colorado, 223 miles. Throughout this distance the stream flows through a plain interspersed with ridges and mountain peaks all denuded of vegetation, and extremely arid and sterile.

From the crossing of the Colorado to the San Gorgonio Pass, 133 miles in a direct line over the Colorado desert, where there is no grass, the railroad will have to pass. From the summit of the Pass to San Pedro, on the Pacific coast, the soil is good, and can be irrigated.

The climate throughout this entire route, from Red River to the Pacific Ocean, is salubrious, the heat due to its southern latitude being tempered and modified by its great altitude. It is seldom that snow falls more than three or four inches upon any part of the route, and rarely remains long upon the ground.

A striking feature in the physical geography of this section is the great elevation of the table-lands, which cover 1200 miles upon the line of the road.

The general characteristic of extreme sterility pertaining to the section lying between the Rio Grande and the western border of the Colorado basin is confirmed by the fact that the constituent elements of the greater part of the soil in this region are not conducive to fertility; and the most of that part which possesses the elements of fertility, owing to the absence of rains, is equally uncultivable with the other.

The entire distance from where this road leaves the Red River to the Pacific coast at San Pedro is 1618 miles.

From Red River for about 350 miles west the country has a very desirable diversification of prairies and timbered lands, which are bountifully watered with pure spring branches. The soil is of the richest and most productive character, and this section is doubtless destined to contain a large farming population. But from thence to the Pacific, as I have mentioned before, with the exception of a very insignificant fraction along the narrow valleys immediately bordering the few streams that are encountered, the country can not be made available for agriculture, and the greater part of the land I regard as valueless.

The small portion of New Mexico susceptible of irrigation (and this is the only part that can be cultivated) is now, and has been for more than a century, occupied and cultivated by Spaniards and Indians, and it has augmented its population but little since we acquired possession of it in 1847. Moreover, it is thought by many that if the troops and Indians were withdrawn from that territory, but few of our people would think of remaining there. As it is now, the Army and Indian contracts, with other government patronage, enables many of them to gain a livelihood, and some to make fortunes.

In view of the facts I have adduced, the conclusion seems to my mind inevitable that New Mexico can never become an agricultural state of much importance.

There are, doubtless, rich mines in this territory that will be developed and worked to advantage as soon as the railroad is completed; but up to this time the inhabitants of New Mexico, with a few prominent exceptions, have exhibited a feeble spirit of enterprise in developing the mineral resources of their country.

If the traveler, on reaching the eastern border of Arizona, could close his eyes, and make an aerial leap of some 500 miles, landing upon the summit of the San Gorgonio Pass, he might remain in happy ignorance of the character of the region he had passed over; but, unfortunately, our powers of locomotion are not as yet equal to the achievement of such gigantic strides as this; and as it is necessary for the traveler in this section to move cautiously, and keep his eyes wide open to guard against the attacks of those ubiquitous and relentless Bedouins of the desert, the Apaches, he can not avoid beholding, and he must admit that he is traversing the most unattractive, barren, desolate, God-forsaken, and (except for its mines) worthless region within the limits of our entire possessions.

The face of the country here is characterized by features of extreme sterility and aridity, and with an almost total absence of wood, water, and grass; and it is only here and there, at huge intervals, that a few small spots are found where the land is cultivable.

As a significant evidence of the future prospects of this territory, it is only necessary to advert to the fact that this section commenced settling more than twenty years ago, and, with all the patronage of the government in carrying on the territorial machinery, and in purchasing supplies for the troops and Indians, as well as employing mechanics and laborers, the territory is said to contain at this time less than seven thousand inhabitants, many of whom, either directly or indirectly, receive their subsistence from the government; and unless the development of the mines shall augment the population, Arizona is not, in my judgment, destined to become of much more significance than it is now.

The supplies for the troops in Arizona are brought from great distances out of the territory, and cost enormous prices.

There are, however, many rich silver mines here, which have not been worked with profit on account of the depredations of the Indians, and the difficulty of procuring supplies and labor in these remote and dangerous localities. The railroad would, without doubt, tend to bring these mines into notice, and the development of them might materially swell the aggregate of population, but this territory can never be of the slightest significance as a farming locality.

As an evidence of this, there is between the Rio Grande and the head of the San Pedro, a distance of 223 miles, upon this route but one spot that can be cultivated, and that is a narrow strip of land along the Mimbus Creek, where about a dozen farms might be made.

ROUTE NEAR THE 35TH PARALLEL OF LATITUDE.

This route does not seem to have met with favorable consideration from Congress or capitalists, yet it possesses some advantages over the route upon the 32d parallel. Commencing at Fort Smith, Arkansas, this route follows up the Valley of the Canadian River for about 600 miles, passing over a section which I explored in 1849.

For the first 350 miles it traverses a splendid agricultural section, lying exclusively within the Choctaw Reservation.

At about the 99th meridian of longitude the character of the country, except along the banks of the streams, at once changes from the highest degree of fertility to that of absolute sterility.

The only points upon the route west of this where cultivable soil is found are on the Pecos, Rio Grande, Zuni, Colorado - Chiquito, San Francisco Rivers, and upon the Colorado of the West, where small areas of land, with the aid of irrigation, can be made productive, but the greater part of all the country west of the meridian of 99° is similar to that upon the

32d parallel west of the meridian of 102°, a succession of elevated, arid, and barren plateaus.

Generally these plains are covered with nutritious grasses, but there are extensive tracts where none is found.

From thè Rio Grande this route traverses a district of country where the mountains are more wooded than upon the other route, although there are portions where no fuel is found. The greatest distance over which there is a total absence of fuel is between the Colorado and Mohave Rivers, 115 miles.

From what has been stated, it will be evident that, with the exception of the limited areas that have been specified along the water-courses, the physical geography of the country in the vicinity of the 35th parallel of latitude is such as to preclude the probability of its ever possessing much agricultural importance.

THE NORTH PACIFIC RAILROAD.

What inducements could have influenced the authorities controlling the road in locating its eastern terminus at Duluth was a mystery to me on visiting that place during the past season.

The only advantage this place possesses over others upon the west shore of Lake Superior, so far as I could learn or conjecture, is in the fact that it is the most westerly point of the lake; but this advantage is, in my judgment, greatly overbalanced by many other adverse considerations, some of which I will proceed to mention.

1st. This place has no natural harbor, and no other protection for shipping but a breakwater, which it is not believed will afford secure anchorage against the easterly gales which occasionally sweep with tremendous force across the entire length of the lake.

2d. Situated as Duluth is at the bottom of a deep bay, into which the ice, in immense masses, is driven during winter storms, and does not melt or drift away for some considerable time after it has disappeared from other portions of the lake, which materially retards the opening of navigation at this point.

3d. The outlet of the large River St. Louis is only seven miles below here, opposite Superior City, where there is a much better site for a town (as Duluth is a very bad one). Moreover, large expenditures have already been made by the government in throwing out breakwaters and improving the entrance to this harbor.

4th. Bayfield, which has incomparably the best natural harbor on the lake, only eighty miles below Duluth, and directly on the transit line to the Sault de St. Marié, could easily have been reached as the eastern terminus of this road, and this, without a dollar's expenditure upon the harbor, would have been an excellent shipping point for all time.

Notwithstanding the improvements which have been made at Duluth, and the high figures at which real estate is held there at the present time, I, at the risk of incurring the displeasure of the inhabitants of the place, venture the prediction that the relative advantages of the two places will ultimately carry the terminus of the road to Bayfield.

On departing from Duluth, the North Pacific Railroad runs along the bank of the St. Louis River for twenty-six miles to the junction of the St. Paul Road, when it bears to the right, and strikes the Mississippi above Crow-wing River. I passed over a portion of this road in September last, and carefully observed the character of the adjacent country, which, from the junction, consists of low sandy ridges and tamarack swamps, with a considerable portion covered with water. Wherever the surface appears above the water the soil is very thin, cold, and unproductive; and I can candidly assert that I did not, in the whole distance I passed over, see a single spot where a tolerable farm could be made. My observations upon the country bordering the road which connects Duluth with St. Paul, and which is similar in features with that along the North Pacific Road, together with the information I obtained from others, lead to the belief that the same character of country continues upon the last-mentioned road to near the Mississippi River.

The swamps covering a great part of this section are for the most part clothed with dense thickets of small tamaracks, and the remaining surface grows white birch, maple, oak, and pine, the latter not in dimensions or quantity sufficient to make it of much value for lumbering purposes. My own opinion of this particular section, condensed into a very few words, is, that any person purchasing it at sixpence an acre would have a huge elephant on his hands, for I can imagine no possible use to which it could be applied. From the Mississippi River to near Otter-tail Lake, about seventy-five miles, the soil is shallow and sandy, but from thence to Red River it presents a more favorable aspect; and the Red River Valley, having a belt of rich bottom land from five to thirty miles wide, with an abundance of good hard timber along the stream, is admirably adapted to agriculture. The soil is an unctuous black alluvium four feet deep, sustaining a most exuberant growth of natural grasses, and the same characteristics continue to the British possessions.

As the North Pacific Railroad runs directly across Red River, comparatively little of its fertile valley will be in easy access with it. The road will then ascend the eastern border of the "Coteau du Missouri," which is a vast plateau from 1000 to 2000 feet above the sea, extending entirely across the country from Red to the Missouri River some 400 miles, and containing but few small streams, with occasional shallow ponds, many of them having salt or unpalatable water, and with only a few stunted trees at wide intervals upon it.

This plain is covered with short grass, but, in consequence of the scanty supply of wood and water, but a small fraction could be made available for agriculture or pasturage.

From the crossing of the Missouri along the Yellowstone River (should the road take that track) to Bozeman's Pass, estimated at something like 400 miles, but little is known of the country; but the general features of the adjacent sections justify the inference that, with the exception of that portion which can be irrigated, it is uncultivable.

The soil upon the head waters of the Yellowstone, as well as that in the bottom lands of the three principal forks of the Missouri, the Gallatin, Madison, and Jefferson, receiving the wash from the surrounding mountains, is fertile, and, with artificial irrigation, produces good crops, as the flourishing farming settlements already established in the last-named valleys fully attest.

Admitting that this region is capable of sustaining an extensive farming community, I doubt, in view of the fact that it is over a thousand miles from Duluth, if its products would bear transportation to Eastern markets, passing, as they will, directly through the much more favored agricultural section of Minnesota, so that the producers would be compelled to depend solely upon home consumption, and this would be confined to the limited wants of the miners.

From "Jefferson Fork," the road, as I understand, will probably cross the summit of the Rocky Mountains through "Deer Lodge Pass," and thence down Clarke's Fork to the Columbia, descending that river to the ocean, or to Puget's Sound.

The space between the Rocky Mountains and the Cascade range, the western slopes of which approach near the borders of Puget's Sound, within the latitudes of 45° and 49°, is an alpine region, mainly occupied by mountain masses, and the elevated basaltic plain of the Columbia, which is 150 by 200 miles in extent.

The upper valleys of the tributaries of the Columbia along this section of the route, such as Clarke's Fork, Bitter Root, Hell Gate Rivers, etc., are productive, but their lower valleys are for the most part uncultivable. The fertile areas are exceptional to the general conditions of the soil between the two ranges of mountains mentioned.

The greater part of this section is mountainous, and a large portion of it covered with pine timber, growing upon a thin and sandy soil.

The Secretary of War, in his summary upon the reports of the surveys of this route for a railroad in 1855, says: "The country west of the Rocky Mountains may likewise be described as one of general sterility. The sum of the areas of cultivable soil in the Rocky Mountain region does not exceed, if it equals, 1000 square miles. West of the Cascade Mountains there are rich river bottoms, clay formations that are arable, and prairies, affording good grazing," etc.

The tertiary and cretaceous formations extend over that portion of this route included within the 97th meridian of longitude and the eastern base of the Rocky Mountains, which formations are unfavorable for successful agriculture, even if rains were abundant. But very few summer rains fall over this section.

A good deal has been said by the champions of this route about the small amount of snow that falls upon it. Nevertheless, I was assured by the army officers at Forts Totten and Stevenson, which are directly upon the line of the road, that during the winter of 1867–8 it was impossible, in consequence of the drifting snow-storms upon the "Coteau de Missouri," to transport the mails with horses or mules. They were transmitted exclusively by means of dog-trains under charge of half-breeds, and several of these hardy and experienced voyageurs perished during that winter.

My own guide, Joe Roulette, informed me that he was obliged, during the preceding winter, in one of those terrific snow-storms which sweep with great violence over the Coteau, to crawl into a snow-bank, and remain for three days, with his dogs, one of which he was compelled to kill for subsistence during the time.

Such storms as these would, it strikes me, offer serious obstacles to the passage of railway trains.

The Secretary of War, in the report before alluded to, gives his opinion in regard to the character of the country along the route from St. Paul to Puget's Sound in the following summary, viz.:

"From St. Paul to Red River, 275 miles, the soil is fertile.

"From thence to the 99th meridian, 66 miles, the change from fertility to an uncultivable condition takes place.

"Thence to the crossing of Sun River, 752 miles, the prairie is uncultivable; the river bottom of the Missouri in part, those of Jacques River, Mouse River, and of other streams possessing a cultivable soil.

"We then have mountain region of 404 miles, a well-wooded district to the Spokane River, with mountain valleys of partly cultivable soil, and prairies of the same character.

"From the Spokane River to the crossing of the Columbia, 10 miles above Fort Walla-Walla, over the barren plain of the Columbia, 142 miles.

"Thence to the Cascades, an uncultivable though grazing district, about 192 miles.

"Thence over cultivable land, about 192 miles, to Puget's Sound."

From the foregoing it will be seen that of the 2025 miles of country extending from St. Paul to Puget's Sound, 1086 is regarded by the secretary as uncultivable excepting in the river bottoms.

If the North Pacific Railroad, instead of passing over the Coteau in Missouri, was turned down the valley of the Red River to Fort Garry, at the mouth of the Assinniboin River, and thence up that stream about seventy-five miles, and across to the Saskatchawan River, following this valley to where it debouches from the Rocky Mountains, the road to this point would traverse a continuous highly productive section, which is eminently adapted to agriculture and pasturage.

The Saskatchawan River, flowing into Lake Winnipeg, is said to have 1000 miles of steam-boat navigation upon its waters; and although this locality is considerably north of the arable portion of the Atlantic region, yet the climatic combinations of this section are such that the isothermal belt of Northern Illinois and Ohio passes directly through it. Indeed, good wheat has been grown at the Hudson Bay Company's factories upon Liard and Pearl Rivers, tributaries of the Arctic Ocean, in the high latitude of 58°.

The road over this route would, after leaving Pembina, be entirely within British territory, but the arable country upon it extends much nearer the Pacific than upon any of the more southerly roads.

UNION AND CENTRAL PACIFIC RAILROAD.

This road, throughout the greater part of its course, runs between the 40th and 42d parallels of latitude. From Omaha it follows the Platte River Valley for about 250 miles to the forks, and for this distance the wide and level strip of bottom land along the river is productive, and much of it already occupied and cultivated; but there is no woodland to speak of save a narrow fringe of cottonwood bordering the stream.

From the forks the road runs along the valley of the South Platte for about seventy miles, where there is no wood. Thence it bears to the right up Lodge-pole Creek, striking into an elevated arid plain, and for five hundred miles traverses a district of country where but very few small cultivable patches of ground occur, until entering the Great Salt Lake Basin, within the limits of which there is a considerable area of land that by the aid of irrigation is arable.

But as the water in most parts has to be brought from sources several miles distant, the irrigating canals require unremitting care and labor to keep them in repair, which augments the expense of producing crops very materially. I was told by some of the Mormon farmers in Salt Lake Valley that it requires the constant labor of one hand to cultivate four acres of wheat in that locality. If this is correct, I doubt if our Eastern farmers could be induced to migrate to that section from a region where the rains of heaven irrigate the soil, and where one man can cultivate five times as much ground.

The truth is, the Mormons, men, women, and children, labor hard, and up to this time they have found a ready market, with high prices, for all their surplus produce among the emigrants and miners who traverse the country. Notwithstanding this, I have seldom seen more abject destitution and poverty than I encountered in some of the Mormon settlements in 1858.

Nearly all the arable land in the Salt Lake Valley is occupied.

From the head of Salt Lake the road crosses the Humboldt divide or pass, and enters the Humboldt (sometimes called St. Mary's) River Valley, which it traverses for 190 miles, to its terminus in a marshy lake called the "Sink of the Humboldt."

The River Valley varies in width from two to twenty miles, but, except immediately along the stream, it is a sandy plain, without grass, wood, or cultivable soil.

From the lake the road passes over the desert for about a hundred miles, and, crossing the Sierra Nevada, finds its way through the mountains to Sacramento and San Francisco.

The Secretary of War, in his summary of the surveys upon this route in 1855, says, "From the 98th or 99th meridian to the western slopes of the Sierra Nevada, a distance of about 1400 miles, the soil is uncultivable, excepting the comparatively limited area of the Mormon settlements, and an occasional river-bottom and mountain valley of small extent."

In this opinion I fully concur.

From what has been stated in regard to the features of the country upon the different lines of Pacific Railroads, with a careful and intelligent reading of the map of the United States, it will be seen that the central and western portions of our domain upon this broad continent are traversed from nearly north to south by an undulating belt of elevated table-land, the greater part of which is arid, sterile, and treeless.

This plateau, with its summit level nearly midway between the Mississippi River and the Pacific coast, forms the great watershed that drains our entire possessions west of the Mississippi Valley.

The crest of this vast extent of table-land is, in latitude 32°, 5200 feet; in latitude 42°, 7490 feet; and in latitude 47°, 5100 feet above the ocean level.

Its greatest elevation, so far as determined, is near latitude 38°, where it rises to 10,000 feet above the sea.

It is intersected by the Missouri, Platte, Arkansas,

Red, Brazos, Colorado, and Del Norte Rivers on the eastern slope, by the Colorado and Columbia Rivers on the western slope, and by Mackenzie's and the Saskatchawan Rivers on the northern slope, all taking their rise near the summit of the plateau, and flowing off in deep channels to almost every point of the compass, into the Gulf of Mexico, the Pacific and Arctic Oceans, and into Hudson's Bay.

The facts herein adduced will, in my judgment, fully establish what I proposed to show, namely, that the greater part of this continent, lying between latitudes 32° and 47°, and between longitude 99° and the Sierra Nevada chain of mountains, is destitute of arable soil, wood, and water, and does not, therefore, possess the essential requisites for the establishment and development of agricultural states. But if the character of this section was different, and it possessed equally favorable conditions of soil, timber, and water with the most attractive lands in Illinois, would our farmers, as a general rule, be willing to pass over the vast areas of excellent unoccupied lands in the more easterly districts, where they are in close proximity to navigable rivers and railroads, affording easy and cheap access to markets, and migrate far back into the interior, entirely out of reach of markets, and where a bushel of wheat might not, perhaps, serve to purchase an ounce of tea or sugar?

As it is now, I am informed that the farmers in some of the remote populated districts of Kansas find it difficult to sell their corn for fifteen cents a bushel.

Up to this time, the number of farmers in the mining districts of Utah and our other new territories has been so small, compared with the entire populations, that they have realized remunerative prices for their products; but, should the preponderance of population become largely the other way, I think they would find agriculture not very profitable.

THE END.

LOSSING'S FIELD-BOOK OF THE REVOLUTION. Pictorial Field-Book of the Revolution; or, Illustrations, by Pen and Pencil, of the History, Biography, Scenery, Relics, and Traditions of the War for Independence. By BENSON J. LOSSING. 2 vols., 8vo, Cloth, $14 00; Sheep, $15 00; Half Calf, $18 00; Full Turkey Morocco, $22 00.

LOSSING'S FIELD-BOOK OF THE WAR OF 1812. Pictorial Field-Book of the War of 1812; or, Illustrations, by Pen and Pencil, of the History, Biography, Scenery, Relics, and Traditions of the Last War for American Independence. By BENSON J. LOSSING. With several hundred Engravings on Wood, by Lossing and Barritt, chiefly from Original Sketches by the Author. 1088 pages, 8vo, Cloth, $7 00; Sheep, $8 50; Half Calf, $10 00.

WINCHELL'S SKETCHES OF CREATION. Sketches of Creation: a Popular View of some of the Grand Conclusions of the Sciences in reference to the History of Matter and of Life. Together with a Statement of the Intimations of Science respecting the Primordial Condition and the Ultimate Destiny of the Earth and the Solar System. By ALEXANDER WINCHELL, LL.D., Professor of Geology, Zoology, and Botany in the University of Michigan, and Director of the State Geological Survey. With Illustrations. 12mo, Cloth, $2 00.

WHITE'S MASSACRE OF ST. BARTHOLOMEW. The Massacre of St. Bartholomew: Preceded by a History of the Religious Wars in the Reign of Charles IX. By HENRY WHITE, M.A. With Illustrations. 8vo, Cloth, $1 75.

ALFORD'S GREEK TESTAMENT. The Greek Testament: with a critically-revised Text; a Digest of Various Readings; Marginal References to Verbal and Idiomatic Usage; Prolegomena; and a Critical and Exegetical Commentary. For the Use of Theological Students and Ministers. By HENRY ALFORD, D.D., Dean of Canterbury. Vol. I., containing the Four Gospels. 944 pages, 8vo, Cloth, $6 00; Sheep, $6 50.

ABBOTT'S FREDERICK THE GREAT. The History of Frederick the Second, called Frederick the Great. By JOHN S. C. ABBOTT. Elegantly Illustrated. 8vo, Cloth, $5 00.

ABBOTT'S HISTORY OF THE FRENCH REVOLUTION. The French Revolution of 1789, as viewed in the Light of Republican Institutions. By JOHN S. C. ABBOTT. With 100 Engravings. 8vo, Cloth, $5 00.

ABBOTT'S NAPOLEON BONAPARTE. The History of Napoleon Bonaparte. By JOHN S. C. ABBOTT. With Maps, Woodcuts, and Portraits on Steel. 2 vols., 8vo, Cloth, $10 00.

ABBOTT'S NAPOLEON AT ST. HELENA; or, Interesting Anecdotes and Remarkable Conversations of the Emperor during the Five and a Half Years of his Captivity. Collected from the Memorials of Las Casas, O'Meara, Montholon, Antommarchi, and others. By JOHN S. C. ABBOTT. With Illustrations. 8vo, Cloth, $5 00.

ADDISON'S COMPLETE WORKS. The Works of Joseph Addison, embracing the whole of the "Spectator." Complete in 3 vols., 8vo, Cloth, $6 00.

ALCOCK'S JAPAN. The Capital of the Tycoon: a Narrative of a Three Years' Residence in Japan. By Sir RUTHERFORD ALCOCK, K.C.B., Her Majesty's Envoy Extraordinary and Minister Plenipotentiary in Japan. With Maps and Engravings. 2 vols., 12mo, Cloth, $3 50.

ALISON'S HISTORY OF EUROPE. FIRST SERIES: From the Commencement of the French Revolution, in 1789, to the Restoration of the Bourbons, in 1815. [In addition to the Notes on Chapter LXXVI., which correct the errors of the original work concerning the United States, a copious Analytical Index has been appended to this American edition.] SECOND SERIES: From the Fall of Napoleon, in 1815, to the Accession of Louis Napoleon, in 1852. 8vols., 8vo, Cloth, $16 00.

BALDWIN'S PRE-HISTORIC NATIONS. Pre-Historic Nations; or, Inquiries concerning some of the Great Peoples and Civilizations of Antiquity, and their Probable Relation to a still Older Civilization of the Ethiopians or Cushites of Arabia. By JOHN D. BALDWIN, Member of the American Oriental Society. 12mo, Cloth, $1 75.

BARTH'S NORTH AND CENTRAL AFRICA. Travels and Discoveries in North and Central Africa: being a Journal of an Expedition undertaken under the Auspices of H.B.M.'s Government, in the Years 1849-1855. By HENRY BARTH, Ph.D., D.C.L. Illustrated. 3 vols., 8vo, Cloth, $12 00.

HENRY WARD BEECHER'S SERMONS. Sermons by HENRY WARD BEECHER, Plymouth Church, Brooklyn. Selected from Published and Unpublished Discourses, and Revised by their Author. With Steel Portrait. Complete in Two Vols., 8vo, Cloth, $5 00.

LYMAN BEECHER'S AUTOBIOGRAPHY, &c. Autobiography, Correspondence, &c., of Lyman Beecher, D.D. Edited by his Son, CHARLES BEECHER. With Three Steel Portraits, and Engravings on Wood. In 2 vols., 12mo, Cloth, $5 00.

BELLOWS'S OLD WORLD. The Old World in its New Face: Impressions of Europe in 1867-1868. By HENRY W. BELLOWS. 2 vols., 12mo, Cloth, $3 50.

BOSWELL'S JOHNSON. The Life of Samuel Johnson, LL.D. Including a Journey to the Hebrides. By JAMES BOSWELL, Esq. A New Edition, with numerous Additions and Notes. By JOHN WILSON CROKER, LL.D., F.R.S. Portrait of Boswell. 2 vols., 8vo, Cloth, $4 00.

BRODHEAD'S HISTORY OF NEW YORK. History of the State of New York. By JOHN ROMEYN BRODHEAD. 1609-1691. 2 vols. 8vo, Cloth, $3 00 per vol.

BROUGHAM'S AUTOBIOGRAPHY. Life and Times of HENRY, LORD BROUGHAM. Written by Himself. In Three Volumes. 12mo, Cloth, $2 00 per vol.

BULWER'S PROSE WORKS. Miscellaneous Prose Works of Edward Bulwer, Lord Lytton. 2 vols., 12mo, Cloth, $3 50.

BULWER'S HORACE. The Odes and Epodes of Horace. A Metrical Translation into English. With Introduction and Commentaries. By LORD LYTTON. With Latin Text from the Editions of Orelli, Macleane, and Yonge. 12mo, Cloth, $1 75.

BULWER'S KING ARTHUR. King Arthur. A Poem. By EARL LYTTON. New Edition. 12mo, Cloth, $1 75.

BURNS'S LIFE AND WORKS. The Life and Works of Robert Burns. Edited by ROBERT CHAMBERS. 4 vols., 12mo, Cloth, $6 00.

REINDEER, DOGS, AND SNOW-SHOES. A Journal of Siberian Travel and Explorations made in the Years 1865-'67. By RICHARD J. BUSH, late of the Russo-American Telegraph Expedition. Illustrated. Crown 8vo, Cloth, $3 00.

CARLYLE'S FREDERICK THE GREAT. History of Friedrich II., called Frederick the Great. By THOMAS CARLYLE. Portraits, Maps, Plans, &c. 6 vols., 12mo, Cloth, $12 00.

CARLYLE'S FRENCH REVOLUTION. History of the French Revolution. Newly Revised by the Author, with Index, &c. 2 vols., 12mo, Cloth, $3 50.

CARLYLE'S OLIVER CROMWELL. Letters and Speeches of Oliver Cromwell. With Elucidations and Connecting Narrative. 2 vols., 12mo, Cloth, $3 50.

CHALMERS'S POSTHUMOUS WORKS. The Posthumous Works of Dr. Chalmers. Edited by his Son-in-Law, Rev. WILLIAM HANNA, LL.D. Complete in 9 vols., 12mo, Cloth, $13 50.

COLERIDGE'S COMPLETE WORKS. The Complete Works of Samuel Taylor Coleridge. With an Introductory Essay upon his Philosophical and Theological Opinions. Edited by Professor SHEDD. Complete in Seven Vols. With a fine Portrait. Small 8vo, Cloth, $10 50.

CURTIS'S HISTORY OF THE CONSTITUTION. History of the Origin, Formation, and Adoption of the Constitution of the United States. By GEORGE TICKNOR CURTIS. 2 vols., 8vo, Cloth, $6 00.

DRAPER'S CIVIL WAR. History of the American Civil War. By JOHN W. DRAPER, M.D., LL.D., Professor of Chemistry and Physiology in the University of New York. In Three Vols. 8vo, Cloth, $3 50 per vol.

DRAPER'S INTELLECTUAL DEVELOPMENT OF EUROPE. A History of the Intellectual Development of Europe. By JOHN W. DRAPER, M.D., LL.D., Professor of Chemistry and Physiology in the University of New York. 8vo, Cloth, $5 00.

DRAPER'S AMERICAN CIVIL POLICY. Thoughts on the Future Civil Policy of America. By JOHN W. DRAPER, M.D., LL.D., Professor of Chemistry and Physiology in the University of New York. Crown 8vo, Cloth, $2 50.

DAVIS'S CARTHAGE. Carthage and her Remains: being an Account of the Excavations and Researches on the Site of the Phœnician Metropolis in Africa and other adjacent Places. Conducted under the Auspices of Her Majesty's Government. By Dr. DAVIS, F.R.G.S. Profusely Illustrated with Maps, Woodcuts, Chromo-Lithographs, &c. 8vo, Cloth, $4 00.

DOOLITTLE'S CHINA. Social Life of the Chinese: with some Account of their Religious, Governmental, Educational, and Business Customs and Opinions. With special but not exclusive Reference to Fuhchau. By Rev. JUSTUS DOOLITTLE, Fourteen Years Member of the Fuhchau Mission of the American Board. Illustrated with more than 150 characteristic Engravings on Wood. 2 vols., 12mo, Cloth, $5 00.

DU CHAILLU'S AFRICA. Explorations and Adventures in Equatorial Africa: with Accounts of the Manners and Customs of the People, and of the Chase of the Gorilla, the Crocodile, Leopard, Elephant, Hippopotamus, and other Animals. By PAUL B. DU CHAILLU. Numerous Illustrations. 8vo, Cloth, $5 00.

DU CHAILLU'S ASHANGO LAND. A Journey to Ashango Land, and Further Penetration into Equatorial Africa. By PAUL B. DU CHAILLU. New Edition. Handsomely Illustrated. 8vo, Cloth, $5 00.

EDGEWORTH'S (MISS) NOVELS. With Engravings. 10 vols., 12mo, Cloth, $15 00.

GIBBON'S ROME. History of the Decline and Fall of the Roman Empire. By EDWARD GIBBON. With Notes by Rev. H. H. MILMAN and M. GUIZOT. A new Cheap Edition. To which is added a complete Index of the whole Work, and a Portrait of the Author. 6 vols., 12mo, Cloth, $9 00.

GROTE'S HISTORY OF GREECE. 12 vols., 12mo, Cloth, $18 00.

HALE'S (MRS.) WOMAN'S RECORD. Woman's Record; or, Biographical Sketches of all Distinguished Women, from the Creation to the Present Time. Arranged in Four Eras, with Selections from Female Writers of each Era. By Mrs. SARAH JOSEPHA HALE. Illustrated with more than 200 Portraits. 8vo, Cloth, $5 00.

HALL'S ARCTIC RESEARCHES. Arctic Researches and Life among the Esquimaux: being the Narrative of an Expedition in Search of Sir John Franklin, in the Years 1860, 1861, and 1862. By CHARLES FRANCIS HALL. With Maps and 100 Illustrations. The Illustrations are from Original Drawings by Charles Parsons, Henry L. Stephens, Solomon Eytinge, W. S. L. Jewett, and Granville Perkins, after Sketches by Captain Hall. 8vo, Cloth, $5 00.

HALLAM'S CONSTITUTIONAL HISTORY OF ENGLAND, from the Accession of Henry VII. to the Death of George II. 8vo, Cloth, $2 00.

HALLAM'S LITERATURE. Introduction to the Literature of Europe during the Fifteenth, Sixteenth, and Seventeenth Centuries. By HENRY HALLAM. 2 vols., 8vo, Cloth, $4 00.

HALLAM'S MIDDLE AGES. State of Europe during the Middle Ages. By HENRY HALLAM. 8vo, Cloth, $2 00.

HILDRETH'S HISTORY OF THE UNITED STATES. FIRST SERIES: From the First Settlement of the Country to the Adoption of the Federal Constitution. SECOND SERIES: From the Adoption of the Federal Constitution to the End of the Sixteenth Congress. 6 vols., 8vo, Cloth, $18 00.

HARPER'S NEW CLASSICAL LIBRARY. Literal Translations.

The following Volumes are now ready. Portraits. 12mo, Cloth, $1 50 each.

CÆSAR.—VIRGIL.—SALLUST.—HORACE.—CICERO'S ORATIONS.—CICERO'S OFFICES, &C.—CICERO ON ORATORY AND ORATORS.—TACITUS (2 vols.).—TERENCE.—SOPHOCLES.—JUVENAL.—XENOPHON.—HOMER'S ILIAD.—HOMER'S ODYSSEY.—HERODOTUS.—DEMOSTHENES.—THUCYDIDES.—ÆSCHYLUS.—EURIPIDES (2 vols.).—LIVY (2 vols.).

HUME'S HISTORY OF ENGLAND. History of England, from the Invasion of Julius Cæsar to the Abdication of James II., 1688. By DAVID HUME. A new Edition, with the Author's last Corrections and Improvements. To which is prefixed a short Account of his Life, written by Himself. With a Portrait of the Author. 6 vols., 12mo, Cloth, $9 00.

HELPS'S SPANISH CONQUEST. The Spanish Conquest in America, and its Relation to the History of Slavery and to the Government of Colonies. By ARTHUR HELPS. 4 vols., 12mo, Cloth, $6 00.

JAY'S WORKS. Complete Works of Rev. William Jay: comprising his Sermons, Family Discourses, Morning and Evening Exercises for every Day in the Year, Family Prayers, &c. Author's Enlarged Edition, revised. 3 vols., 8vo, Cloth, $6 00.

JEFFERSON'S DOMESTIC LIFE. The Domestic Life of Thomas Jefferson: compiled from Family Letters and Reminiscences by his Great-Granddaughter, SARAH N. RANDOLPH. With Illustrations. Crown 8vo, Illuminated Cloth, Beveled Edges, $2 50.

JOHNSON'S COMPLETE WORKS. The Works of Samuel Johnson, LL.D. With an Essay on his Life and Genius, by ARTHUR MURPHY, Esq. Portrait of Johnson. 2 vols., 8vo, Cloth, $4 00.

KINGLAKE'S CRIMEAN WAR. The Invasion of the Crimea, and an Account of its Progress down to the Death of Lord Raglan. By ALEXANDER WILLIAM KINGLAKE. With Maps and Plans. Two Vols. ready. 12mo, Cloth, $2 00 per vol.

KINGSLEY'S WEST INDIES. At Last: A Christmas in the West Indies. By CHARLES KINGSLEY. Illustrated. 12mo, Cloth, $1 50.

KRUMMACHER'S DAVID, KING OF ISRAEL. David, the King of Israel: a Portrait drawn from Bible History and the Book of Psalms. By FREDERICK WILLIAM KRUMMACHER, D.D., Author of "Elijah the Tishbite," &c. Translated under the express Sanction of the Author by the Rev. M. G. EASTON, M.A. With a Letter from Dr. Krummacher to his American Readers, and a Portrait. 12mo, Cloth, $1 75.

LAMB'S COMPLETE WORKS. The Works of Charles Lamb. Comprising his Letters, Poems, Essays of Elia, Essays upon Shakspeare, Hogarth, &c., and a Sketch of his Life, with the Final Memorials, by T. NOON TALFOURD. Portrait. 2 vols., 12mo, Cloth, $3 00.

LIVINGSTONE'S SOUTH AFRICA. Missionary Travels and Researches in South Africa; including a Sketch of Sixteen Years' Residence in the Interior of Africa, and a Journey from the Cape of Good Hope to Loando on the West Coast; thence across the Continent, down the River Zambesi, to the Eastern Ocean. By DAVID LIVINGSTONE, LL.D., D.C.L. With Portrait, Maps by Arrowsmith, and numerous Illustrations. 8vo, Cloth, $4 50.

LIVINGSTONE'S ZAMBESI. Narrative of an Expedition to the Zambesi and its Tributaries, and of the Discovery of the Lakes Shirwa and Nyassa. 1858–1864. By DAVID and CHARLES LIVINGSTONE. With Map and Illustrations. 8vo, Cloth, $5 00.

MARCY'S ARMY LIFE ON THE BORDER. Thirty Years of Army Life on the Border. Comprising Descriptions of the Indian Nomads of the Plains; Explorations of New Territory; a Trip across the Rocky Mountains in the Winter; Descriptions of the Habits of Different Animals found in the West, and the Methods of Hunting them; with Incidents in the Life of Different Frontier Men, &c., &c. By Brevet Brigadier-General R. B. MARCY, U.S.A., Author of "The Prairie Traveler." With numerous Illustrations. 8vo, Cloth, Beveled Edges, $3 00.

M'CLINTOCK & STRONG'S CYCLOPÆDIA. Cyclopædia of Biblical, Theological, and Ecclesiastical Literature. Prepared by the Rev. JOHN M'CLINTOCK, D.D., and JAMES STRONG, S.T.D. *3 vols. now ready.* Royal 8vo. Price per vol., Cloth, $5 00; Sheep, $6 00; Half Morocco, $8 00.

MOSHEIM'S ECCLESIASTICAL HISTORY, Ancient and Modern; in which the Rise, Progress, and Variation of Church Power are considered in their Connection with the State of Learning and Philosophy, and the Political History of Europe during that Period. Translated, with Notes, &c., by A. MACLAINE, D.D. A New Edition, continued to 1826, by C. COOTE, LL.D. 2 vols., 8vo, Cloth, $4 00.

MACAULAY'S HISTORY OF ENGLAND. The History of England from the Accession of James II. By THOMAS BABINGTON MACAULAY. With an Original Portrait of the Author. 5 vols., 8vo, Cloth, $10 00; 12mo, Cloth, $7 50.

NEVIUS'S CHINA. China and the Chinese: a General Description of the Country and its Inhabitants; its Civilization and Form of Government; its Religious and Social Institutions; its Intercourse with other Nations; and its Present Condition and Prospects. By the Rev. JOHN L. NEVIUS, Ten Years a Missionary in China. With a Map and Illustrations. 12mo, Cloth, $1 75.

OLIN'S (DR.) LIFE AND LETTERS. 2 vols., 12mo, Cloth, $3 00.

OLIN'S (DR.) TRAVELS. Travels in Egypt, Arabia Petræa, and the Holy Land. Engravings. 2 vols., 8vo, Cloth, $3 00.

OLIN'S (DR.) WORKS. The Works of Stephen Olin, D.D., late President of the Wesleyan University. 2 vols., 12mo, Cloth, $3 00.

OLIPHANT'S CHINA AND JAPAN. Narrative of the Earl of Elgin's Mission to China and Japan, in the Years 1857, '58, '59. By LAURENCE OLIPHANT. Private Secretary to Lord Elgin. Illustrations. 8vo, Cloth, $3 50.

OLIPHANT'S (MRS.) LIFE OF EDWARD IRVING. The Life of Edward Irving, Minister of the National Scotch Church, London. Illustrated by his Journals and Correspondence. By Mrs. OLIPHANT. Portrait. 8vo, Cloth, $3 50.

POETS OF THE NINETEENTH CENTURY. The Poets of the Nineteenth Century. Selected and Edited by the Rev. ROBERT ARIS WILLMOTT. With English and American Additions, arranged by EVERT A. DUYCKINCK, Editor of "Cyclopædia of American Literature." Comprising Selections from the Greatest Authors of the Age. Superbly Illustrated with 132 Engravings from Designs by the most Eminent Artists. In elegant small 4to form, printed on Superfine Tinted Paper, richly bound in extra Cloth, Beveled, Gilt Edges, $6 00; Half Calf, $6 00; Full Turkey Morocco, $10 00.

RAWLINSON'S MANUAL OF ANCIENT HISTORY. A Manual of Ancient History, from the Earliest Times to the Fall of the Western Empire. Comprising the History of Chaldæa, Assyria, Media, Babylonia, Lydia, Phœnicia, Syria, Judæa, Egypt, Carthage, Persia, Greece, Macedonia, Parthia, and Rome. By GEORGE RAWLINSON, M.A., Camden Professor of Ancient History in the University of Oxford. 12mo, Cloth, $2 50.

RECLUS'S THE EARTH. The Earth: a Descriptive History of the Phenomena and Life of the Globe. By ÉLISÉE RECLUS. Translated by the late B. B. Woodward, and Edited by Henry Woodward. With 234 Maps and Illustrations, and 23 Page Maps printed in Colors. 8vo, Cloth, $5 00.

SMILES'S LIFE OF THE STEPHENSONS. The Life of George Stephenson, and of his Son, Robert Stephenson; comprising, also, a History of the Invention and Introduction of the Railway Locomotive. By SAMUEL SMILES, Author of "Self-Help," &c. With Steel Portraits and numerous Illustrations. 8vo, Cloth, $3 00.

SMILES'S HISTORY OF THE HUGUENOTS. The Huguenots: their Settlements, Churches, and Industries in England and Ireland. By SAMUEL SMILES. With an Appendix relating to the Huguenots in America. Crown 8vo, Cloth, $1 75.

SHAKSPEARE. The Dramatic Works of William Shakspeare, with the Corrections and Illustrations of Dr. JOHNSON, G. STEEVENS, and others. Revised by ISAAC REED. Engravings. 6 vols., Royal 12mo, Cloth, $9 00.

SPEKE'S AFRICA. Journal of the Discovery of the Source of the Nile. By Captain JOHN HANNING SPEKE, Captain H. M.'s Indian Army, Fellow and Gold Medalist of the Royal Geographical Society, Hon. Corresponding Member and Gold Medalist of the French Geographical Society, &c. With Maps and Portraits and numerous Illustrations, chiefly from Drawings by Captain Grant. 8vo, Cloth, uniform with Livingstone, Barth, Burton, &c., $4 00.

SPRING'S SERMONS. Pulpit Ministrations; or, Sabbath Readings. A Series of Discourses on Christian Doctrine and Duty. By Rev. GARDINER SPRING, D.D., Pastor of the Brick Presbyterian Church in the City of New York. Portrait on Steel. 2 vols., 8vo, Cloth, $6 00.

STRICKLAND'S (MISS) QUEENS OF SCOTLAND. Lives of the Queens of Scotland and English Princesses connected with the Regal Succession of Great Britain. By AGNES STRICKLAND. 8 vols., 12mo, Cloth, $12 00.

THE STUDENT'S SERIES.
France. Engravings. 12mo, Cloth, $2 00.
Gibbon. Engravings. 12mo, Cloth, $2 00.
Greece. Engravings. 12mo, Cloth, $2 00.
Hume. Engravings. 12mo, Cloth, $2 00.
Rome. By Liddell. Engravings. 12mo, Cloth, $2 00.
Old Testament History. Engravings. 12mo, Cloth, $2 00.
New Testament History. Engravings. 12mo, Cloth, $2 00.
Strickland's Queens of England. Abridged. Engravings. 12mo, Cloth, $2 00.
Ancient History of the East. 12mo, Cloth, $2 00.
Hallam's Middle Ages. 12mo, Cloth, $2 00.
Lyell's Elements of Geology. 12mo, Cloth, $2 00.

TENNYSON'S COMPLETE POEMS. The Complete Poems of Alfred Tennyson, Poet Laureate. With numerous Illustrations by Eminent Artists, and Three Characteristic Portraits. 8vo, Paper, 75 cents; Cloth, $1 25.

THOMSON'S LAND AND THE BOOK. The Land and the Book; or, Biblical Illustrations drawn from the Manners and Customs, the Scenes and the Scenery of the Holy Land. By W. M. THOMSON, D.D., Twenty-five Years a Missionary of the A.B.C.F.M. in Syria and Palestine. With two elaborate Maps of Palestine, an accurate Plan of Jerusalem, and several hundred Engravings, representing the Scenery, Topography, and Productions of the Holy Land, and the Costumes, Manners, and Habits of the People. 2 large 12mo vols., Cloth, $5 00.

TICKNOR'S HISTORY OF SPANISH LITERATURE. With Criticisms on the particular Works, and Biographical Notices of Prominent Writers. 3 vols., 8vo, Cloth, $5 00.

TYERMAN'S WESLEY. The Life and Times of the Rev. John Wesley, M.A., Founder of the Methodists. By the Rev. LUKE TYERMAN, Author of "The Life of Rev. Samuel Wesley." Portraits. 3 vols., Crown 8vo.

VAMBÉRY'S CENTRAL ASIA. Travels in Central Asia. Being the Account of a Journey from Teheran across the Turkoman Desert, on the Eastern Shore of the Caspian, to Khiva, Bokhara, and Samarcand, performed in the Year 1863. By ARMINIUS VÁMBÉRY, Member of the Hungarian Academy of Pesth, by whom he was sent on this Scientific Mission. With Map and Woodcuts. 8vo, Cloth, $4 50.

WOOD'S HOMES WITHOUT HANDS. Homes Without Hands: being a Description of the Habitations of Animals, classed according to their Principle of Construction. By J. G. WOOD, M.A., F.L.S. With about 140 Illustrations. 8vo, Cloth, Beveled Edges, $4 50.

WILKINSON'S ANCIENT EGYPTIANS. A Popular Account of their Manners and Customs, condensed from his larger Work, with some New Matter. Illustrated with 500 Woodcuts. 2 vols., 12mo, Cloth, $3 50.

ANTHON'S SMITH'S DICTIONARY OF ANTIQUITIES. A Dictionary of Greek and Roman Antiquities. Edited by WILLIAM SMITH, LL.D., and Illustrated by numerous Engravings on Wood. Third American Edition, carefully Revised, and containing, also, numerous additional Articles relative to the Botany, Mineralogy, and Zoology of the Ancients. By CHARLES ANTHON, LL.D. Royal 8vo, Sheep extra, $6 00.

ANTHON'S CLASSICAL DICTIONARY. Containing an Account of the principal Proper Names mentioned in Ancient Authors, and intended to elucidate all the important Points connected with the Geography, History, Biography, Mythology, and Fine Arts of the Greeks and Romans; together with an Account of the Coins, Weights, and Measures of the Ancients, with Tabular Values of the same. Royal 8vo, Sheep extra, $6 00.

DWIGHT'S (REV. DR.) THEOLOGY. Theology Explained and Defended, in a Series of Sermons. By TIMOTHY DWIGHT, S.T.D., LL.D. With a Memoir and Portrait. 4 vols., 8vo, Cloth, $8 00.

ENGLISHMAN'S GREEK CONCORDANCE. The Englishman's Greek Concordance of the New Testament: being an Attempt at a Verbal Connection between the Greek and the English Texts: including a Concordance to the Proper Names, with Indexes, Greek-English and English-Greek. 8vo, Cloth, $5 00.

FOWLER'S ENGLISH LANGUAGE. The English Language in its Elements and Forms. With a History of its Origin and Development, and a full Grammar. Designed for Use in Colleges and Schools. Revised and Enlarged. By WILLIAM C. FOWLER, LL.D., late Professor in Amherst College. 8vo, Cloth, $2 50.

GIESELER'S ECCLESIASTICAL HISTORY. A Text-Book of Church History. By Dr. JOHN C. L. GIESELER. Translated from the Fourth Revised German Edition by SAMUEL DAVIDSON, LL.D., and Rev. JOHN WINSTANLEY HULL, M.A. A New American Edition, Revised and Edited by Rev. HENRY B. SMITH, D.D., Professor in the Union Theological Seminary, New York. Four Volumes ready. (*Vol. V. in Press.*) 8vo, Cloth, $2 25 per vol.

HALL'S (ROBERT) WORKS. The Complete Works of Robert Hall; with a brief Memoir of his Life by Dr. GREGORY, and Observations on his Character as a Preacher by Rev. JOHN FOSTER. Edited by OLINTHUS GREGORY, LL.D., and Rev. JOSEPH BELCHER. Portrait. 4 vols., 8vo, Cloth, $8 00.

HAMILTON'S (SIR WILLIAM) WORKS. Discussions on Philosophy and Literature, Education and University Reform. Chiefly from the *Edinburgh Review*. Corrected, Vindicated, and Enlarged, in Notes and Appendices. By Sir WILLIAM HAMILTON, Bart. With an Introductory Essay by Rev. ROBERT TURNBULL, D.D. 8vo, Cloth, $3 00.

HUMBOLDT'S COSMOS. Cosmos: a Sketch of a Physical Description of the Universe. By ALEXANDER VON HUMBOLDT. Translated from the German by E. C. OTTÉ. 5 vols., 12mo, Cloth, $6 25.

www.ingramcontent.com/pod-product-compliance
Lightning Source LLC
LaVergne TN
LVHW020112110826
845151LV00001B/131